An Ethic of Hospitality

Contrapuntal Readings of the Bible in World Christianity

Series Editors: K. K. Yeo, Melanie Baffes

Just as God knows no boundaries and incarnation happens in shared space, truth does not respect borders and its expression in various contexts is kaleidoscopic. As God's church is birthed forth from local cultures, it is called into a catholic community—namely world Christianity. This series values the twofold identity of biblical interpretations that seek to engage in contextual theology and, at the same time, become part of a global and "many-voiced" conversation for the sake of mutual understanding. By promoting contrapuntal readings that hold contextual and global biblical hermeneutics in tension, this series celebrates interpretations in three movements: (1) those based on the biblical text that honor multiple and interacting worldviews (reading the world biblically/theologically); (2) those that work at the translatability of the biblical text to uphold various dynamic vernaculars and faithful hermeneutics for the world (reading the Bible/theology contextually); and (3) those that respect the cross-cultural and shifting contexts in which faithful communities are embedded, and embody, real-life issues.

International Advisory Board

Walter Brueggemann, William Marcellus McPheeters Professor Emeritus of Old Testament, Columbia Theological Seminary (US)

Adela Yarbro Collins, Buckingham Professor of New Testament Criticism and Interpretation, Yale Divinity School (US)

Kathy Ehrensperger, Research Professor of New Testament in Jewish Perspective, University of Potsdam (Germany)

Justo L. González, Emeritus Professor of Historical Theology, Candler School of Theology, Emory University (US)

Richard A. Horsley, Distinguished Professor of Liberal Arts and the Study of Religion Emeritus, University of Massachusetts— Boston (US)

Robert Jewett, Emeritus Professor of New Testament, Heidelberg University (Germany)

Brigitte Kahl, Professor of New Testament, Union Theological Seminary (US)

Peter Lampe, Professor of New Testament Theology, Heidelberg University (Germany)

Tremper Longman III, Robert H. Gundry Professor Emeritus of Biblical Studies, Westmont College (US)

Daniel Patte, Professor Emeritus of Religious Studies, New Testament, and Christianity, Vanderbilt University (US)

Volumes in the Series (2018–2020)

Volume 1: *Text and Context: Vernacular Approaches to the Bible in Global Christianity*, edited by Melanie Baffes

Volume 2: *What Has Jerusalem to Do with Beijing? Biblical Interpretation from a Chinese Perspective* (Twentieth Anniversary Edition), K. K. Yeo

Volume 3: *Chinese Biblical Anthropology: Persons and Ideas in the Old Testament and in Modern Chinese Literature*, Cao Jian

Volume 4: *Cross-textual Reading of Ecclesiastes with Analects: In Search of Political Wisdom in a Disordered World*, Elaine Wei-Fun Goh

Volume 5: *The Cambridge Dictionary of Christianity*, 2 vols., edited by Daniel Patte

Volume 6: *An Ethic of Hospitality: The Pilgrim Motif in Hebrews and the Refugee Problem in Kenya*, Emily Jeptepkeny Choge

Volume 7: *Diffused Story of the Foot-Washing in John 13: A Textual Study of Bible Reception in Late Imperial China*, Yanrong Chen

An Ethic of Hospitality

The Pilgrim Motif in Hebrews and
the Refugee Problem in Kenya

Emily Jeptepkeny Choge

FOREWORD BY
William Dyrness

◆PICKWICK *Publications* • Eugene, Oregon

AN ETHIC OF HOSPITALITY
The Pilgrim Motif in Hebrews and the Refugee Problem in Kenya

Contrapuntal Readings of the Bible in World Christianity 6

Copyright © 2020 Emily Jeptepkeny Choge. All rights reserved. Except for brief quotations in critical publications or reviews, no part of this book may be reproduced in any manner without prior written permission from the publisher. Write: Permissions, Wipf and Stock Publishers, 199 W. 8th Ave., Suite 3, Eugene, OR 97401.

Pickwick Publications
An Imprint of Wipf and Stock Publishers
199 W. 8th Ave., Suite 3
Eugene, OR 97401

www.wipfandstock.com

PAPERBACK ISBN: 978-1-5326-9934-4
HARDCOVER ISBN: 978-1-5326-9935-1
EBOOK ISBN: 978-1-5326-9936-8

Cataloguing-in-Publication data:

Names: Choge, Emily Jeptepkeny, author. | Dyrness, William, foreword.

Title: An ethic of hospitality : the pilgrim motif in Hebrews and the refugee problem in Kenya / Emily Jeptepkeny Choge ; foreword by William Dyrness.

Description: Eugene, OR: Pickwick Publications, 2020. | Contrapuntal Readings of the Bible in World Christianity 6. | Includes bibliographical references and index.

Identifiers: ISBN 978-1-5326-9934-4 (paperback). | ISBN 978-1-5326-9935-1 (hardcover). | ISBN 978-1-5326-9936-8 (ebook).

Subjects: LCSH: Bible. Hebrews—Criticism, interpretation, etc. | Hospitality in the Bible. | Strangers in the Bible. | Hospitality—Religious aspects—Christianity. | Bible—Hermeneutics. | Africa—Refugees.

Classification: BS2775.52 C46 2020 (print). | BS2775.52 (ebook).

Manufactured in the U.S.A.   07/14/20

In the blessed memory of my father,
Rev. Job A. Choge,
and my mother,
Mary Jelagat Choge

Contents

Foreword by William Dyrness | ix
Acknowledgments | xiii
Introduction | xv
Abbreviations | xxi

1. A Hospitality Ethic of Pilgrims for Kenyan Refugees | 1
2. The Refugee Situation in the Horn of Africa | 15
3. Responses to the Refugee Problem | 38
4. Kenya: A Refugee-hosting Country | 59
5. The Pilgrim Motif in the Book of Hebrews | 94
6. The Role of the Church in Kenya and the Refugee Problem | 138
7. Recommendations and Conclusion | 185

Appendix A: Definition of Key Terms | 203
Appendix B: Interview Questions | 208
Appendix C: Letter to the Refugees | 210
Bibliography | 215
Author Index | 235
Subject Index | 237
Scripture Index | 241

Foreword

WHEN PEOPLE IN EUROPE and North America consider the "refugee problem" in 2020, they are likely to think about the recent influx of Africans into Europe or the caravans of refugees from Central America camped on America's doorstep. What they are less likely to think about is the back story of these migrations and the devastation and displacement in developing countries that has given rise to these desperate journeys. This is the story that Emily Choge tells in this important study. Though the study focuses on her home country of Kenya, she frames the flight of refugees as a global problem that in its modern incarnation dates back to the hordes of "displaced peoples" triggered by the desolation of the Second World War. The United Nations High Commission for Refugees (UNHCR), which figures prominently in Emily's study, was founded in 1951—with an initial three-year term!—to deal with that crisis. The irony of that three-year term is due to a Western history that overlooks the horrific realities of the middle passage of enslaved Africans and the many internal migrations of slaves in the early history of America. Emily is not afraid to point out that the struggles she documents of Kenya's refugee problems are the bitter fruit of this history of colonialism.

But if we take seriously the methodology that Emily uses, that of her late mentor Glen Stassen, the first responsibility of the Christian seeking to respond to this history is "perception": that is, the discipline of seeing things as they are, including a clear-eyed view of how things came to be as they are. But even before developing this methodology, it is clear from Emily's patient description of the situation on the ground, that this "seeing" means drinking tea with them and *seeing with them* the violence that sparked the refugees' flight. She describes how the indigenous practices of African hospitality, in the period since Kenya's independence (in the 1960s), have welcomed thousands of internally displaced people but, beginning in the 1990s with the wars in Ethiopia and Somalia, have struggled under the load.

Since we are made to see things from the refugees' point of view, we can easily see the limitations of the UNHCR's insistence that only fear of persecution qualifies one for refugee status; such limitation violates the call to deep perception of these neighbors that Emily insists upon. But identification with these neighbors carries an additional benefit. Since we are made to join in their sense of life in the refugee campus and the innovative (and often multi-ethnic) Christian response in these places, we are discouraged from seeing this simply as a "problem to be solved." Rather, we are able to see these camps as places where God already is at work, where God's reign of justice and righteousness already is on display, and where Christians' salt and light already is doing its work.

To the natural question of how this can be, Emily moves to show how the book of Hebrews provides a map of the central New Testament call to develop a "pilgrim identity." Though Emily is modest in pointing out how revolutionary this perspective might be in our treatment of others, what she is doing is allowing our experience of walking alongside these neighbors, stranded so far from home in camps strategically placed in arid wastelands far from urban populations, to remake our view of our faith. These refugees, in their worship and service, including their forming of associations and schools, become our teachers.

They give us eyes to rediscover our own Scripture, where a pilgrim identity nurtures a faith that requires endurance in community. It hardly needs stressing how counter-cultural this appears in an environment where evangelical faith is marketed as a simple belief in Jesus to assure one of eternal life. Since the refugee church harbors no illusions of political power or cultural influence, it actually is liberated to serve its neighbors. And so, it turns out that an exercise in perception becomes, in the hands of this author, a journey of biblical and theological construction, allowing us to move deeply into a more capacious understanding of the Christian journey.

One of the principles enshrined in the United Nations practice of responding to refugees is *non-refoulement*, which forbids a country receiving refugees from returning them to their home country if they would be at risk of persecution because of their "race, religion, nationality, or membership in a particular social or political group."[1] This struck me deeply. Though we struggle to define and parse these categories, it strikes me that what we seek is the central notion of hospitality that God displays toward the world: Throughout Scripture, God's love and provision is defined by a special concern for the alien and stranger, an experience Israel had known first-hand in Egypt. As Emily shows, our call to entertain the stranger is meant to reflect, however imperfectly, that divine impulse.

The book of Hebrews offers one further gift to the refugee church from which we can learn. That gift is the hope that throughout history has

---

1. Trevisanut, "International Law and Practice," 661.

sustained the heroes of faith, many of them in situations not unlike today's refugees. All of these, the writer of Hebrews tells us, "died in faith not having received the promises, but from a distance they saw and greeted them" (Heb 11:13). Though, like Abraham, today's refugees have set out without knowing where they are going; they too, by faith are looking forward "to the city that has foundations, whose architect and builder is God" (v. 10).

William Dyrness
Epiphany 2020
San Jose, Costa Rica

Acknowledgments

As I walked the pilgrim path for six years (1999–2004) at Fuller Theological Seminary, there were several people who walked the path with me and cheered and encouraged me along. They are "the cloud of witnesses" to whom Hebrews refers.

First, I would like to thank my mentor, the late Glen H. Stassen, who was more than a mentor to me. He welcomed me as a stranger into his home during my early days in Pasadena. These were crucial and formative years for me. He walked alongside me, helping me to learn what it means to be a Christian ethicist and the importance of subjecting issues to thorough scrutiny. Thanks to Dot, his wife and David, his son, who also have been companions along the way and included me into the family.

This work would not have been possible without the generous financial support of John Stott Ministries. Thank you, Uncle John, Merrit Sawyer, and David Jones. My deep gratitude also goes to my support group and church family, Abundant Life Christian Fellowship, Palo Alto, for their prayers and financial support. Thank you to members of the GO missions' team, especially Eben and Arthur, for accompanying me to the refugee camp. I am truly grateful to have been part of this loving family.

My friends and "sisters on the wall"—Marion, Paula, Tina, and Gloria—have helped to form my spiritual dimension, providing fuel when I could not continue. Thanks also go to my housemate Christine, who joined me in the pilgrimage to the camp, and to Scott, for letting me tap into his knowledge of Hebrews.

My church family, First Baptist Pasadena, have prayed for me every week through the writing of this dissertation. They have experienced the entire process with me and, for that, I am truly grateful.

I will not forget those who have taught me literally what it means to be a pilgrim, my brothers and sisters at Kakuma Refugee Camp. You welcomed me into your fellowship and let me share some of your experiences, even in the small way that I did. Thanks to Pastor Tito, Pastor Gatera, Pastor Simon, Pastor Namuya and sister Florence. Thank you also, Rejoice and Dominic, for being part of my life and for letting me join in yours.

Gratitude to my friend and prayer partner, Esker Harris, for holding my hand and praying me through the whole process. Thank you, Alice, for hosting me in your house during the critical time of writing the dissertation and for introducing me to the Kenyan pilgrim community in the Bay area, who exemplified in reality what it means to have a pilgrim faith.

Thanks also to my family members, Dad and Mum (both now in glory), my brothers, sisters, nieces and nephews who, though far away in Kenya, have kept in touch and prayed for me consistently.

My wholehearted thanks and gratitude, of course, go to the pilgrim *par excellence*, Jesus, who pioneered this idea and brought it to completion. My prayer and hope is that this remains the attitude of my life and mind.

Introduction

THE REFUGEE SITUATION HAS reached alarming proportions in Kenya. Though there have been historical and sociological studies focusing on the problem, there has never been a biblical theological reflection that addresses the issue. This work provides a biblical theological response to the problem based on the pilgrim motif in Hebrews. It begins with a historical analysis, highlighting the fact that the root causes of the problem of refugees in the Horn of Africa lie in the unequal relationship between the North and South. This relationship began with the slave trade, continued through colonialism, and now exists in the form of powerful multinational companies that deplete the resources of Africa. Following independence, Kenya hosted refugees who came through its borders in an exemplary manner. But since 1992, the numbers have increased and, due to social, economic, and political challenges, the Kenya government has not applied the wisdom of the saying, *Mgeni siku ya kwanza; siku ya pili mpe jembe* (One is a guest is for two days; on the third day give him/her a hoe). The refugees have been confined in the camps for over ten years, and there seems to be no solution in sight.

As a framework for my biblical and theological reflection, I call on multiple understandings of what it means to be a refugee. According to the 1951 UN Convention Relating to the Status of Refugees—and its 1967 Protocol, which extended the Convention's provisions to current refugees, including individuals fleeing persecution in the post-war era—a refugee is defined as:

> Any person who owing to a well-founded fear of being persecuted for reasons of race, religion, nationality, membership of a particular social group or political opinion, is outside the country of his nationality and is unable or, owing to such fear, unwilling to avail himself of the protection of that country, or who, not having a nationality is outside the country of his former habitual residence, is unable or, owing to such fear, is unwilling to return to it.[1]

---

1. UNHCR, *Convention and Protocol Relating to the Status of Refugees*, 14.

Elizabeth Ferris notes three important exclusions in this definition.[2] First, it excludes those individuals who have been displaced by violence or warfare and who have not been singled out for individual persecution. It also excludes those whose have been displaced because of violence and have not left the country of origin. Third, it excludes those whose livelihoods are threatened by economic conditions in their countries, forcing them to search for a better existence. It also leaves out those for whom environmental situations have caused them to move to other places. For those in the third-world countries, political, economic and environmental conditions intertwine, causing refugee flows both within and outside the country. And there is internal displacement for those who do not cross international borders.[3]

Recognizing the limitation of this definition, in 1969, the Organization of African Unity (OAU) developed the Convention Governing the Specific Aspects of Refugee Problems in Africa. The OAU definition therefore includes:

> Every person who, owing to external aggression, occupation, foreign domination, or events seriously disturbing public order in either part or the whole of his country of his nationality, is compelled to leave his place or habitual residence in order to seek refuge in another place outside his country of origin or nationality.[4]

This convention reflects the reality of the African situation, but it still excludes internally displaced people or those who are uprooted by economic disasters. To find a definition that will include everyone is difficult, and of course, there is a danger that if the definition is too broad it will not serve the neediest people. According to Elizabeth Ferris, Christian organizations such as World Council of Churches (WCC) and other NGOs have always had the liberty to extend the definition, and, as she says, they have "shown greater flexibility in working with uprooted people, including internally displaced people, than either governments or intergovernmental organizations."[5]

I call on both the UN and OAU definitions because refugees are a clearly defined group within our borders. From the situations in African countries, it is obvious that Africans have suffered all sorts of deprivations arising from diverse situations—political, environmental, and economic. However, because tribal affiliations in Africa have been used to separate people, whether they belong to the same nation or not, we need to use the

---

2. Ferris, *Beyond Borders*, 12. These would still fall under the category of refugees.

3. Though I recognize those internally displaced as refugees, my focus in on refugees from outside.

4. *OAU Convention Governing the Specific Aspects of Refugee Problems in Africa.*

5. Ferris, *Beyond Borders*, 20.

word "refugee" also to refer to those who suffer internal displacement. This includes those who suffered as a result of tribal clashes in 1992 as well as in 2007/2008 in Kenya.[6] It should be noted that when we focus on the needs of refugees, it does not mean we do not have our own needy people to attend to. I know Kenyans struggle with the issue of how we can respond to refugees, some of whom appear well-to-do, when we have our own pressing needs. But the presence of refugees in our country is a unique opportunity that should sensitize us to their unique dilemma and should also make us concerned about those who are needy among our own people.

In this work, I explore the refugee crisis through the lens of pilgrimage. In its most classic and generic usage, the word "pilgrim" has a twofold dimension. It means one who makes a journey to a sacred place. But it also gives the sense that all of life is a pilgrimage. More specifically, the word "pilgrim" is rooted in a very rich religious tradition. Upon hearing the word, one immediately gets the visual image of a band of people on a journey, with their hearts set on a goal or destination, which is usually an earthly sacred place. Such a journey is purposeful because it is usually planned and deliberately arranged for, and in most cases, it is undertaken along with a group of people who share the same purpose.

The concept of Christian pilgrimage has biblical roots in both the Old and New Testaments. Thus, I would like to use this word in two ways: first, to refer to the Christian life as a whole. The physical journey of the Israelites from Egypt to the Promised Land is equated to the Christian walk of faith from the kingdom of darkness to the kingdom of light, or the journey from earth to our heavenly destination.

Second, more particularly, I would use the word to refer to the refugees as those who have set their hearts on a pilgrimage. If they have espoused the Christian life, then they are not just refugees living a haphazard existence, but they are pilgrims journeying towards a specific destination. Most of them did not deliberately set out on the physical journey, but if they view their existence in this manner—not just as helpless victims who were pushed out of their land, but as purposeful pilgrims on a journey of faith, both literally and figuratively— then this brings an added dimension of purpose and meaning to their existence. It can transform the hopeless, dreary existence at the refugee camp to a life of hopeful expectation—not just for the durable solutions of the UNHCR, but for the ultimate manifestation of the kingdom of God. Thus, the word "pilgrim" denotes more than the physical experience of merely existing in a foreign land; it includes a sense

---

6. I have not given a detailed analysis of the ethnic clashes in Kenya except insofar as they affected the response to the refugees who came from outside Kenya. However, I believe the guidelines for a Christian response to strangers, whether internal or external, remains the same.

of purpose and psycho-spiritual awareness that radically alters the quality of that existence. This understanding, therefore, is that although life on earth is temporary and fleeting, it also has a dimension of purpose that should inform everything the pilgrims do.

That said, I hope this Christian goal is not seen just as a pie-in-the-sky idea. It is a life of determination and expectation that, by clinging to faith, refuses to give in to the despair of what is around it. This is a life that is caught in the reality of the worst thing that could happen to anyone, and the hopeful expectation that there is a better world awaiting that they can call home. They know they have lost what they call home here on earth, temporarily or permanently, and yet they anticipate a place they will call home, both physically and spiritually. And because they are caught in that ongoing tension of the "now and the not yet," they are the ones who can best exemplify to Christians everywhere the essence and meaning of eschatological expectation. That is why I hope the Christians in Kenya can learn from the refugees what it means to live as aliens, exiles and pilgrims who are looking for a city whose architect and founder is God. The refugees are a part of the "cloud of witnesses" that the epistle to the Hebrews talks about, who urge the rest of the world to run the race with perseverance.

This work is a call to Christians in Kenya to provide an alternative ethic to the refugee crisis. Armed with the rich resources of African hospitality and taking seriously their pilgrim identity as manifested in the book of Hebrews, they will be able to deal with the situation courageously, compassionately, and creatively.

Hospitality in both the biblical and the African tradition is not just about entertaining family and friends; it reaches to the arena of one who is the "other," the stranger, the outsider, the foreigner. In most African languages, the same word is used for both stranger and guest. To show how hospitality was built into the structure of life of the Kipsigis people, Adam Chepkwony tells us that whenever a meal was prepared, it was normal to leave one portion, known as *"kimyet ab lakwa,"* set aside, so that if a stranger showed up after an evening meal, there would be something to offer.[7] It is also a normal practice in most African homes to prepare more food than for those who regularly eat because there is the expectation that a stranger will arrive.

Christians have a rich biblical heritage of hospitality. For ancient Israel, it was one of the central pillars of their identity as the people of God. Abraham, who is considered the father of the nation and of the faithful, is lifted up as the prime practitioner of hospitality. In the book of Hebrews, Christians are urged not only to emulate Abraham's example of faith (Heb 11:11–17), but also his practice of hospitality (Heb 13:2).

---

7. Chepkwony, "African Religion in the Study of Comparative Religion."

Therefore, as Christine D. Pohl shows us, although throughout the history of the church the practice has lost this radical meaning of reaching out to those on the margins of society, we can still recover the essence of this virtue to be practiced within the Christian church.[8] I contend that those who need this hospitality the most are "those who are disconnected from basic relationships that give a secure place in the world."[9] I agree with Pohl that "this condition is most clearly seen in the state of the homeless people and the refugees."[10] Thus, this work focuses on how we can be hospitable to one specific category of people, the refugees.

Hospitality as a practice is potentially subversive, upsetting the status quo, and it is full of risks. It is about giving those who have been displaced a legitimate place to belong and to be. It is not about making a people constantly dependent on handouts, as some have done, thus making them more vulnerable than when they started. Rightfully applied, this practice can be a tool for empowerment, restoration, and transformation for those who have been excluded. In recovering this concept, especially in the public arena of the nation and the church, we also are recovering our rich biblical heritage and church history and a traditional African practice. The Kiswahili proverb mentioned earlier—*Mgeni siku ya kwanza, siku ya pili mpatie jembe*, which literally means "one is a guest for only two days; on the third day, give him/her a hoe to dig"—addresses the protracted refugee situations that seem to be prevalent all over Africa. Such is the wisdom we need in our complex world, where insecurities thrive, and people are not sure who is a genuine stranger.

The main components of an ethic for refugees are following Jesus, the pilgrim *par excellence,* and a community of faith characterized by hospitality, courage, and hope in the face of adversity. Drawing upon Yoder and Okullu, we note that the mission of the church has a four-fold dimension: to announce the Lordship of Jesus Christ over and against all powers, to be a community that transcends national and ethnic boundaries, to be a paradigm for society, and to serve the community in its multiple functions.[11] Thus, a church that will own its pilgrim identity will respond to refugees in caring and compassionate ways and will lead the nation towards creative life-transforming solutions.

---

8. Pohl, *Making Room*, 13.
9. Ibid.
10. Ibid.
11. See Okullu, *Church and Politics in East Africa*; Okullu, *Church and State in Nation Building*; and Okullu, *Quest for Justice*. Yoder's works include: *The Priestly Kingdom*; *The Politics of Jesus*; *For the Nations*; *The Christian Witness to the State*; *Body Politics*; and *Royal Priesthood*.

Abbreviations

AACC	All Africa Conference of Churches
AEA	Association of Evangelicals of Africa
ALARM	African Leadership and Reconciliation Ministries
BEST	Bangui Evangelical School of Theology
CARE	CARE International
CLMC	Christian Learning Materials Centre
FECCGLAHA	Fellowship of Christian Councils in the Great Lakes Area and Horn of Africa
GTZ	Deutsche Gesellschraft für Technische Zusammenarbeit
ICARA	International Conference on Assistance for Refugees in Africa
ILO	International Labor Organization
IRC	International Rescue Committee
JRS	Jesuit Refugee Service
KISOM	Kakuma Interdenominational School of Mission
LWF/DWS	Lutheran World Federation/Department of World Service
MSF	Medecins Sans Frontieres—Belgium
NEGST	Nairobi Evangelical Graduate School of Theology
NCCK	National Christian Council of Kenya
OAU	Organization of African Union
UN	United Nations
UNHCR	United Nations High Commissioner for Refugees
WV (K)	World Vision Kenya

1

A Hospitality Ethic of Pilgrims for Kenyan Refugees

> The refugee is a product of our errors, his predicament an indictment of our conduct as peoples and nations. He exists for our education and as a warning.
>
> —SADRUDDIN AGA KHAN, UNHCR HIGH COMMISSIONER 1965–1977

Introduction

THE PROBLEM OF REFUGEES is worldwide.[1] When the United Nations High Commission for Refugees (UNHCR) was launched in 1951, it was given a three-year mandate. Its specific task was the resettlement of more than two million European refugees after the Second World War. In 2001, as the UNHCR celebrated fifty years, it was evident that the organization had expanded to meet the needs of refugees, and today it assists some twenty-two million people from all over the globe. Reflecting on these fifty years in the foreword of the book, *The State of the World's Refugees: Fifty Years of Humanitarian Action*, the present High Commissioner had this to say:

> It takes only a glance at some of the chapter titles of this book to understand why UNHCR's 50th anniversary is not a cause for celebration... As we enter the new millennium, the fact that the world still finds a need for UNHCR should serve as a sobering reminder of the international community's continuing failure to prevent prejudice, persecution, poverty and the root causes of conflict and displacement.[2]

---

1. For a better understanding of terms such as "pilgrim," "refugee," and "hospitality," see Appendix A.

2. Cutts, *The State of the World's Refugees*, x; see also UNHCR, *State of the World's Refugees 2016*, xii.

The State of the Problem

Until recently Africa has borne the greatest burden of the refugee problem, and it is still true that the ratio of refugees in proportion to its total population is the highest compared to all other continents. A positive note in this grim picture is that those who have hosted the refugees in Africa have done so relentlessly, amidst very dire circumstances. They have been willing to give, even when it has been difficult to feed their own populations. This generosity of heart has been attributed to the African spirit of hospitality. In support of this, one of Africa's esteemed leaders, Mwalimu Julius Nyerere, the first president of Tanzania, wrote extensively on African socialism as rooted within the extended family and this manifested in hospitality to all people. Another writer has aptly put it this way:

> One hears of the traditional African hospitality, now and then of African Socialism. Never before in the annals of history have a people with so little agreed to share with so many, nor has such an opportunity to be one's brother's keeper ever presented itself on such a grand scale and been willingly accepted.[3]

However, there is evidence that this generosity of spirit is being increasingly challenged due to the social, political and economic constraints facing many of the African countries.[4] Kenya is not an exception to this challenge. Her experience with hosting large numbers of refugees has been recent. Veney reports:

> After independence in 1963, Kenya did not become a refugee-producing or refugee-receiving country. At the end of 1972, Kenya had only 2,500 refugees, 3,500 in 1981; 3,400 in 1982. However, this is no longer the case. More than 300,000 Somalia refugees alone fled to Kenya from 1990–1993, victims of violence, anarchy, and famine. They joined thousands of others from Ethiopia, Sudan, Rwanda, Uganda, and Zaire.[5]

Another report shows that, at the peak of the influx in December 1992, 420,000 refugees had entered the country in search of asylum. Thankfully,

---

3. Kironde, "African Evaluation of the Problem," 106. It is interesting that this book was written in 1970 and even at that time the problem was acute. It worsened in the 1990s.

4. Kibreab, *African Refugees*, 67–83. He has argued strongly that this spirit of African hospitality should not be used as an excuse by Western countries not to help African countries in the burden of hosting refugees. He also says that hospitality is a myth when there are no resources to share.

5. Veney, "The Politics of Refugee Relief Operations in Kenya," 46.

the return of relative peace in parts of Somalia in the last four years, and the resolution of conflict in Ethiopia, have facilitated the voluntary return of more than 200,000 refugees, mainly from these two countries. This allowed the closure of thirteen refugee camps across Kenya. The only two camps now open are Dadaab in the eastern part, which houses over 120,000 refugees, mainly of Somali origin, and Kakuma in the northern region, which is the home of nearly 80,000 refugees, mainly from Sudan, though other countries also are represented.[6]

Though Kenya, like other African nations, has hosted these refugees in an exemplary way, her own internal problems such as ethnic clashes have caused internal displacement of the populations within the country. The economic hardships sustained due to the debt crisis, lack of rain, and leadership problems have made this burden too hard to bear. The result is that, in these later years, the refugees have been seen as a burden and have been subjected to harsh treatment by the government and the local population.[7] In a nation that is said to be 80 percent Christian, such reports are very distressing. One can see that if the general atmosphere in the country is hostile to strangers, it is also difficult for Christians to exercise hospitality. My research then is an attempt to address these questions:

- How can Kenyan Christians continue to exercise their Christian calling of being hospitable to the stranger in the midst of social, economic and political hardships?
- What are the factors that have influenced their response to the refugee problem?
- How can a study of the pilgrim motif in the book of Hebrews inform a Christian response to the refugee problem?
- What can Kenyan Christians learn from the book of Hebrews on how to live as the pilgrim people of God?
- What can we learn from the presence of refugees in our midst about how to live a pilgrim existence?

---

6. See Rawlence, *City of Thorns*, ix–xiv, for maps of: 1) The Horn of Africa; 2) the Kenya-Somalia Border; 3) Dadaab Refugee Complex; 4) Ifo Refugee Camp; and 5) Hagadera Refugee Camp.

7. I lived in Nairobi from 1987 to 1990, and I constantly witnessed the harassment of strangers. This was especially evident in public vehicles. If a stranger had obvious foreign features (like Somalis or Ethiopians), did not have enough money to pay, or did something else to draw attention to themselves, many unkind and rude remarks were uttered, not only by the owners of the vehicle but also the passengers.

- How can the church in Kenya be a prophetic voice in addressing the root causes of the refugee problem and yet, at the same time, support refugees in their pilgrim walk?

Purpose of the Study

This study hopes to provide a biblical-theological response to the refugee problem in Kenya. Specifically, I hope to show that the book of Hebrews can provide Kenyan Christians ethical guidelines on how to respond to the refugee problem. I also seek to prove that refugees living a pilgrim existence have much to teach us about what it means to live as pilgrims and exiles in this world. Finally, I draw attention to the plight of the refugees so that the Christian community both locally and internationally, including their governments, can work toward better policies for the treatment of refugees, who have a special place in the household of God.

The State of the Study

The problem of refugees around the world, which has preoccupied the UN-HCR for more than fifty years, has only recently become a fertile field for academic study. It has attracted scholars from various disciplines, especially political and social scientists and economists. Scholars also have focused on specific geographical areas in order to see how the problem affects particular places around the world. For my specific area, Kenya, four dissertations have been written on this topic,[8] and these works serve me well in analyzing the problem from a political, cultural, social, and economic perspective.

Nonetheless, studies that have focused specifically on Christian theological reflection about the refugee problem are still few and far between. It is evident, therefore, that a comprehensive study of this topic from a Christian theological perspective is needed. The studies that have come close to what I intend to do in this work are Michael Anthony Evans' work, "An Analysis of U.N. Refugee Policy in the Light of Roman Catholic Social Teaching and the Phenomena Creating Refugees."[9] He has done comprehensive analysis that critiques the United Nations' limited definition of a refugee. His aim is to show that the United Nations' refugee policy and the international response to the

---

8. Bariagaber, "Political Violence, Refugee Solutions"; Veney, "The Politics of the Refugee Relief Operations in Kenya"; Okoro, "Africa's Refugee Problem"; and Hydman, "Geographies of Displacement."

9. Evans, "An Analysis of U.N. Refugee Policy."

refugee crisis are inadequate in light of the phenomena that create refugees and in light of the Roman Catholic teaching on refugees. He suggests strongly that the UN definition of refugees, which is based on Europe's post-World War situation, is obsolete and narrow in addressing conditions that create refugees, especially in regions far from Europe. His questioning of this definition is based on the Roman Catholic teaching that gives clear guidance on the rights and duties expected of the international community toward those who are displaced. Thus, he gives a thorough assessment of the papal encyclicals and their special attention to refugees. He sums it up this way:

> R.C. social teaching posits basic rights for refugees, displaced persons, and migrants including a limited right to emigration and immigration. These rights are based on human dignity and *imago Dei*, the rights to bodily integrity, subsistence, private property and usufruct, as well as political and religious freedom rights. The right to migration is limited and tempered by considerations of the common good, including the common good of both the country of emigration as well as that of immigration.[10]

He also uses the case studies of Sudan and Ethiopia to demonstrate the complexity of the factors that cause refugee flows. In his discussion on the ethical responsibility of the international community to respond to refugee rights based on the teachings of Henry Shue and John Langan, he "challenges the commonly accepted wisdom that nation-states et al. may respond to refugee situations, if they wish or they are strategically expedient, out of a sense of generous humanitarianism and largesse." But he goes on to argue that "while this may be the case for occasions of natural disaster, our analysis suggests that in many cases refugee assistance is owed out of justice. It is not a matter of voluntary charity."[11] Thus, he calls for policy considerations that are intended for all audiences, the UN system, the international community, churches and church-sponsored Non-governmental Organizations (NGOs), and all men and women of faith and good will. The refugee crisis is so large that it calls for an extensive audience. He calls on the UN to change policy in order to adapt to the contemporary refugee situation. The definition of the refugee must be broadened so that it includes those who are internally displaced and are victims of civil war, famine, and genocide. I use his work to provide a backdrop for the refugee problem in Kenya, especially his thorough analysis of the situation in Ethiopia and Sudan, areas that have generated refugees that are hosted in Kenya. My work, however, differs from his in that I draw ethical

---

10. Ibid., 161–62. Also, Oka, "Coping with the Refugee Wait," 23–37.
11. Ibid., 369.

guidelines for the church in Kenya not from Catholic teaching but from the pilgrim motif in the epistle to the Hebrews.

Another scholar who has attempted to provide an ethical response to the refugee problem is Thadei Mwereke in her work, "The Problem of Refugees in Africa South of the Sahara: The Legacy of Foreign Intervention."[12] Her argument is that Africa's refugee problems lie in the foreign interference in Africa that came through the avenue of colonialism and the entry of Christianity. She says:

> Before foreign intervention, Africa reached the pinnacle of achievement in all aspects of life—in the economy, in culture and in the promulgation of laws and so on. It was only afterwards, especially with foreign intervention, that Africa's destiny was destroyed. Foreign intervention made the people of Africa experience a lot of setbacks economically, politically and socially.[13]

She also argues strongly that "with the coming of colonialism and Christianity, Africa's hope and aspirations for development and integrity were shattered."[14] This resulted in the destruction of the African way of life and of the coherence of the community. Religion in Africa influenced every aspect of life, even the search for social justice. She says the solution for the church in Africa is to adopt inculturation, which will open the way for Africa to regain her dignity and rights.

I think Mwereke has put her finger on the key issue that underlies the refugee problem in Africa, and that is foreign interference. However, she has not given a thorough analysis of how the Christian church, which she considers a big part of the problem, should spearhead the changes that would make this inculturation a reality in Africa. I also think that she has painted too glowing a picture of the African past without critically assessing some of the inherent cracks within the African system that gave a foothold to some of the evil practices. Some of these include class differentiation and tribal hostilities that the colonialists exploited to the maximum by their use of the policy of "divide and rule." I hope that my work pays attention to these loopholes as I seek to provide some practical solutions, especially on how the church should respond, drawing on the rich cultural heritage of the practice of hospitality in Africa.

In order to provide a theoretical framework of Christian involvement in the political sphere, I use the works of John H. Yoder, in particular *The*

---

12. Mwereke, "Problem of Refugees in Africa South of the Sahara."
13. Ibid., 34.
14. Ibid.," 36.

Politics of Jesus, For the Nations, A Priestly Kingdom, and *Body Politics.* Yoder is a Christian ethicist who argues that, if the church follows Jesus seriously, it will demonstrate a public ethic that will impact the community for its own good. In *Body Politics,*[15] Yoder shows how the church can actually use five practices as a symbolic witness:

1. Baptism of Jews and Gentiles shows that all racial and ethnic barriers have been defeated.
2. Forgiveness in the community through binding and loosing is the demonstration of what conflict resolution is like in the world.
3. The breaking of bread as a symbol of meeting the needs of the poor is a form of economic justice.
4. The openness of people to talk is a symbol of democracy.
5. Universality of giftedness shows that everyone has a role in the body of Christ, which goes against hierarchism.

In his work *For the Nations,*[16] Yoder states that the mission of the church in the world is to be a witness to the nations. He proposes the paradigm of the Jews in exile, whom Jeremiah encouraged to "pray for the peace of the city." He argues that this is possible because the calling of the people of God is no different from the calling of all humanity. The difference between the human community as a whole and the faith community is a matter of awareness, knowledge, commitment, or celebration, but not of ultimate destiny.[17]

I use these reflections about the role of the church in the world to guide my discussion regarding what the Christian response to the refugees in Kenya should be, and especially toward unearthing the real causes and lasting solutions to the problem. No doubt God's call to Christians to live as exiles and yet to influence the affairs of the nations in which they live will have great value to Christians already experiencing these conditions, both as refugees and hosts to refugees.

In his books, *Church and State in East Africa, Church and State in Nation Building and Human Development,* and *A Quest for Justice: An Autobiography of Bishop Henry Okullu,* the late Kenyan Anglican Bishop Henry Okullu is a pioneer in showing a Christian approach to social and ethical issues from a Kenyan perspective. In his book, *Church and Politics in East Africa,*[18] he speaks very strongly against the view that the church should

15. Yoder, *Body Politics.*
16. Yoder, *For the Nations.*
17. Ibid., 24.
18. Okullu, *Church and Politics in East Africa.*

keep away from politics. He parts ways with the gospel inherited from the missionaries that separates the spiritual from the physical, the secular from the sacred. He says, "Christianity was planted in East Africa along these very lines, emphasizing that the church's duty was solely that of curing the soul. It had nothing to do with the social life of the people and politics was a sin of the first order."[19] Contradicting this notion, he says:

> Men and women are saved and liberated for the bodily as well as the spiritual service of their fellow men. God is not a God of souls only, but of the body as well. There is no department of life which he does not enter. A true Christian is the one who is truly in the world without being of the world, who is truly "holy" and truly "worldly."[20]

In his second book, *Church and State in Nation Building and Human Development*,[21] he continues to argue that the church cannot be divorced from the public sphere. He says:

> I cannot think of theology except in the context of a hungry child crying for food, Ugandan refugees running from Amin's tyranny, a coup d'etat in Ethiopia, a parent in Kenya with two young children who have failed their national examinations, a villager without water and proper sanitation, a beggar in the streets of Nairobi, the forest of buildings in Lagos, hunger and death in the Sahel.[22]

Thus, he advocates strongly for the church to teach people human rights and even encourage external intervention in order to curb the excesses of some of the rulers in Africa. In the call to aim toward the root causes of Africa's problems, he says, "Churches must therefore always be ready and willing to stand up and be counted where the God given liberties are violated by whomsoever. We cannot allow ourselves only to be ambulance services caring for the refugees, without asking about the cause of the casualty."[23]

However, Okullu and previous scholars have not tackled the problem of refugees in a significantly in-depth way, and this is where I hope to make my contribution. I do this by using the pilgrim motif in the book of Hebrews to draw ethical guidelines for how the church should address this issue in Kenya. I chose the book of Hebrews because of its motif of the pilgrim or

19. Ibid., 12.
20. Ibid., 6.
21. Okullu, *Church and State*.
22. Ibid., xiv.
23. Ibid., 140.

alien—which is what a refugee is—an exhortation for Christians to be patient in suffering. It takes seriously the example of Jesus not only as the one who has gone ahead but also as one who provides the way of deliverance. The image of the Christian life as a journey is evident throughout the Bible and also in Christian literature. In the Old Testament, the Israelites are told to care for those who live an alien existence because they, too, once lived as such in Egypt. The book of Hebrews reiterates the pilgrim/alien motif, especially when it refers to the pioneers of faith as aliens and exiles (Heb 11:13–16). I also hope this can be an encouragement to refugees who have been forced to flee their homeland.

Articles, books, and commentaries that have focused on the church as the pilgrim people of God are brought to bear on this topic, and especially the works by Käsemann,[24] Townsend,[25] Lane,[26] deSilva,[27] Jewett,[28] Johnsson,[29] and Nash.[30] Arowele's article, "The Pilgrim People of God (An African Reflection on the Motif of Sojourn in the Epistle to the Hebrews)" is a very insightful article that has attempted to link the pilgrim motif in Hebrews to the African refugee problem. It is a useful backdrop to this study. However, unlike Arowele, I provide a more comprehensive study of the problem of refugees in Kenya and a thorough study of the pilgrim motif in an attempt to provide useful and practical ethical guidelines to address the issue.

One of the practices that I hope the church can adopt in response to the refugee problem in Kenya is hospitality. Christine Pohl[31] has written a thorough and comprehensive work documenting the practice of hospitality within the biblical text and the Christian church over the centuries. She shows how this practice shaped the identity and life of the people of God, both in the Bible and in the history of the church. She also gives concrete suggestions on how this practice can be incorporated not only within the life of the church but also within institutions such as hospitals and hotels offering that service. She also makes mention of how the practice of hospitality can provide needed guidance on how to respond to refugees at various levels. She says:

24. Käsemann, *The Wandering People of God*.
25. Townsend, *Hebrews*.
26. Lane, *Hebrews*.
27. DeSilva, *Perseverance in Gratitude*; similarly, Whitlark, *Enabling Fidelity to God*.
28. Jewett, *Letter to the Pilgrims*.
29. Johnsson, "The Pilgrim Motif in the Book of Hebrews," 239–51.
30. Nash, *The Church as a Pilgrim People*.
31. Pohl, *Making Room*.

> Even if we think only about the needs of refugees, we quickly see the necessity of hospitable responses at various levels. Refugees need a compassionate response from the international community; they also depend on individual nations, communities, churches and families to be willing to make a place for them.[32]

Pohl has not, however, given more detailed guidance as to what this compassionate response toward the refugees would look like. My work fills this gap by showing how the church in Kenya can indeed care for refugees in a hospitable way, providing guidance for international bodies and the church universal.

Gaim Kibreab, in *African Refugees: Reflections on the African Refugee Problem,* also has provided a challenge to the practice of hospitality. He says that, although this practice has been lauded as the ideal solution to the refugee problem, it is often contrary to what has been observed in practice. He says:

> In present-day Africa it is erroneous to assume that the so-called traditional hospitality and assistance will alleviate the plight of refugees. The tradition, like the tribe, has become a museum piece and there is a catalogue of evidence that shows that African refugees are not always given welcome emanating from "tribal" tradition, but they are subjected to harassment, exploitation, etc. and when they receive warm welcome, it was mainly due to the advantages the local population hoped to enjoy as a result of such an influx.[33]

I do agree with Kibreab that to exercise hospitality in the midst of dire poverty is difficult, and it poses many societal challenges. But I hope to encourage the church in Kenya that the accompanying economic hardships should not be used as an excuse to be hostile to refugees. And as I recognize the exemplary way in which the church in Africa has responded hospitably, especially in the face of such insurmountable odds, I hope this would challenge the Western church to do the same or better. I acknowledge the need to pay attention to Kibreab's work, which helps to dispel any romantic notions that being hospitable is a simple task. But I hope my work helps to restore hospitality from being a "museum" piece to the practical daily experience of the Christian community—not only in Kenya but also in the church worldwide, for whom the problem has become acute.

---

32. Ibid., 151.
33. Kibreab, *African Refugees,* 68.

There is a need for cooperation and coordination among all partners that work with refugees. In her book, *Beyond Borders: Refugees, Migrants and Human Rights in the Post-Cold War Era,* Elizabeth Ferris has focused on how NGOs, and especially churches, have provided invaluable assistance in response to the refugee influxes. Her emphasis on the theme of exile is insightful. She says:

> The Bible is full of stories of people in exile. The theme of exodus, of a people wandering in the wilderness, is central to both the Jewish and Christian faiths. Christ's own homelessness and his universal message create a Christian imperative for responding to refugees and exiles. Throughout the Bible, people are called to offer hospitality to strangers and exiles. Moreover, the refugees bring messages for those who choose to hear and have much to teach those who respond to their voices.[34]

This book is a helpful resource as I attempt to show how the church can listen more keenly to refugee voices and can also help other partners to listen better and to make humane changes in the system that provides for accurately addressing the needs of those displaced.

Reflecting on the fifty years of work of the UNHCR, *The State of the World's Refugees: Fifty Years of Humanitarian Action* calls for lasting solutions to this problem. I hope the response to that call, one that attempts to address the root causes of the problem and give some theological answers, will in some way move us toward producing some significant and sustainable solutions to this problem.

Significance of the Study

Africans, and more particularly Kenyans, have a rich heritage in the practice of welcoming strangers and in their understanding of life as pilgrimage. This is demonstrated by the way they have hosted many refugees over the years. The word for stranger and guest is the same in most Kenyan languages.[35] For example, in my language, Nandi, "*toot*" stands both for guest and stranger. In Kiswahili, the word "*mgeni*" is used for both. Adam Chepkwony also demonstrates in his dissertation, "African Religion in the Study of Comparative Religion: A Case Study of the Kipsigis Religious Practices," that among

---

34. Ferris, *Beyond Borders,* xxvii.

35. I have not done extensive research in this field, but inquiries from Bantu speakers who are a majority in Kenya seem to show that the various words are related in root form to the Kiswahili word "mgeni."

the Kipsigis of Kenya, one of the key religious practices was hospitality or *ayebindo*.[36] He shows how this is rooted in the belief in a supreme being, *Asis*, who is considered to be the source of all things. He says, "*Asis* provides all things willingly and freely and mankind is likewise expected to reciprocate the good deeds of *Asis* by sharing with others. To give to others is thus considered a blessing while inhospitality calls for a curse . . . It is therefore a moral obligation to be hospitable to others and even more so to strangers."[37] One way to demonstrate this hospitality was to eat meals outside the house so that those who passed by could be invited to share in the meal. All these examples demonstrate how richly the practice of hospitality permeated the life of the community. However, as I mentioned earlier, this practice has come under modern challenge. So, my goal for this work is to show how this ancient practice can be kept alive.

It is interesting to note that not only is hospitality rooted in the African heritage, it also has a long tradition within the history of the Christian church,[38] as shown by Christine Pohl. In line with that long and rich tradition, this study shows the role the practice of hospitality has played within the Christian church in Kenya, particularly as it is reflected in its response to the refugee problem. It also analyzes and assesses the challenges that have faced the practice in light of the contemporary social, economic, and political situation in Kenya. It also seeks to provide new alternatives and avenues for how this practice can be continued in the midst of the complex refugee and migrant problem facing most countries around the world.

Over the years, the church in Africa has contributed significantly by being a shelter and by providing for the material needs of those who are constantly displaced from their homes. It has also been an advocate and a voice for those who are displaced. However, in interviews[39] I conducted with some Kenyan pastors and Christians, it was evident that they are at a loss as to how to respond to this great need. They are not sure what their role is, especially alongside international bodies like the UNHCR, All Africa Conference Churches (AACC), or the Kenya government. Therefore, my goal is to empower the church in Kenya to go further than it has done so

---

36. Chepkwony, "African Religion in the Study of Comparative Religion," 158.

37. Ibid., 158; cf. Whitlark, *Enabling Fidelity to God*, 1–7.

38. See also Oden, ed., *And You Welcomed Me*. This book takes excerpts from the early church and shows how hospitality played a key role in faith and life.

39. See Appendix B for interview questions. Cf. Kalisha, "Writing the In-between Spaces," 55, regarding "seeing pedagogy" and "writing phenomenologically" in working with refugees; Ngugi, *Baseline Report*, 26–54 on another study regarding the methodology and findings of Kenya refugees. On Ghana's Buduburam refugee camp, see Holzer, *The Concerned Women of Buduburam*.

far, by creating communities whose self-identities are evidenced by their sense of pilgrimage. The church in Kenya needs to form people who will foster hospitality, reconciliation, solidarity, and acceptance across different communities, so that the problem of refugees is tackled from its roots. It is sad that a continent that has seen such great expansion in the growth of Christianity should not also be in a situation to deter the factors that fuel war. I hope this work provides guidelines so that Christians in Africa will influence their communities toward greater democratic governance, equitable sharing of resources, and respect for human rights.

The refugee problem in Africa affects so many people. Efforts from NGOs, governments and international bodies have been commendable. However, durable solutions have not been forthcoming. We find that refugee interventions that were meant to be temporary have stretched on for many years. For example, when Kakuma camp was established in 1992, it was meant only as a temporary shelter. In order to rectify this ongoing colossal problem, efforts from all parties need to be encouraged. Therefore, this work attempts to go beyond the analysis of the problem from a sociological and political perspective. It is an attempt to show how the church in Kenya can help provide lasting solutions to the refugee situation from a spiritual perspective as well. I hope this work leads to some answers to this intractable human crisis that has been very elusive, even to the UNHCR.

Methodology

I combine several methods in approaching this work because the subject matter encompasses many fields. I apply descriptive historical analysis as I survey the causes of the refugee situation, both in the past and in the present. I do an exegetical analysis of Hebrews 11:3–16, as well as a thematic study of the pilgrim motif in the book of Hebrews. But above all, since this study is prescriptive in nature, in analyzing what the role of the church should be in this situation, I apply the four dimensions (perception, reason, passion, and conviction) of the method of concreteness in Christian ethics as developed by Glen Stassen.[40] The strength of this method is that it pays close attention to the perception of the social context that influences the outcome in Christian ethics. It also takes seriously the role of the church in the formation and the living out of the Christian life. This method also helps me to develop concrete values and practices to motivate the church in Kenya to treat the refugees in a wholesome way.

40. Stassen, "Critical Variables in Christian Social Ethics," 57–76. This method has been updated and reworked in Stassen and Gushee, *Kingdom Ethics*, 55–124.

However, this study would not be complete without hearing the lived stories of refugees and Kenyan Christians as they journey and interact in their pilgrimage. Therefore, I incorporate some field study consisting of participant observations from within the refugee churches. I also use recorded interviews of key church leaders, both from among the refugee population and from among the Kenyan Christians. I hope the field study sheds light on how this problem impacts individuals and leads to more compassion and care for those in this dire situation.

2

The Refugee Situation in the Horn of Africa

> It is the refugee who reveals to us the defective society in which we live. The refugee is a mirror through whose suffering we can see the injustices, the oppression and the maltreatment of the powerless by the powerful.
>
> —MELAKU KIFLE, WORLD COUNCIL OF CHURCHES[1]

Introduction

THE REFUGEE SITUATION IN Africa has reached alarming proportions. One report says, "While Africans constitute around 12 percent of the global population, around 28 percent (i.e., 3.2 million) of the world's 11.5 million refugees and just under 50 percent (9.5 million) of the world's 20 million internally displaced persons are to be found in Africa."[2] Also, among the "top 20 refugee-producing countries in the world nine are to be found in Africa. Twenty-five African states have refugee populations in excess of 10,000, while 11 of those countries are currently hosting refugee populations of 100,000 or more."[3] The region that is mostly affected by this problem is the Horn of Africa.[4] It has not only suffered through armed conflict that has produced a huge displacement of populations, but also the situation has been made worse by environmental disasters that have caused

---

1. Evans, "An Analysis of U.N. Refugee Policy," 1.
2. Crisp, "Africa's Refugees," 2.
3. Ibid.
4. The Horn of Africa technically refers to the countries that converge toward the northeastern tip of Africa, bordering the Red Sea. These countries are Sudan, Ethiopia, Eritrea, Djibouti, Somalia, and Kenya. However, in my discussion of the region, I will cover the countries of Uganda, Rwanda and Burundi because there is a close interrelationship among these countries. What happens in one seems to flow into another.

the loss of many lives through famine, hunger, drought, and disease.[5] It is therefore evident that concerted and urgent efforts are required from all fronts to figure out solutions to this human tragedy.

Africa's refugee problem has persisted and escalated because of the reluctance by the international community to address the root causes of the problem. Humanitarian aid has been forthcoming, but this has only served to curb the symptoms for a brief moment before the next outburst begins. The real cause of the problem is the powerful socio-political and economic imbalance between the northern and the southern countries. This was first felt when European interference in Africa began through the transatlantic slave trade. This unequal relationship persisted through the era of colonialism, and it has continued into the present through the powerful presence of multinational corporations.

This chapter traces the history of the refugee problem in the Horn of Africa, through three historical eras: pre-colonial, colonial, and post-independence. I also give a brief overview of the countries that have been ravaged by war, namely Sudan, Ethiopia, Somalia, Uganda, Rwanda, and Burundi. I hope to highlight those factors that have served to widen the gap between the north and south, thereby fueling the refugee problem. My argument is that though the causes that lie behind the refugee problem may seem varied and multifaceted, it is clear that these problems have stemmed from the legacy of European intervention in Africa.

A Historical Survey of the Refugee Problem in Africa

The scholarly study of African's refugee problem has been recent, covering a span of about thirty or forty years. The fascinating thing is that this study has been multidisciplinary. There have been those who have analyzed it from the political angle, discussing issues of ethnicity and relationship to the state. A good example of this is John Markakis in his three books: *Resource Conflict in the Horn of Africa*,[6] the volume he edited with Katsuyoshi Fukui; *Ethnicity and Conflict in the Horn of Africa*;[7] and the book he edited with Mohammed Salih, *Ethnicity and State in Eastern Africa*.[8] Some have attempted a socio-economic assessment of the problem, such

---

5. Elizabeth Ferris has described this situation in the Horn of Africa as "One of the world's largest, most intractable and most complex human tragedies." (Ferris, *Beyond Borders*, 136.) See also, Ngugi, *Baseline Report*, 14–19.
6. Markakis, *Resource Conflict in the Horn of Africa*.
7. Fukui and Markakis, *Ethnicity and Conflict in the Horn of Africa*.
8. Salih and Markakis, *Ethnicity and State in Eastern Africa*.

as Gaim Kibreab in his two books: *African Refugees: Reflections on the African Refugee Problem* and *Refugees and Development: The Case of Eritrea*. Others have focused on the effects of the problem on the host countries, such as Robert F. Gorman, *Coping With Africa's Refugee Burden: A Time for Solutions*[9] and the book edited by Howard Adelman with John Sorenson: *African Refugees: Development and Repatriation*.[10] Two older books give a historical coverage of the refugee problem in Africa in the 1960s and 1970s; one is edited by Sven Hamrell, *Refugee Problems in Africa*,[11] and the other is edited by Hugh C. Brooks and Yassin El-Ayouty, *Refugees South of the Sahara: An African Dilemma*.[12] The books and papers[13] issued by UNHCR are of course very pertinent sources of this material. In this category is the two-volume older work by Louise W. Holborn, *Refugees: A Problem of Our Time, The Work of United Nations High Commissioner for Refugees 1951–1972*.[14] The second volume gives coverage to the problem in Africa through a country-by-country survey. This work is updated in the recent volume edited by Mark Cutts, *The State of the World's Refugees: Fifty Years of Humanitarian Action*.[15] Two attempts have been made to give a theological and ethical response to the problem. Michael Anthony Evans' PhD dissertation, "An Analysis of UN Refugee Policy in the Light of Roman Catholic Social Teaching and the Phenomena Causing Refugees,"[16] shows how Catholic teaching provides a wider framework for response to the refugees, rather than the narrow UN definition. Thadei Mwereke's LST thesis rightly entitled, "The Problem of Refugees in Africa South of the Sahara: The Legacy of Foreign Intervention," argues that Africa's refugee problem can be traced to European interference in Africa.[17] All these sources provide useful information as I analyze the historical context of Africa's refugee problem in three broad phases: pre-colonial, colonial and post-independence. This will not be an exhaustive coverage but an attempt to highlight recurring themes and patterns that have great bearing on refugee influxes in Africa and, more specifically, the Horn of Africa.

9. Gorman, *Coping with Africa's Refugee Burden*.
10. Adelman and Sorenson, *African Refugees*.
11. Hamrell, *Refugee Problems in Africa*.
12. Brooks and El-Ayouty, *Refugees South of the Sahara*.
13. UNHCR produces working papers called "New Issues in Research," which continually bring up to date the problem of refugees in various parts of world, Africa included. An example of this is Working Paper No. 28 by Crisp, "Africa's Refugees."
14. Holborn, *Refugees*.
15. Cutts, *The State of the World's Refugees*.
16. Evans, "An Analysis of U.N. Refugee Policy."
17. Mwereke, "Problem of Refugees in Africa South of the Sahara."

Pre-colonial

The displacement of Africa's population in the pre-colonial era was mainly due to intertribal wars and famine, but this did not create huge influxes of refugee movements as it has in the present day. However, one huge population displacement in this era was due to the slave trade. One author has argued that the refugee phenomenon in Africa can be traced to the European and Arab slave trade and to colonialism.[18] Slave trade was a great loss to Africa in several ways: "It deprived a large number of African societies of many of their best producers, the youngest and the strongest of their men and women; and it did this not spasmodically but continuously over several centuries."[19] The constant raids and disruption of the population meant that stable and viable economies could not be established. In his analysis of this historical period, Hatch laments that the "effects of depopulation were of less significance to African society than other aspects of European economic influence."[20] He argues that when Europe first made contact with Africa, developments of some parts of African society were almost parallel to those in Europe.[21] He mentions socio-economic centers like Timbuktu and Sofala that may be compared to Genoa and Venice.[22] He also cites the flourishing textile industry and the metal craft mining and agriculture in the West African coast. But he says this balance of power was upset when the commodity for trade changed to that of human beings. "Because, for three-hundred years African society right down to the West coast concentrated on collecting and delivering human beings as its major commodity, and receiving in exchange firearms and manufactured goods, metalware, hardware, and cloth from Europe, the whole socio-economic development of African society was stunted."[23] Yet this effect went even deeper because it disrupted African social and political structures. He says:

> In a period of warfare, insecurity, obsession with the human commodity, the power of authority was greatly increased. What had been a rough means of checks and balances between authority and bureaucracy, and the mass of people within each African

---

18. Rodney, *How Europe Underdeveloped Africa*, 157.
19. Davidson, *Africa in History*, 221.
20. Hatch, "Historical Background," 6.
21. Ibid.
22. Hatch, "Historical Background," 6. See also Mazrui, *The African Condition*, 29. He argues that the part of West Africa from which the British took the slaves was the most thickly populated and most economically developed.
23. Hatch, "Historical Background," 7.

society, was perceptively channeled into increasing degrees of authoritarianism.[24]

This shows clearly how deeply slave trade affected the African landscape and brought the imbalance between the northern and southern countries. No wonder Davidson also says, "This was the period in which the foundations for Africa's dependence on Europe, whether economic or political, began to be laid."[25]

Colonial

The colonial era was a time when Africa's social, political, and economic systems were interrupted completely. Hatch comments, "The partition of continent, which had already seen its progress slowed and distorted over the past 300 to 400 years, was the final blow to any possibility that an African society might develop in what we may term "the natural growth from African traditions."[26] Wars of conquest displaced huge populations and the establishment of colonial boundaries divided different groups in an arbitrary manner. "These new frontiers were drawn in Europe, by the Europeans according to European balance of power, often dependent on whose army arrived in the area first. There was no reference to anything African, to the geographic, economic, social and political elements of the African life."[27] The tragic nature of the results of such a venture can be seen in what happened to the Somali people. They were divided into five groups: British East Africa, British Somaliland, Ethiopia, Italian Somaliland, and Djibouti. This might explain the reason there have been many problems in Somalia, for despite the fact that they are a homogeneous group, there has been extensive strife among them. To make it worse, peoples who had no previous relationship were brought together as nations and are now having to try hard to forge unity. One author describes this problem in this way:

> Before 1885 there was no Nigeria, no Congo, no Zambia. The borders of these nations were to a large extent the results of inter-European rivalries and agreements made in Europe. Britain dreamed of a Cape-to-Cairo network of countries, while France struggled for a trans-Saharan control. The result was a series of arbitrary borders, often, straight lines, plotted from a

24. Ibid.
25. Davidson, *Africa in History*, 7.
26. Hatch, "Historical Background," 8.
27. Ibid., 8.

T-square in the meeting rooms of Europe with no correlation to geography.[28]

The evils of colonialism also extended to the destruction of the economy of Africa. Kibreab notes: "After the ending of slave trade, there followed colonial conquest completing the political subjection and the economic subordination of the African people and the relations were particularly tailored to suit the accumulation need of European capitalism."[29] The settlers took most of the land and Africans were forced to work on these lands as cheap labor. In central Kenya, for example, 60,000 acres were taken from Gikuyu families and given to European settlers.[30] Africans also were forced to produce cash or commercial crops but did not have control over the sale or purchase.[31] Furthermore, in order to escape the colonial insistence on forced labor, the expropriation of land, poll taxes, and hut taxes, many people went into exile.[32] In the 1970s, for example, the former Portuguese colonies produced the highest number of refugees.

The wars of independence, when African people sought to rid themselves of colonial rule, began to produce a new wave of refugees in the 1950s and 1960s. Among the first of these was the Algerian War of Independence from 1954 to 1962. This was one of the bloodiest wars in which an estimated 300,000 were killed and more than a million European settlers were forced to flee the country.[33] Thousands of Algerians also fled over the border to Tunisia and Morocco. This led to the involvement of UNHCR in the problems of Africa, where it has been engaged ever since. A resolution of the problems of Algeria was reached with the help of negotiations, and this led to the repatriation of refugees from Morocco and Tunisia in 1962. Following this involvement in the African refugee problems, the UNHCR had to expand its scope by drawing up the UN Refugee Convention in 1967. "The 1967 Protocol Relating to the Status of Refugees" removed the time limitation of "events occurring before 1 January 1951," which had been written into the 1951 UN Refugee Convention's definition of a refugee.[34]

The Algerian situation was not the only one that generated refugees in Africa. There were many other civil wars after the independence of several nations all over Africa. First was the secessionist struggle of the Katanga

28. Brooks and El-Ayouty, *Refugees South of the Sahara*, xii.
29. Kibreab, *African Refugees*, 17.
30. Ross, *Kenya from Within*, 70.
31. Kibreab, *African Refugees*, 17.
32. Ibid., 18.
33. Cutts, *The State of the World's Refugees*, 38.
34. Ibid., 53.

region in the Congo, which also coincided with the events in Rwanda that sent many fleeing into neighboring countries for refuge. Because the international community was preoccupied with the problems that were in the Congo, they did not give adequate attention to the Rwandan situation and this sowed the seeds for the genocide of 1994.[35] Then there was the Biafran war in Nigeria in 1966, in which the eastern part of Nigeria sought to break away from the rest of the country. More than 50,000 Nigerians were displaced and many fled into the neighboring countries. These were helped by the UNHCR. By 1965, there were some 850,000 refugees in Africa and, by the end of the decade, there were approximately one million.[36] This situation caused the Organization for African Unity (OAU) to draft its own regional convention on refugees. The OAU secretariat agreed with UNHCR that the African instrument should be the regional complement to the 1951 Convention. The 1951 Convention needed to be expanded because it had confined the definition of a refugee to the events that had occurred in Europe before 1951. The preamble to the 1969 *OAU Convention Governing the Specific Aspects of Refugee Problems in Africa* recognizes the 1951 Convention as constituting the basic and universal instrument relating to the status of refugees.[37] However, it defines the refugee as someone who has a well-founded fear of persecution according to the 1951 Convention, but it also includes those who have fled as a result of external aggression, foreign occupation or domination, or events disturbing public order in their countries of origin.[38]

Post-Independence

One would have thought that with the attainment of political independence, the problem of refugees would have ceased. It is evident that in the period of the 60s and 70s, some of the countries that gave rise to refugee flows were still in the hands of colonial masters such as South Africa, Angola, Rhodesia, Namibia, Mozambique, and Guinea-Bissau. However, it is also evident that those countries that had gained independence also produced refugees. In this section, I attempt to address the countries of the Horn of Africa—all of which had attained independence by 1960 and yet have been some of the worst in producing refugees that have been hosted in Kenya. This region also has suffered immensely from environmental disasters. Markakis gives

35. Ibid., 49.
36. Ibid., 52.
37. See ibid., 55. Box 2.3 lists in detail the articles of the 1969 OAU Convention.
38. Ibid., 55–57.

a graphic description: "In recent years an enormous toll in lives has been taken by war, famine and disease, as the Four Horsemen of the Apocalypse crisscrossed the region, leaving few communities unscathed."[39] There also has been heavy interest from external forces in this region. One author has argued that "the reason for this interest is not so much for economic as much as geographic strategic importance." He says further:

> The Horn commands the Red Sea and the northwestern quadrant of the Indian Ocean. It looks across the Red Sea and the Gulf of Aden to the Arabian Peninsula. All maritime commerce bound for the Suez Canal and the Mediterranean from Asia, the Persian Gulf and East Africa must transit through the narrow waterway at Bab el Mandeb. This is the reason why both superpowers, as well as Western Europe and Japan, cannot but be keenly interested in the Horn.[40]

The strategic significance of the Horn was perceived in the nineteenth century, when the British, the French, and the Italians began to have footholds in the area. The countries I study from the Horn are Sudan, Somalia, Ethiopia, Uganda, Rwanda, and Burundi. The last three are not strictly considered to be in the Horn, but they have generated many refugees who have fled to Kenya. Although Kenya also has refugees from the Congo, I do not address them because they extend far beyond our geographical scope.

Sudan

Sudan is one of the largest countries in Africa. It shares boundaries with eight nations in Africa. It is a country of diverse climatic conditions, but the North predominantly is dry and with the least rainfall, while the South has a tropical climate and more rainfall and vegetation cover. The population has diverse ethnic and cultural backgrounds, but one superficial division is that residents of the North are mainly of Arab descent and Islamic, while those in the South are mainly Christian and animist. The sad and unfortunate thing is that it has had civil war for the last forty years, with a brief respite between 1972 and 1982. Sudan's history is very interesting in that it is both a refugee-hosting as well as a refugee-producing country. In

---

39. Markakis, *Resource Conflict in the Horn of Africa*, 7. Evans also notes that the Horn of Africa has been the scene of invasions of locusts and other pests, floods, earthquakes and other natural calamities. He cites a source that shows that, from the thirteenth century, Ethiopia has recorded about fifty periods of drought. Evans, "An Analysis of U.N. Refugee Policy," 206.

40. Dougherty, *Horn of Africa*, 2.

the 1980s, before the problem of refugees was very acute in Africa, it was hosting approximately 500,000 refugees from the surrounding nations, mainly from Ethiopia, Eritrea, Uganda, Chad, and the Congo. In his study, Naid Mohammed Suleiman has argued that refugees always have formed the mainstay of Sudan's economy. They have been a constant source of migrant labor over the years.[41]

The causes that fuel the refugee crisis are very complex and enormous. One can only hope to scratch the surface of the problem. Some of the causes seem to have deep roots in the colonial past, but they have been fueled and magnified by the present political and economic policies of the Khartoum government. Sudan came under British rule almost by default, not because the British valued it. The British wanted to protect their interests in Egypt, where the Nile was centered. But even then, the interior of Sudan functioned as a cheap supply of some raw materials like cotton when the Gezira Irrigation Scheme was opened. The South also served as a source of slave labor, a sore spot that remains to the present. One of the main colonial legacies is the rift that has been created between Southern and the Northern Sudan. The British left the South in the hands of missionaries, while the North was predominantly Islamic and thus protected from any missionary influence. It did not seem to enter the minds of the British how the two isolated regions were to function at independence. This rift is the root of the civil war that started in 1956. The South was not satisfied with the arrangement of the British and the Arabs, so a mutiny ensued and it broke away.

The policies and decisions of the subsequent Northern governments continued to estrange the South from coming to the negotiating table. It was not until 1972, when President Numeiry offered the South a form of regional government, that the Addis Ababa agreement was reached. This truce lasted ten years. In these years, the Northern government made promises it did not keep. There were two policies in which it seems to have erred. First, it constructed the Jonglei Dam without anticipating the geographic and economic ramifications for the pastoral and agricultural population.[42] Second, it attempted to avert the building of an oil refinery for the rich petroleum resources that were discovered in the South. The first move by the government in this project was to try to change the boundaries so that these resources would be located in the North rather than in the South. Upon failure to do so, the government decided to construct a pipeline to the Port of Assam, on the Red Sea, in order to transport oil

---

41. Suleiman, "A Historical Basis of Sudanese Refugee Problems," 101.
42. Markakis, *Resource Conflict in the Horn of Africa*, 120.

abroad to be refined. The claim of the government was that it was cheaper to refine the oil outside, rather than within, the country.[43]

All these government attempts to sideline and deplete the South of any development activity have made the Southerners feel that they have no part within the Khartoum government. This was worsened by the enforcement of Islamic law on the population in the South. The disruption of viable economic activity, coupled with the absence of rainfall in 1988, meant that the drought was followed by severe famine. The attempt by relief organizations to reach displaced populations that have been ravaged by continuous war and famine have not been fruitful, mainly due to the actions by government forces to cut off the food supplies. On the other hand, there have been claims that the Sudan People's Liberation Army (SPLA), the group that is fighting for self-government of the South, also has stood in the way of food supplies in order to isolate the areas that are still in the government hands. The result of all this is untold misery and suffering for the innocent people, mainly women and children.

The Western nations are not exempt from contributing to the activities that have generated refugee influxes in Sudan. The US government supported the Islamic government, giving them weapons to ward off the Soviet Union's influence in Ethiopia during the period of the Cold War until 1989, when it was evident that these activities were undermining the rule of law in the country. Some relief organizations have been shown to serve the interests of the US government rather than the people for whom they should have been working. The motive of multinational companies like Chevron also has been evident in their attempt to negotiate for the prospects of oil rather than for peace in Sudan.

All these have happened in the midst of civil unrest in which the SPLA has attempted to get the upper hand in the situation in the South while government forces have made counter moves, sometimes even bombing villages they suspect are hosting rebels of SPLA. This has meant that over 500,000 people have fled the country and several hundred thousand have been internally displaced. Reports are that several people have fled to Khartoum in order to find shelter and relief from the famine and war. Markakis notes that, in the 1990s, there were more than 1.5 million people living in appalling conditions outside the city. The military government performed its routine practice known as *Kasha*, expelling these people forcefully and destroying their temporary shelters.[44]

43. Ibid.
44. Markakis, *Resource Conflict in the Horn of Africa*, 20.

The civil war has been going on for these years without any sign of ceasing. The former President Moi of Kenya chaired six meetings of IGADD (Inter-Governmental Authority on Drought and Development), which was founded in 1988 by six member states: Djibouti, Ethiopia, Kenya, Somalia, Sudan, and Uganda. It was joined by Eritrea in 1993. The IGADD member states have common borders and form one bloc, sharing natural resources and socio-economic concerns.[45] This body has spearheaded talks between the Khartoum government and the SPLA, but not many peace initiatives have been forthcoming. About 80,000 Southern Sudanese people live in the Kakuma refugee camp in Kenya, and several thousand live in the urban areas. Their desire to see an end to this ongoing war was tangibly expressed when they staged a peaceful demonstration during UN Secretary General Kofi Annan's visit to Nairobi in April 2001. The report says that about one hundred tearful Sudanese stood along the UN complex, chanting slogans and waving banners. They hoisted a coffin large enough to carry a child, as a symbol of the killings of tens of thousands of innocent Southern Sudanese children who have died in the civil war.[46] Some of the slogans read, "Kofi, we believe in you. Stop the war in Sudan. We are tired of war. To be a refugee is not just. Multinational interest in the Sudan oil is killing us. Stop slavery in Sudan."[47] The summary of their petition to the UN read:

> We believe that member nations of the United Nations are aware of human rights violations in the Sudan but have not officially advocated for its adherence to Article Twenty-Five (25) of the Geneva Convention. Therefore, we strongly appeal to you and to the UN Security Council to be duty bound and see to it that freedom, justice and human rights are upheld in Sudan.[48]

It is the desire of the people to see that this war is stopped because it has done untold damage to the people and the land. UNHCR efforts are laudable as they have intervened and done very much to relieve the suffering by providing safety and shelter.

For now, it is clear and evident that more than emergency relief is necessary for providing solutions to this intractable problem. The Sudanese churches also have been involved in this region, and later we will see what they have done and what still needs to be done. The problem is too large for only one organization to be involved, so it has to be tackled from all sides, and especially by the church.

45. Ibid., 157.
46. *Refugee Insights*, 7.
47. Ibid.
48. Ibid.

Ethiopia

Ethiopia is a country in the Horn of Africa that has suffered from environmental disasters as well from the ravages of war. Though Ethiopia did not go through the colonial burden, it seems to have made up for this lack through all the upheavals that have engulfed the country since the collapse of the imperial regime in 1974. As early as 1974, there were 663,200 Ethiopian refugees in the Sudan, another 350,000 in Somalia, and an additional 1,500,000 who were internally displaced. The refugee influxes have both internal and external instigation. Early in the nineteenth century, Menelik's expansionist policies of the imperial regime did not please the Eritrean peoples in the North, the Oromo speakers in the South, and the Somali speakers in the East. The repeated government efforts to put down these rebellious forces have been the cause of the refugee influxes. Eventually, when the borders were settled in 1908 in the Tripartite Agreement that Ethiopia made with Britain and France, the boundaries were as arbitrary as those set by the colonial powers, and they laid the ground for the problems that Ethiopia later faced.[49]

Three key internal factors have continuously generated refugees and thus challenged the Ethiopian government. First was her relationship with Eritrea. Eritrea was a colony of Italy between 1890 and 1941, but after the Second World War it came under the protection of the British. Eritrea's future became the focus for the East-West rivalry. On the one hand, the Soviet Union favored the independence of Eritrea, but the US convinced Ethiopia to give it a federal status. This was proposed to the UN General Assembly on December 2, 1950, and it came to force in 1952. Eritrea gained control of its domestic affairs through the executive, legislative, and judicial branches of the government, while Addis Ababa took control of the defense, foreign affairs, finance, and trade.[50] At the same time, Ethiopia signed a treaty with the US to offer them a military naval base (Kagnew Station) situated near Asmara, the provincial capital of Eritrea.[51] The US, in return, provided military and economic assistance worth nearly $450 million to Ethiopia over the next two decades. It was the largest military support that any country had ever received.[52] This enabled Ethiopia to suppress the conquered areas. It

---

49. Evans, "An Analysis of U.N. Refugee Policy," 173. See also Clay and Holcomb, *Politics and the Ethiopian Famine, 1984–1985*, 11, 14. They show how Menelik's conquests and the boundaries that he established did not differ much from those created by the colonial powers. These divisions have contributed to the tension in this region.

50. Evans, "An Analysis of U.N. Refugee Policy," 175.

51. Ibid., 176.

52. Ibid.

also may have sown the seeds of the present-day civil wars and population displacement. In 1962, Haile Selassie blatantly dispensed with any pretense and annexed Eritrea as part of the provinces of Ethiopia.[53] The Eritreans did not receive this well and they intensified their resistance; however, the government fought back with US-supplied military weapons. This sent many Eritrean refugees into Sudan, where they were well received. Eventually, the US supply of weapons ended when Ethiopia fell out of favor with the US government at the end of Haile Selassie's rule. During this period of unrest in Ethiopia, between 1974 and 1977, the Eritrean Liberation Front (ELF) made headway in their resistance against Ethiopia. The only thing that gave power to the Ethiopians was the fact that Mengistu, the head of the revolutionary government, appealed to the Soviet Union to provide arms that continued to fuel this conflict. One report says that the Soviet Union provided military equipment estimated to be five times greater than all US aid delivered to Ethiopia since 1953.[54] Throughout the 1980s, the Eritreans built up their support with the peoples and eventually captured so many areas from the government that they were granted self-rule in 1991.[55] Though reconstruction work has begun, it will take years because the conflict has created so many refugees and displaced peoples.

Ethiopia's conflict with Somalia is another incident that has created refugees. The Ogaden region has always been an issue of contention between Somalia and Ethiopia. The Somalis always have considered it part of their territory and have always looked for an opportunity to reclaim it. In 1977, while Ethiopia was having border clashes with Sudan as a result of Sudan's support of the Eritrean rebels, Somalia took the opportunity to attack Ethiopia and to attempt to regain control over the Ogaden. Mengistu appealed to the Soviet Union and their allies for support. The war lasted until the Ethiopians drove the Somalis back to the border. But this was not before a large refugee influx went into Somalia. This has been a sore spot that has kept coming back. In 1988, there was again some fear that war might begin here. But at the end of the decade, the Ethiopian government was forced to come to the negotiating table.

The wars against Eritrea and Somalia have produced population displacement, but all these were worsened by agricultural reforms. Starting with Haile Sellasie's government, land alienation was an issue in Ethiopia.

53. Ibid., 178.
54. Dougherty, *Horn of Africa*, 32.
55. See Kibreab, *African Refugees*, 49–51. He shows how Eritreans' sense of nationalism and the fight for self-determination gave them the persistence to resist Ethiopia's domination for a long time. In his other book, *Refugees and Development in Africa*, he has shown how Eritrean refugees contributed to the economy of Sudan.

Farmers were forced to give up their parcel of land so that they could be mechanized in the form of modernized agriculture. Self-sufficient peasants were driven into marginal lands, and as they continued to farm these lands in an inappropriate manner it led to land degradation, erosion of topsoil, and deforestation.[56] This meant that when the drought hit the land, people were already very vulnerable because they had nothing to fall back on. Drought and famine befell the country both in 1974 and 1984, and many people suffered and died as a result. The government took advantage of the situation to subdue the discontented population, and to introduce forced villagization and settlements under the pretext that land was needed for capital-intensive agriculture.[57] Before 1984, about 250,000 people were resettled in eighty-seven sites but no single site was self-sufficient in food production, even after ten years.[58] Food incentives promised to the starving population helped the process of resettlement, while at the same time they aided the government to consolidate its control in the countryside.[59]

All these internal factors were compounded by external influences. We have seen earlier that the strategic actions of the superpowers in this region meant that they competed in trying to get their interests protected. With the aid of the military assistance that was given to Ethiopia, first by the US and then the Soviet Union, the government was able to subdue the rebel forces and continue its oppressive policies against the populations without making any political reforms. The process of forced settlements attempted to modernize agriculture through the "Green Revolution,"[60] accelerating the displacement of populations.[61] Some of the Christian relief organizations participated in the forced settlement projects, thinking they were helping to aid the government in tackling the problem of starvation, but in truth they were causing havoc to innocent people. Thus, as Evans argues, the relief organizations and NGOs became the source of the refugee problem that they sought to solve and provide relief for.[62]

---

56. Evans, "An Analysis of U.N. Refugee Policy," 178–79.

57. Ibid., 223–24.

58. Ibid., 212.

59. Ibid., 213–18.

60. These reforms were encouraged by international aid organizations such as the World Bank, USAID, and the FAO. See Evans, "An Analysis of U.N. Refugee Policy," 207 and 209; Nzau, *Transitional Justice*, 22–60, 116–99.

61. Evans, "An Analysis of U.N. Refugee Policy," 207.

62. Ibid., 220. He has argued in great length about how some NGOs were taken in to support these government settlement policies without inquiring about the long-term consequences of these schemes.

Somalia

In 1978, Somalia became a major refugee-hosting country after the Ogaden war. But ten years later, following the war between the government and the Sudan National Movement (SNM), it was a major refugee-producing country. This war produced more than 350,000 refugees. The Somali government armed the Ethiopian refugees to fight against rebel forces and, in turn, the rebel forces invaded refugee camps in an attempt to root out the armed refugees.[63]

A major influx of refugees in Kenya came in 1991 when two movements, the United Somali Congress and the Somali Patriotic Movement, decided to oust Mohammed Siad Barre from the country. But even when he had been ousted, there was no peace. The two movements that had fought to get Barre out of the country continued to fight in order to get the power. The fighting was organized along clan lines and the result has been the breakdown of civil authority, the terrorizing of the civil population, and the fleeing of thousands because of the chaos. Within Mogadishu, the conditions continued to worsen until they drew the attention of the Western media. The US government decided to send a force in 1992 that was meant to provide humanitarian assistance. But Somali warring factions continued their terrorist acts, and the US forces were forced to withdraw in March 1994. Peace initiatives have failed to bring a resolution to these warring factions. In addition to dealing with the war situation, the country has experienced drought and famine, which means that the people are in continuous need of food and protection from wars. Many Somali have been displaced, but they do not find favorable treatment in the host country of Kenya. However, since November 2002, Somali warring forces have been meeting in Eldoret, Kenya to discuss peace initiatives, and they are making progress.

Uganda

At the time of independence, Uganda was the most economically promising and favored country. It was known as the "pearl of Africa." But soon it plunged into civil war as it suffered both political and economic unrest. First, Prime Minister Milton Obote ousted the traditional king, Kabaka Mutesa, and forced him into exile in 1967. In 1971, Obote was ousted from power by the infamous military regime of Idi Amin Dada. This dictator plunged the country into much chaos, starting with the expulsion of all Indians, who were the economic backbone of the Ugandan economy. Then

---

63. Veney, "The Politics of Refugee Relief Operations," 55.

he began to systematically get rid of all political opposition. Church leaders who stood in his way, like Anglican archbishop Janani Luwum, were murdered. Many Ugandans at this time were forced into exile to neighboring countries, especially Kenya. Because most of the Ugandans were well educated, the refugees who came to Kenya fit well into the urban areas and they also filled the gap by being teachers in many Kenyan schools. Most of the refugees were hosted hospitably. The bulk of refugees in Kenya in the 1970s were from Uganda.

Uganda's security situation improved with the coming of Yoweri Museveni to power in 1986. As a result, many were repatriated. Kenya has traditionally been hospitable to refugees from Uganda, but there was a forcible repatriation of 237 Ugandans in 1988, following the outbreak of violence at Thika camp. This was instigated by the arrival of Alice Lakwena, the leader of the Holy Spirit movement, who had been fighting against Museveni's government.[64] This repatriation also was motivated by the fact that the Ugandan government felt that Kenya was hosting their rebels. But the current relations between Kenya and Uganda have improved with the reestablishment of the East African Cooperation, and this has meant the restoration of economic and political ties. Those refugees who chose to continue to live in Kenya are few in number. They come from the northern side of Uganda, where Museveni's government has continued to face opposition from a rebel movement known as the Lord's Resistance Army.

Rwanda

Rwanda has seen much turmoil and displacement of its population for over three decades. The two main communities are the Hutu and the Tutsi.[65] The Hutu are traditionally agriculturalists, while the Tutsi are pastoralists. Even before the advent of European influence, there was a power hierarchy, and a Tutsi dynasty ruled for a long time. But there was a sharing of power through the client-patron relationship of *buhake* that ensured good relations between the two. However, with the advent of colonization, first by the Germans and then by the Belgians, the Tutsi hegemony was

---

64. Ibid., 60.

65. A conversation with a pastor from Rwanda helped me to understand the power relations between these two main groups. He told me that the two communities are not tribes or ethnic groups, because the separation is through class differentiation resulting from livelihood and occupation rather than from language or customs. The pastoralists were the ruling class while the agriculturalists were the servants. These differences were well negotiated before the colonial entry, but the Belgians came and exploited the differences to serve their own ends.

strengthened.⁶⁶ They were given the education and the economic wherewithal so that they could be the ruling class. In 1959, a revolution, assisted by priests, brought the Hutu to power. They made it clear that they would not share power with the Tutsi even when they gained independence. So, in 1962, with the independence of Rwanda, many Tutsi were driven into exile because of massacres by the ruling Hutu. Those Tutsi who were in exile never let go of the longing to return home. They decided that if they did not go peacefully, they would use any means available to them. The UNHCR laments that if a durable solution had been found for the Rwandan refugee situation in 1962 or immediately after that, there would never have been the bloodbath that occurred in 1994.⁶⁷

In summary, the history of this region is told by the UNHCR:

> Ethnic tensions and armed conflict in the Great Lakes region of Central Africa have been the cause of repeated instances of human displacement. The pattern of events in the last 50 years is rooted in a long history of violence, but it is also a history of missed opportunities, on the part of local actors and the international community in general. Failure to pursue just solutions to old grievances has in all too many cases, decades later, led to a recurrence of violence and bloodletting on an even greater scale than before.⁶⁸

The Tutsi who had fled to Uganda and neighboring countries plotted to come back. They joined the National Resistance Army of Yoweri Museveni in order to be trained militarily. Then they formed their own force of resistance from the outside, known as the "Rwandese Patriotic Front" (RPF). In 1990, they attacked Rwanda but, after much guerilla fighting between the government forces and this army, the Arusha Agreement was signed in 1993. The tensions continued to mount however, culminating with the assassination of Burundi president Melchior Ndadaye in 1993.⁶⁹ This also led to mass killings of Tutsi, and then of Hutu. This was worsened even further with the deaths of Presidents Juvenal Habyarimana of Rwanda and Cyprien Ntryamira of Burundi in an unexplained plane crash on April 6, 1994. The Hutu extremists used this event to seize power and to attack the

---

66. Refer to Prunier, *The Rwanda Crisis*, 5–9. He shows how the rift between the Hutu and Tutsi was widened by the propagation of the Hamitic myth that promoted Tutsi superiority.

67. Cutts, *The State of the World's Refugees*, 245.

68. Ibid., 246.

69. Events in the Great Lakes Region are interconnected. Ndadaye's death broke the peace attempts in the region and opened the way for genocide in Rwanda.

Tutsi population in what became known as the Rwanda genocide. The UN force that had been placed in Rwanda was recalled before the genocide occurred, and this meant that the culprits did not have any restraints. But the RPF forces gained control of Kigali, and it was now the turn of the Hutu to flee. Over two million of them went into the same countries to which they had forced the Tutsi to flee thirty years earlier. By late August 1994, the UNHCR estimated that there were about two million refugees in neighboring countries, including some 1.2 million in what was then Zaire,[70] 580,000 in Tanzania, 270,000 in Burundi, and 10,000 in Uganda.[71] Those who fled to Zaire faced two difficulties, especially in the camps: the regrouping of the former forces in the camps (Hutu militia or *interahamwe*) and also the outbreak of cholera, which killed several thousand. The Zairean government at this time was too weak to control military activity in some of the refugee camps. The events in this region between 1994 and 1998 were very confusing, with refugees caught in armed conflict with both the ousted Hutu forces and the rebel Zairean forces. Then several hundred refugees were forced to be repatriated back into Rwanda from Zaire and Tanzania. The efforts of UNHCR in this messy situation are to be lauded. The words of UNHCR confirm the widespread remorse:

> The failure to halt the genocide in Rwanda in 1994, the failure to prevent the militarization of the refugee camps at Goma in 1994–96, and the failure to monitor effectively the dispersal of the Rwanda Hutu refugees driven into Zaire and to protect and assist them, have shown that if civil conflict and forced human displacement are not addressed promptly, the longest term consequences can be catastrophic . . . Only an international response which is better orchestrated and brings in the process of peace keeping and diplomatic pressure into the same frame as humanitarian assistance, can hope to improve the flawed record of the last decade.[72]

The Rwanda genocide shocked many people because this country has been a stronghold of Christianity.[73] Many questioned how a country

---

70. Until 1997, the name for present-day Democratic Republic of Congo was Zaire. I use it here because the events happened during this time period.

71. Ibid.

72. Ibid., 272–73; on the issue of refugee militarization in Africa, see Muggah, ed., *No Refuge*, chapters 1 and 5.

73. Christians have discussed and reflected on where and how the Rwandan church failed to stand against the genocide atrocities. This is seen in literature that is now being produced to help enhance unity and reconciliation among Christians. Among such works are Gatwa's, "Mission and Belgian Colonial Anthropology in Rwanda," 1–20;

that has hosted the East African Revival could become engulfed in such massive atrocities. This startling reality makes it even more urgent for the church to look for lasting solutions to this problem. Recent concern by church organizations and relief agencies has led to work on the restoration of peaceful relations within the area.

Burundi

Burundi is a small country on the northern shores of Lake Tanganyika. It lies just south of the equator and is completely cut off from the sea. It has an area of 10,747 square miles and is dwarfed by its neighbor to the west, the Democratic Republic of the Congo, which is eighty-five times its size.[74] Other bordering countries are Rwanda to the north, and Tanzania to the east and the south. Like Rwanda, it was under Belgian rule until 1961. The population comprises three main groups: the Hutu, who are mainly agriculturists; the Tutsi, who are pastoralists and the rulers; and the Twa, who are hunters and gatherers. Though there have been distinctions between these groups, Burundi has not suffered the same reprisal as Rwanda because social contact and intermarriage between the groups have been encouraged.[75] Burundi did not experience wars early in its independence because of a relatively stable monarchy that gave power to both the Hutu and the Tutsi. But in 1966, the monarchy was dissolved, and Burundi became a republic under a president who was of mixed Hutu and Tutsi parentage. In the years that followed, the Hutu became increasingly sidelined in the ruling regime, until 1972, when they openly revolted, which resulted in massacres of the Hutu.[76] As a result, thousands left the country to the neighboring states, namely Tanzania, Congo, and Rwanda. This was the first major wave of violence that generated several refugees, but since then the country has been relatively stable. The recent spate of violence came after 1993 when the president Melchior Ndadaye was assassinated, and in 1994, with the mysterious crash of the plane carrying the two presidents of Rwanda and Burundi. Burundi has served as a refugee-producing country as well as a host to hundreds of refugees from Rwanda and the Congo.

Aguilar, *The Rwanda Genocide*. See also a recent assessment regarding the failure of Christians to halt the genocide in Gushee, "Remembering Rwanda: Church Failure," 28–31.

74. Holborn, *Refugees*, 985.

75. Ibid., 987. See also Gatwa, "Mission and Belgian Colonial Anthropology in Rwanda," 10.

76. Holborn, *Refugees*, 987.

A Summary of the Causes of the Refugee Problem in Africa

The above analysis has shown that the attempt to determine refugee status for political reasons alone is arbitrary and does not make sense in Africa because social, political, and economic causes all combine, causing refugee influxes and forced migrations. Though each era and each country exhibit a variety of causes, still it is evident that there are similar threads common to all of them. While it is true that conditions that caused refugee influxes during the colonial era and immediately after independence, during the Cold War era, and those in the post-Cold War era are different, one can also say that the same causes manifest themselves differently over the decades, and that there are also patterns that are persistent over the years. It is to these common patterns and threads that we now turn.

External Interference

Thadei Mwereke has quite appropriately entitled her thesis, "The Problem of Refugees in Africa South of the Sahara: The Legacy of Foreign Intervention." Most scholars are in agreement that the key factor that has caused huge displacement of populations in Africa stems from Africa's relations with Europe from the time of the slave trade to the present. The greatest interference came with the creation of the colonial boundaries during the Berlin Conference of 1884. It is clear that boundary making was done without the consultation of the communities that were going to be affected. As mentioned earlier, this has created border disputes all over Africa. For example, Somalia has gone to war with Ethiopia, claiming the Ogaden region, and also has had a grudge with Kenya over territory that they think is their own. As a result of this, one cannot give a clear answer to the question, where do the Somali people belong? Is it in Ethiopia, Kenya, Djibouti, or Somalia? Another similar question is; where do the Rwanda people belong, especially with all the Banyarwanda speakers in the surrounding nations of Congo, Burundi, and Tanzania? The Belgians confined them to the small area they now occupy. This arbitrary division of boundaries not only has divided people but also has placed incompatible groups together, such as those in northern and southern Sudan. These two areas have been at war for the last four decades, trying to resolve whether to be together or apart. All over Africa, this story has been repeated over and over again. The OAU report had this to say: "As a result of the rather arbitrary manner in which the continent of Africa was carved out among the colonial powers, most of the present nation states of Africa consist of a medley of different ethnic, cultural and tribal groups, and very often refugees are the products of clashes between these groups."[77]

Thadei also has shown that external interference has contributed not only to the emergence of conflicts but also to the destruction of traditional values that accompanied the spread of Christianity that came with colonialism. Unlike Thadei, I will not buy wholesale the fact that African life in the past was without its flaws. She has painted an idealized picture of Africa before the colonial intervention that does not tally with reality. However, I still agree with her that the spread of a gospel that did not contextualize its message to its listeners did more harm than good with regard to conflict and refugee-causation. By "contextualize," I mean a positive appreciation of the values within the African culture and, at the same time, a critique of some of the weaknesses and faults within the system—warranted by the homily and paraenesis characters of the book of Hebrews.[78] It is equally true that there were already unjust practices within the African traditional societies that were exploited by the coming of colonialism. An example of this is the feudalistic hierarchical system that favored one ruling group over another and perpetuated an entrenchment of a superior attitude among some people while relegating others to the subservient role. This was common in countries that had monarchies prior to colonial rule. Among these were countries such as Rwanda, Burundi, Uganda, and Ethiopia, to mention a few. There were also animosities between the communities, even before the coming of Christianity, that were not addressed. At independence, artificial communities then had to come together and try to forge unity. This has been a great challenge in most African countries because they did not exist as countries prior to this time. It is a wonder that there is some measure of unity now. The Organization of African Unity (OAU) decided not to interfere with the boundaries, as this would have created more chaos. Still, the lack of clarity on boundaries has entrenched a legacy of war on the continent.

This external interference did not cease with the coming of independence. Kinoti echoes what many African scholars assess when he says:

> . . . the colonial powers never really surrendered power to the Africans at independence: all they did was to adopt a more subtle form of colonialism, namely neo-colonialism, which strongly

---

77. Aderanti, "The Dimension of the Refugee Problem in Africa," 24–25, citing the Organization of African Unity, *Final Report*, 10.

78. See Berquist, "Critical Spatiality and the Book of Hebrews," 181–93; Aitken, "The Body of Jesus Outside the Eternal City," 193–237; Cockerill, *Epistle to the Hebrews*, 11–40.

linked the political interests of Africa's ruling classes with those of the ruling classes in the West.[79]

It was continued with the Cold War era as African countries again were divided along external interests of the East and West bloc countries. These external countries supplied weapons that empowered dictators who served their own interests. They did not care for the needs of their people but were concerned about amassing personal wealth.

Human Rights Violations and a Legacy of Bad Leadership

It is evident that, even after independence, most African leaders did not have a good record of accountable, transparent, fair and just governments. There was hardly any preparation for democratic governance, and that did not help the newly independent countries in their search for unity. The political systems were too fragile and new, and they yielded to the pressure and creation of one-party systems that were divided along ethnic lines. Those countries that still had colonial domination caused refugee influxes to the newly independent countries, thus putting even more strain upon the fragile economies. With the collapse of the Cold War, African countries were caught in the throes of more conflicts as the dictators and their supporters were overthrown in the 1990s. These upheavals produced the largest influxes of refugees of all time. The collapse of these governments was accompanied by the downfall of greedy, authoritarian leaders who had collaborated with external powers in order to enrich themselves at the expense of their subjects. Every region of Africa had its share of dictators, such as Bokassa, Mobutu, and Siad Barre. Such leaders not only accelerated the deterioration of the externally driven export economies, which were in themselves a legacy of colonialism, but also they benefited from it. The injustice of the world economy is that it benefits the countries of the North while destroying the economies of Africa. No wonder there is competition for the scarce resources through the intense wagers for political power and influence.[80] In the post-Cold War era, economic injustice has continued through the introduction of the Structural Adjustment Programs (SAPs) instituted by the IMF and the World Bank, which have continued to further impoverish nations already ravaged by war.[81]

79. See Kinoti, *Hope for Africa*, 29.

80. Bayart has appropriately named the search for power for personal enrichment in Africa as "The politics of the belly." His analysis of Africa's political systems after independence is very deep and insightful. See Bayart, *The State of Africa*, xvii. Kimuyu calls it the "grab" culture. See also Kimuyu, "A Christian Response to the Economic Crisis in Africa," 111.

81. See Olofin, "The African Economic Crisis," 63–103.

Environmental Disasters

These countries that were already vulnerable due to wars were not spared the ravages of environmental disasters. In the Horn of Africa, the countries that have been affected by war have also suffered through famine and drought. Furthermore, the failure to grow crops was due to the lack of peace among the people; peacetime would have given incentive for a thriving agriculture. The focus on external trade was not wise because food crops were the ones affected whenever drought hit, and not the huge plantations of cash crops.[82] The irony of environmental tragedy culminated most recently in the Kivu area, in Congo, when a volcano erupted over huge camps of refugees, who had to be relocated. This shows how various factors have combined to create or worsen the plight of refugees. These factors are all interrelated, and it is naïve to think that one factor can be isolated over against the other in the interest of determining refugee status.

Conclusion

It is clear from this overview that Africa's refugee problem stems from the unjust international economic system that continues to put Africa at a disadvantage in its relationship with Western countries. The exploitation of Africa's resources started with the slave trade and it has continued through the multinational corporations of the present. Violation of human rights and the legacy of bad leadership in African countries have contributed to the crisis that sends Africa's peoples across borders for refuge. This bitter consequence is evident in the words of an African proverb, "The elephants have fought and the grass has suffered." Truth is, those who suffer mainly in these wars are women, children, and elderly people. What we need now are creative interventions that will serve to stem the tide of vicious cycle of violence, death, displacement of populations, and even more violence.

In the next chapter, I assess solutions and responses offered by the UNHCR, the implementing partners, and the asylum countries. To echo the sentiments of Jeremiah, the Old Testament prophet, have they provided the right "balm" for the healing of my people?

---

82. In Kenya, only three percent is arable land, and almost half of this is devoted to cash crops such as tea and coffee. When drought hits, these cash-crop plantations are not affected, and yet people cannot eat them as food.

3

Responses to the Refugee Problem

> Humanitarian assistance has been used as a fig leaf hiding a lack of political will to address the root cause of conflict.[1]
>
> —Kofi Annan, UN Secretary-General

Introduction

IN THIS CHAPTER, WE explore how the refugee problem has been handled both by the directly receiving asylum countries and also by the international community, best represented by the UNHCR but including the cooperating partners. I evaluate which of these efforts have been effective as well as those that have been counter-productive, so that we can work toward long-lasting solutions. It is evident that this is needed because the problem has gone from bad to worse and there is an urgent concern from all sectors as to how these vicious cycles of violence, bloodshed, and displacement of populations can be broken. I believe that the problem is not just an African problem; instead, as has already been seen, the protection of strategic interests by the superpowers in the Horn of Africa has played into the problems of the individual countries, thus aggravating the situation. First, I begin with the host countries and then deal with external help.

Second, I assess the response to this problem both from the international community and from the countries of asylum. I inquire whether this has helped to alleviate the situation or made it worse. There is so much humanitarian effort that has gone into trying to respond to the problem, but what has been the result? What are alternative measures that are being tried now?

---

1. Wilkinson, "Quote Unquote," 24.

The Host Countries

The countries that have borne the burden of the refugee problem have been those immediately bordering the scenes of war and violence. Most countries in Africa have either been affected by war or have been recipients of the refugees. Some countries like Sudan, Uganda, Somalia, the Congo, and Ethiopia have been both refugee-generating as well as refugee-hosting countries. It also is important to note that most of the refugees in Africa are rural populations. There are also refugees who are educated and can fit into an urban setting, but these are in the minority. When war, fear of political reprisals, and drought occur, the first reaction is to move people to the next country, primarily to those that are somehow related to them on the other side of the border. We now look at different ways host countries have received refugees.

Hospitality of the Host Countries

Most of the host countries in Africa are among the poorest nations of the world, but they are the ones that have opened the doors to these refugees. Researchers have attributed this to the African concept of hospitality because nothing else can explain how huge populations are able to coexist with one another with barely anything to eat. African hospitality is intrinsic to African culture and is evident in the way most African languages use the same word for stranger and guest.[2] Commenting in regard to the refugee phenomenon, a UNHCR report notes:

> African hospitality is not simply an attitude: at the local level it is the matter of people with very little, sometimes pitifully little, sharing what they have with many others. At the governmental level, the hosts have played a leading role in emergency aid and have helped to provide food and medication including hospitalization, as well as transport to move food supplies and medicines from international sources. The already thinly spread government services have been shared as well; and in country after country, land has been given freely to the refugees for their settlement. In relation to resources, the spontaneous hospitality

---

2. In my language, "*Nandi*," the word for "guest" and "stranger" is *toot*. A child born when strangers/guests are around is named *kiptoo* if it's a boy or *cheptoo* if it's a girl. Various languages follow the same pattern of using the same word to mean two "different" things. The Kamba use the word *mueni*; Gikuyu the word *mugeni*; Giriama the word *mjeni*; Luo the word *wendo*. Thanks to Rebecca Mueni Musakwa, who was appropriately named *Mueni* because strangers were in her home at her birth, for supplying the words for the other languages I did not know.

shown to refugees in Africa goes far beyond that in previous refugee situations.³

Gaim Kibreab, however, has cautioned that we should not put much capital on the concept of hospitality as the panacea for the African refugee problem. He has shown that hospitality is indeed waning, especially where the resources are scarce. He says:

> In present-day Africa it is erroneous to assume that the so-called traditional hospitality and assistance will alleviate the plight of refugees. The tradition, like the tribe, has become a museum piece and there is a catalogue of evidence that shows that African refugees are not always given welcome emanating from the tribal tradition, but are subject to harassment, exploitation, etc. and when they receive a warm welcome, it was mainly due to the advantages the local population hoped to enjoy as a result of such an influx.⁴

Kibreab affirms the fact that the concept of openness to strangers is deeply rooted in the culture of African peoples. But he offers a word of caution, emphasizing that if African populations continue in poverty, they will not be able to practice this hospitality in an effective manner. He further states:

> Most of the host countries are among the least developed countries in the world with a very low rate of economic growth. These countries and especially their rural areas are characterized by an abject poverty and no matter how generous the rural people intend to be they have nothing more to offer than their hospitality—and hospitality in a state of wretchedness is like a lamp without electricity, and a myth to say the least.⁵

Mazrui also warns us that "African hospitality" was a concept that was abused through colonialism. He further shows how such a rich practice eventually became perverted, so that instead of serving the good of both the host and the guest it deteriorated into parasitism and exploitation. He says:

> Before colonization indigenous cultures had their own checks and balances between ethnic solidarity and hospitality on one side and the tendency toward parasitism, on the other. Then came colonialism. By its very nature colonial rule was a supreme form of economic parasitism—Europeans living off others. No longer were the Africans able to obey traditional

3. Holborn, *Refugees*, Vol. 1:843.
4. Kibreab, *African Refugees*, 68.
5. Ibid, 69.

wisdom in the Swahili adage, "*Mgeni siku ya pili, siku ya tatu mpe jembe*" ("treat your guest as a guest for two days; but on the third day give him a hoe.") The colonial white man was at best an uninvited guest in Africa, but alas, his African hosts were in no position to force a hoe on him.[6]

No doubt, the root of this generosity toward refugees has been the attitude of openness toward the stranger within the African culture. Indeed, this explains what worked in the early reception of refugees into the host countries. They were integrated into the rural communities that they found themselves in. Tanzania has been an exemplary model in this type of reception. However, with the above warnings in mind, we need to acknowledge and address the socio-economic challenges that this practice is contending with right now and provide an alternative means of reviving it. I believe that we should not give in to despair and think that nothing can be done about it. Since hospitality is a central virtue within the Christian faith, we will examine later how this can be strengthened and continued within the church as part of the ethic for refugees.

Integration within the Local Communities

In the early years of the refugee problem in Africa, i.e., in the 1960s and the 1970s, most refugees settled among the rural communities. This happened in Tanzania, Sudan, Congo, and Malawi, and was possible because the numbers had not escalated at that time. It also was possible because some of the neighboring people shared the same culture and language across the border but had been separated arbitrarily by colonial boundaries. The settling happened not far from the border of the countries they had come from and also in the areas where there were large tracts of land the local population was not using. So, newcomers could easily inhabit this land. This was quite an ideal situation because the external bodies only came in at the initial stage to help refugees erect shelters and to give them the basic tools necessary to function in life. And once this was done, the refugees continued a normal life of subsistence. However, presently this has not been the case as the numbers of refugees has increased, leading to hostilities between local communities and refugees because of the competition for scarce resources of land or water. The integration of refugees with local communities also happened because the situation was thought to be short-term. But the many wars in this region has resulted in a constant influx of refugee populations, so another solution

---

6. Mazrui, *The Africans*, 234–35. See also Healy, *Hebrews*, 98 on Christ's solidarity with the weak.

has to be sought. A UNHCR report notes, "By 1965 there were some 850,000 refugees in Africa. Although many of those who fled during the independent struggles were able to return within a relatively short period, new conflicts created further outflows, and by the end of the decade, the number of refugees in Africa had risen to around one million."[7]

Foreseeing the problem of refugees settling near the border, the OAU drafted the 1969 Convention with an important clause stating that the refugees should not settle near the borders so that they could not be used as rebel forces.[8] It also clearly states that the refugee settlement should not be a training ground in order to attack the country they came from. But this has been the issue that the UNHCR has had to wrestle with in almost all refugee settlements. The trouble that has fueled the situation in the Great Lakes region has been the Rwandan refugees, who fled and have been constantly armed across the border. They have repeatedly made attacks on the government forces across the border, and this has not been safe for other refugees.[9] UNHCR has had to take serious steps in order to disarm these refugees. We now look at what UNHCR and other cooperating bodies have done in order to reach some viable solutions for the problems that have occurred due to refugee settlements.

UNHCR

The United Nations High Commission for Refugees (UNHCR) is the international body that deals with refugees worldwide. The help for refugees in rural Africa has been primarily the responsibility of the countries of asylum with the assistance of the UNHCR. Their involvement started in the 1960s with the Algerian War of Independence, followed by the involvement of the Great Lakes region in the Congo crisis.[10] With the formulation of the 1967 Protocol, the extension of the 1951 mandate for refugees officially included refugees from Africa. The OAU mandate for the refugees served to strengthen these ties. UNHCR is guided by the 1951 Convention on the definition of a refugee:

> The term "refugee" shall apply to any person who as a result of events occurring before January 1951 and owing to the

---

7. Cutts, *The State of the World's Refugees*, 52.
8. *OAU Convention*, Article II, No. 6. See Cutts, *The State of the World's Refugees*, 55.
9. Cutts, *The State of the World's Refugees*, 49. These armed groups are known as the "*inyenzi*" (the cockroaches) made repeated attacks on Rwanda.
10. Ibid., 44–47.

well-founded fear of being persecuted for reasons of race, religion, nationality, membership of a particular social group or political opinion, is outside the country of his [sic] nationality and is unable or owing to such fear, is unwilling to avail himself of the protection of that country; or who not having nationality and being outside the country of his former habitual residence as a result of such events, is unable or, owing to such fear, is unwilling to return to it.[11]

This definition has been criticized by Michael Anthony Evans in his dissertation.[12] His main critique is that, even though many reasons are recognized for the flight of a person, "fear of persecution" is the only condition that would give a person acceptance as a refugee. So, he says:

> No mention, of course, is made of the fear that results from war, civil war or strife (including religious or tribal warfare), or fear from starvation or pestilence. No mention is made of "fear" stemming from economic devastation caused by government genocidal policies, or international trade embargoes, or economic development schemes. Only fear of persecution qualifies one for refugee status.[13]

Most African researchers also argue that this definition is too narrow to address the problems that affect refugees in Africa.[14]

However, it is difficult for the UNHCR to take into consideration all these factors because it is constrained by its mandate and guidelines. For example, the UNHCR cannot go looking for refugees until they have become refugees and the organization is thereby called upon to offer assistance. Due to the large numbers of people in Africa, it was impractical to establish on an individual basis whether one had a well-founded fear of persecution. So UNHCR had to resort to a *prima facie* group determination of refugee status by which, in the light of circumstances that led to the departure from the country of origin, refugees could be identified on a group basis.[15] Though

11. UN 1951 Convention.
12. Evans, "An Analysis of U.N. Refugee Policy," 48.
13. Ibid.
14. See Obeng, "Religious Dimensions of Refugee Suffering," 122–23.
15. Cutts, *The State of the World's Refugees*, 53. See also Hyndman and Nylund, "UNHCR and the Status of *Prima Facie* Refugees in Kenya," 29–39. She argues that refugees suffer human-rights abuses in Kenya because of the *prima facie* status. They are only granted temporary asylum but this "temporary" situation has now lasted for a number of years. In the meantime, their rights are being abused in Kenya. She says, "We argue that the suspension of certain human rights, such as the freedom of movement, the right to gainful employment, and the right to education cannot continue indefinitely."

UNHCR assisted refugees in Africa in the early 1960s, it did so using its "good offices" and not because they were officially recognized as refugees.[16] However, in 1967, the convention was extended to remove the time limit of 1951, so African refugees could be included in this category. They also accepted the OAU Convention that provides guidelines regarding refugees from Africa. Though the UNHCR performs several functions, its chief ones regarding refugees are "protection and durable solutions,"[17] which are stated in the first chapter of paragraph 1 on UNHCR:

> The United Nations High Commissioner for Refugee acting under the authority of the General Assembly shall assume the function of providing international protection, under the auspice of United Nations, to refugees who shall fall within the scope of the present statute and seeking permanent solutions for the problems of refugees.[18]

The objectives of UNHCR are the following:

1. Stabilization of the refugee situation.
2. Prioritization to border sites by accelerating cross-border programs to bring relief to people in their place of origin or in the immediate vicinity of the camps.
3. Voluntary repatriation where possible.
4. Promotion of resettlement in third countries when the cases are eligible.[19]

Organization of African Unity (OAU)

After its inception in 1963, OAU (now known as the African Union) rose to meet the challenge of the refugee problem in Africa. At that time, most of the refugees were from countries still under colonial rule. In 1996, it reaffirmed its desire to give all possible assistance to refugees from any member states on humanitarian and fraternal bases. It was an active participant in the first major international conference on the Legal, Social and Economic Aspects of the African Refugee Problem, held in Addis Ababa in 1967. Then, because of the limitation on the 1951 UN Convention, it produced the Convention

---

16. Cutts, *The State of the World's Refugees*, 53.
17. Okoro, "Africa's Refugee Problem," 216.
18. Ibid., 216. See also UNHCR, *Information Bulletin*, 5.
19. Ibid.

Governing the Specific Aspects of the Refugee Problems in Africa. This was adopted by heads of states and governments and promulgated in 1974. It expands the UN definition of the term "refugee" in this way:

> The term "refugee" shall also apply to every person who owing to external aggression, occupation, foreign domination or events seriously disturbing public order in either part or whole of his country of origin or nationality, is compelled to leave his place of habitual residence in order to seek refuge in another place outside his country of origin or nationality.[20]

It also states clearly that the granting of asylum is a humanitarian act and shall not be regarded as an unfriendly act by any member state.[21] It expands on the guarantee of *non-refoulement* contained in the 1951 Convention, "that no person should be compulsorily or forcibly returned by an African state to the territory he has left and where his physical integrity or liberty would be threatened."[22] The OAU convention also prohibits acts of subversion by refugees against the territory they have left, and exempts criminals from the protection of refugee status.[23] The provision also requires that refugees settle at a reasonable distance from the frontier of their country of origin.[24] UNHCR works with cooperating partners, both church-based and secular. Examples of church-based partners include World Vision International (WVI), Lutheran World Federation (LWF), International Rescue Committee (IRC), Catholic Relief Services (CRS), and so on.

Church-Related Organizations

When the refugee problem became acute in Africa, there were no indigenous non-governmental organizations to respond to the problem as in other countries. The only African institution that has been concerned with

---

20. See Cutts, *The State of the World's Refugees*, 55. *OAU Convention*, Article 1(2). See also El-Ayouty, "The O.A.U. Convention Governing," Appendix V (271–78). Though the OAU definition of a refugee is broader than that of UNHCR, Obeng has noted that this is still narrow because it does not mention the violation of human rights as a cause of refugee status. He argues that the signatories of the treaty may have been responsible for violation of human rights in their countries. See Obeng, "Religious Dimensions of Refugee Suffering," 123.

21. Ibid. *OAU Convention*, Article II (2).

22. Cutts, *The State of the World's Refugees*, 57.

23. Ibid., 55. Article III (1 & 2).

24. Ibid. Article II (6).

the problem of African refugees is the church.[25] This mainly comprises the All Africa Conference of Churches (AACC), as well as a variety of Roman Catholic Organizations. The other organizations are from Europe, such as Lutheran World Federation, Church World Service, Lutheran World Service, Catholic Relief Services, and the World Council of Churches. The major and most active organization in spearheading the refugee programs has been AACC, with the support of the World Council of Churches. In 1965, it launched the Ecumenical Programs for Emergency Action in Africa (EPEAA).[26] The aim was to meet the basic needs of refugees by providing them initially with shelter, food, clothing, and medical care. Their goal also was to assist the local churches in the villages, towns, and cities to provide guidance, pastoral counseling, education and training, and other services to help the refugees help themselves.[27] The eventual aim of the program was to integrate refugees into the country of asylum. In order to achieve these goals, they provided churches with financial assistance to carry out these responsibilities.

Lutheran World Federation (LWF)[28] is another organization that performs invaluable service to the refugees. It operates in individual country programs, under names such as Tanganyika Christian Service or Zambia Christian Refugee Service.[29] These services are operated on behalf of the World Council of Churches and with the consultation of the Christian Councils of the Churches of the countries where the services are rendered. In the decade of the 1980s and 1990s, these services by the church organizations and UNCHR have been through planned settlements in the countries of asylum.

---

25. It is a commendable thing that this can be said about the church right from the start of the refugee problem. See also Pirouet, "The Churches and Refugees in Africa," 82–92. She commends the efforts made by the churches in responding to the refugee, while at the same time analyzing the challenges that such bodies like the NCCK faced in the midst of political loyalties. She commends the efforts by individuals like Bishop Kivengere, who also led the African Evangelistic Enterprise (AEE) to pay attention to social justice as opposed to their previous focus only on evangelism. However, as will be seen later, the involvement of churches seems to have remained at the large organization level and not on the local church and grassroots level. Eriksson et al., *An Analysing Account of the Conference*, 188.

26. See Ankrah, "The Stranger Within the Gates," 125.

27. This may have been done in the 70s and 80s, but my research shows that most of the pastors in Kenya currently need this guidance.

28. I will give more information regarding the work of Lutheran World Federation (LWF) in Kakuma, Kenya in the next chapter.

29. Eriksson et al., *An Analysing Account of the Conference*, 188.

The Refugee Settlements

In the early years of the refugee problem, refugees settled spontaneously among their neighbors and did not call attention to themselves. However, due to the increased influx of refugees and the danger that settlements near the border posed for the countries of asylum, the UNHCR, in cooperation with the host countries, decided to build refugee settlements a little farther away from the border. These settlements have unique problems of their own. They were not established with a long-term intention for the future. Furthermore, UNHCR goals for refugees changed, now that it was not possible to integrate people into communities across the border. Initially, there was hope that settlements would be centers for voluntary repatriation to the countries of origin, but more recently, there have been many discussions regarding the viability of these settlements. The general consensus seems to be that those who settle spontaneously are likely to be self-reliant sooner than those in planned settlements. The main value of planned settlements is that they provide avenues for the host governments to keep track of those refugees who are within the country. Most of these settlements were meant to be temporary, but certain camps have continued in existence for a longer time than they were meant to be because no other solutions are in sight. Kakuma and Dadaab in Kenya have overstayed their limit; they have been in existence for ten years.[30]

Problems Faced by the Settlements

Rogge argues that camps are the least desirable of the options because, "they remain dependent and non-productive. They create environments of discontent and despair and in the long term become major political thorns."[31] Another recent report says, "Today, refugee camps are often prison-like places that no one wants to live in and those who can, escape."[32]

Environmental Degradation

The places in which these settlements are established are not the most habitable parts of the countries. Kenya situates them in peripheral areas so that they do not interfere with the local population. Therefore, they

---

30. Refer to Hyndman and Nylund, "UNHCR and the Status of *Prima Facie* Refugees in Kenya," 33. She asks "How temporary is temporary?"
31. Rogge, "Africans' Displaced Population," 72.
32. Harrell-Bond, "What are Camps Good for?"

need daily provisions like firewood and pasture for their herds. Hence, the land has been overused and rendered almost valueless. Critics have indicated that the Mozambican refugees who had been in Malawi left the place in a very devastated condition. Disease thrives in the ill-prepared environment of the settlements. In 1994 to 1995, after the genocide problem in Rwanda, the refugees that fled into the Kivu area suffered from the outbreak of cholera because of the poor conditions of the camps.[33] The lack of firewood causes constant friction with the local population in Kakuma and Dadaab.[34] The Turkana have complained that the refugees indiscriminately cut trees; they do not heed the government slogan of "cut one plant two," thus causing deforestation.[35]

Security

The problem of the lack of security has threatened the quality of people's lives, especially in the camps near the border areas. Host countries do not want to endanger the lives of their citizens by admitting refugees from a neighboring country at war. The refugee influx has threatened to cause some host countries to go to war themselves. In the Great Lakes region, Rwanda refugees returning from Uganda brought an end to the Hutu government. The huge influx of refugees in the eastern region of the Congo worsened the deteriorating conditions of Mobutu's government. With the failing economic conditions in the host countries, the refugees are always blamed for being threatening, especially if they come armed.[36] This becomes a problem, not only for the host country but also for the security of the refugees. The two refugee camps in Kenya are situated in highly volatile areas characterized by banditry, cattle theft, and violent clashes between the Kenya army and the local armed groups.[37] It is no wonder that the complaint to the Kenya government is that they do not provide enough security.

---

33. See Kibreab, *African Refugees,* 90. He notes that in refugee situations, contagious diseases may spread from the refugees to the local population and vice versa.

34. *Daily Nation,* "How Somali Refugees are Ruining the Environment," 16 September, 1992. See also Okoro, "Africa's Refugee Problem," 135–37, Veney, "The Politics of Refugee Relief Operations," 103; Mwangi, "Securitisation, non-refoulement," 1318–34.

35. Aukot, "'It is Better to Be a Refugee Than a Turkana.'"

36. See, "Illegal Arms Pose Threat to Everyone."

37. See Crisp, "Africa's Refugees," 19. He has documented the various sources of insecurity around the refugee camps.

Relations with the Host Country

The refugees are looked upon as those who impose themselves upon the country, taking over jobs or pasturelands. This creates hostility between local inhabitants and the refugees. Veney argues that a consensus in the literature shows that the local population's hospitality decreases as the economic conditions of the country worsen. She says, "If the economic conditions are poor at the time of the refugees' arrival, assimilation is more likely to be difficult or non-existent."[38] When the refugee settlements are distinct from the habitation of the local population, the local people may view them as having special privilege. In 1998, when there was famine in the northern part of Kenya, it was infuriating for the passersby to see the UN trucks on their way to the refugee camps, while leaving the local population suffering.[39] Such images do not endear the local population to the refugees. Integrated programs of development that pay attention to the host community have, however, helped to alleviate this discrepancy.[40] We will see later how such efforts were to be coordinated through the work of the International Conference on Assistance for Refugees in Africa (ICARA).

Dwindling Support from the Donor Nations

Aid for refugees in rural Africa has been mainly the responsibility of the countries of asylum, with the assistance of the UNHCR. Both have rendered exemplary services in these past years by helping the refugees to resettle. But "donor fatigue" has arisen, especially when there seems to be no end in sight to the refugee problem. Those services that have offered more than emergency relief and aid to the refugees and the neighboring population have been more successful. When the UNHCR, the partners, and the host countries have gone beyond just mere assistance, there have been lasting solutions. The ILO/UNHCR mission report notes: "The need to apply the concept of 'refugee affected areas' requires viewing the refugee problem

---

38. Veney, "The Politics of Refugee Relief Operations," 14.

39. See, Aukot, "'It is Better to Be a Refugee Than a Turkana,'" 75. He shows how humanitarian aid focused only on the refugee population neglecting the host people, the Turkana. He has graphically highlighted other factors that have brought a rift between the host community and the refugees.

40. See Kibreab, *African Refugees*, 95. He supports his argument with the example of the Sudanese refugees, who settled among the Madi in Zaire. The policy of integrating the local population not only in the distribution of land but also in all the amenities such as tools, seeds, schooling, health services, extension services was so attractive to the local population that had started coming back from exile.

within the wider perspective of the national economy. Projects will be successful if they cater for the national and the refugees alike."[41]

We can now examine two examples that have been successful in integrating refugees and making them part of the local development program.

Examples of Successful Settlements

Though the picture of response to the refugee situation in East Africa has not been encouraging, there are some success stories. The Tanzania story shows how planned settlement among local inhabitants promotes peaceful coexistence. While the story of Sudan focuses on the income-generating activities, which alleviates the need for sustainable livelihood for both the hosts and the refugees.

Tanzania

Tanzania has had one of the longest experiences with refugees. This country also has been successful in integrating refugees with the local population as well as in helping them become self-reliant. The first wave of refugees had escaped from Mozambique because of the Portuguese programs to contain the guerilla warfare by creating forced settlements. By the 1970s, about 60,000 Mozambiquans had settled in five villages in Southern Tanzania.[42] Being of the Makonde ethnic group, they fitted in well with their relatives from across the border. Before long, they had achieved self-reliance in food production based on maize, rice, cassava, and poultry. They also grew cash crops like cashew nuts, sesame, and ground nuts.[43] With the help of UNHCR, they built two schools and a health center. The success of this program is proven by the fact that when Mozambique gained independence in 1975, about 20,000 people, one third of the population, decided not to repatriate but to remain as "alien residents."[44]

A similar success is observed with the settlement of Rwandan refugees in the northeastern part of Tanzania. Those who settled spontaneously and those who went into the government schemes achieved self-sufficiency to the extent that 36,000 Rwandans embraced Tanzanian citizenship.[45] Initially,

41. UNHCR/ILO Income Generating Activities for Refugees in the Sudan, 3. Quoted in Kibreab, *African Refugees*, 113. See also Rogge, "Africa's Displaced Population," 68.
42. Rogge, "Africa's Displaced Population," 76.
43. Ibid.
44. Ibid.
45. Ibid. On the issue of refugee self-sufficiency and economic contribution, see the

the refugees were able to settle spontaneously in Kigoma District, which is sparsely populated. They managed to control the tsetse fly problem so that they could achieve some farming. But as the numbers grew, it became evident that they needed government intervention. Thus, the Ulyankulu and Katumba settlements were founded under a tripartite agreement, between the government of Tanzania, the Tanzania Christian Refugee Service, and UNHCR, and became the largest refugee settlements in Tanzania.[46] The government of Tanzania set aside 1,000 square kilometers at Katumba and 550 square kilometers at Ulyankulu for the development of these schemes.[47] The development was carried out in the spirit of Tanzania's founding principles of *Ujamaa*. The people were transported into the villages and were provided with hoes and *pangas* to clear the land. Land clearing was done communally. The refugees built the schools and the clinics with the material supplied by the scheme administrators. They cultivated traditional staples such as maize, beans, and cassava and cash crops such as ground nuts, tobacco, soybeans, and sesame. Katumba was so successful that by 1978, it was handed over to the government for supervision.[48] Ulyankulu suffered the setback of poor soil quality, as well as severe water shortage, and the settlement also had outgrown its original size.[49] A third settlement was established at Mishamo and, in addition to getting the refugees that had been in Ulyankulu, it received an additional 20,000 refugees who had remained in Kigoma district. This settlement also was successful to the extent that, in 1980, the government took it over.[50]

Sudan

Sudan has a long history with refugee migrations, from Congo in the mid-60s, from Eritrea in 1967, from Chad in the mid-70s and again in 1980–1981, and from other regions of Ethiopia since 1976, and most recently from Uganda since 1979.[51] During the civil war, Sudan also has been a refugee-generating nation. However, after the Addis Ababa Agreement of 1972, there was repatriation, rehabilitation, and resettlement. Though Sudan has been very receptive to the refugees, it has put a strain on the Sudanese economy.

---

discussion in *Myths and Truths*, 1–36.
  46. Ibid.
  47. Ibid.
  48. Ibid., 78.
  49. Ibid.
  50. Ibid.
  51. Ibid.

This has been made worse by the concentration of the refugee settlements in two parts of the country that are riddled with problems. In the Kassala region, the ratio of refugees to the local population is four to one. In the Eastern Equatorian province, the ratio is six to one.[52]

In cooperation with UNCHR, the government worked at establishing self-sufficient settlements so that they could discourage spontaneous settlement or migrations into the urban centers. Sudan's settlements were unique in that they were not just rural settlements, but they had wage-earning settlements and semi-urban settlements.[53] Sudan has great agricultural potential, which has been boosted by the mechanized irrigation schemes. The only drawback is that it demands seasonal labor for intensive times like the harvest season. Traditionally, migrant labor from West Africa was able to meet this demand.[54] But due to the urbanization of many Sudanese and the scarcity of migrant labor, there has been a low availability of labor for this work. For this reason, the government established five wage-earning settlements in order to foster this need. Many other refugees from the rural settlements also participate in these seasonal labor flows.

Sudan also has a high number of urban refugees and, to discourage this, they have formed the semi-urban settlement. The objective of these semi-urban settlements is to relocate spontaneously settled urban refugees located near the cities. In this way, the settlements can be administered and serviced as refugee communities while those living there are able to commute to the cities in order to sell their labor. They also are strongly encouraged to sell their labor in the agricultural schemes.

The success of these settlements has been varied. In Southern Sudan where the refugee population was less than three years old, self-sufficiency was achieved faster. In the eastern part in one of the oldest and largest land settlement Qala el Nahal, they had a good start in 1969 and, by 1974, they were almost self-sufficient. But when the project was left to the local authorities, it did not do well and many of the refugees left in order to seek a better life in the urban centers. In 1979, fresh funding by UNHCR was injected in order to rehabilitate the program with the fresh new influx of refugees from Eritrea; by 1982, it was near to achieving economic viability. Progress on the wage-earning and semi-urban settlements has been less successful. The five exclusive wage-earning villages were located near the Es Suki irrigation scheme.[55] This was a poor choice for the settlements because the scheme

---

52. Ibid., 79.
53. Ibid.
54. Ibid.
55. Ibid., 80.

is the least successful of the modern irrigation schemes. Seasonal labor is limited to cotton picking and weeding and these were not particularly attractive to refugees. The other problem is that the wages are too low, and the refugees have complained that they are being discriminated against as compared to the local population. The semi-urban settlements face the hostility of the host community because of the fear of the loss of jobs to the refugees. The cause for fear in a population of 350,000 with a refugee population of 45,000 is understandable. Furthermore, the Ethiopian and Eritrean refugees are ready to work for lower wages.[56]

All the challenges facing refugee camps do not negate the fact that there is a great attempt to make the refugees serve as an opportunity and not as a burden to the host country, and these are good attempts to do that. Thus, it is evident that there has been a move not only to give the refugees shelter in a passive way but also to engage them in gainful employment for their own sake and for the sake of their host countries.

Repatriation

Repatriation is one of the durable solutions pursued by UNHCR as a response to the refugee problem. Most refugees want to go back to their countries as soon as there is reasonable peace. Kibreab says nostalgia, as well as a strong desire to go back to their own countries as soon as the hostilities are over, mark the life of African refugees.[57] Some of them return on their own accord without the assistance of UNHCR but some of the repatriations are organized and funded by UNHCR. There are several good examples where this has happened positively in the past. The Algerians returned home from Morocco and Tunisia after 1962. The Sudanese were repatriated to Southern Sudan after the Addis Ababa Agreement in 1972. Those from Guinea-Bissau and Mozambique were able to go home once Portugal relinquished control in 1974 and 1975 respectively. The Zimbabweans also returned home in record time. There have been close to a million of Africa's refugees who have returned to their countries of origin in the last twenty-five years. However, repatriation is not taking place as fast as it had been anticipated. In Kenya, for example, the return of peace in Somalia allowed for the closure of several refugee camps. In the recent past, UNHCR forcefully repatriated refugees and they have been criticized for such violations. A good example of this is the case of Rwandan refugees in 1997. The Tanzania government did not want these refugees anymore

56. Ibid., 81.
57. Kibreab, *African Refugees*, 51.

and though there was not at that time reasonable evidence that there was sufficient peace in Rwanda, the refugees were forcefully repatriated.[58] Some fled to other neighboring countries because they did not want to endanger their lives. Repatriation also has worked where the refugees have been helped to settle back into life in their countries.[59]

Refuge Aid or Development: ICARA I and ICARA II

In order to move beyond humanitarian aid and emergency response to the refugee problems in Africa, there are discussions about how the host countries can be assisted in developmental needs so that they can bear the burden. This happens because the uniqueness of African refugees is that most of them cannot find a place for resettlement in a third country. Though repatriation is seen as the ideal solution, it has not been applicable and appropriate in many cases. This has meant that refugees remain in the countries of asylum for a long time, which exerts much pressure on the poor economies and the infrastructure of the host communities. Thus, there is the need to study the impact of refugee populations on the development of African host countries. The realization that there is a call for much more than emergency response to the needs of the refugees has been long delayed.

The efforts by the African countries and UNCHR to draw attention of the donor countries to the need for development aid for these host countries has not been easy. It began in 1967 with the Conference on the Legal, Economic and Social Aspects of African Refugee Problems, which was held in Addis Ababa under the auspices of UN, Economic Commission for Africa, the OAU, the UNHCR, and Sweden's Dag Hammarskjöld Foundation.[60] The recommendation of this conference was that African countries hosting refugees should treat refugee-affected areas through a zonal development approach. The intention was that refugee needs should not be dealt with in isolation from the development needs of the area in which they have settled.[61] The host countries were not to bear this responsibility alone.

After a decade, the problem of refugees in Africa had tripled to the point that in May 1979, the Pan African Conference on the Situation of Refugees in Africa was convened in Arusha, Tanzania, also cosponsored by the OAU, the Economic Commission of Africa, and UNHCR. The contribution of this conference to the thinking on refugee-related development

58. See Lee, "Your Kingdom Come," 75–81.
59. Rogge, "Africa's Displaced Population," 72.
60. Kibreab, *African Refugees*, 109.
61. Gorman, *Coping with Africa's Refugee Burden*, 13.

was in the concept of burden-sharing.[62] This concept focused on resettlement of some refugees from the overburdened countries in Africa into other countries. It was later expanded to include international assistance with refugee-related development in the host countries. The Arusha Conference contributed to this process by underscoring the acute impact that refugees, especially spontaneously settled ones, can have on the impoverished areas.[63] Following this, Sudan convened a conference to draw attention to the strains that the refugee population had placed on development resources and their need for additional assistance. The result of this was the General Assembly Resolution, which called for the International Conference on Assistance to Refugees in Africa (ICARA—an acronym that was later revised after a second conference had been held).[64] ICARA I had three purposes: 1) to increase international attention to the refugee situation in Africa; 2) to mobilize resources for refugee relief and assistance; and 3) to consider assistance to asylum countries to help them cope with the additional burdens on their economic and social infrastructure caused by refugees.[65] ICARA I focused on the emergency assistance of refugees but did not address the refugee-development needs of host countries. The donors felt that this was a huge success but the African countries were disappointed. This meant that there was need for another conference that that would fully focus on refugee-related development. Thus, ICARA II was formed with the recognition that "neither refugee assistance that ignores development not development assistance that ignores refugee-related burdens can be effective in the long run."[66] The purpose of ICARA II also was three-fold: 1) to thoroughly review the results of ICARA I; 2) to consider the provision of additional international assistance to refugees in Africa for relief, rehabilitation, and resettlement; and 3) to consider the impact imposed on the national economies of the concerned countries and to provide assistance to strengthen their social and economic infrastructure to cope with the burden of refugees and returnees.[67]

Most donor countries were skeptical about the need for another conference to address the additional costs. The US, the largest contributor to refugee programs in Africa, was even reluctant to attend the conference

62. Ibid., 14. See also Kibreab, *African Refugees*, 112.
63. Gorman, *Coping with Africa's Refugee Burden*, 14.
64. Ibid., 15.
65. Ibid.
66. Ibid., 18.
67. Ibid., 23.

until the last minute.[68] However, when the conference convened, there was a consensus among all those who attended with regard to the need for additional resources to meet the development needs of the countries of asylum strained by the presence of refugees. It also was agreed that this would take several years of work and coordination between the development agencies, UN systems, donor countries, and host countries. The UNHCR would oversee the projects related to the refugees directly and UNDP would oversee the development projects.[69]

Evaluation of the Responses to the Refugee Problem

It is commendable how the African countries have responded to the influx of refugees in light of the scarcity of their resources. As mentioned earlier, many humanitarian organizations have lauded this generosity of spirit. But it has also been noted that this generosity in the midst of poverty can easily turn into hostility and conflict between the host community and the refugees.[70] It is evident that African countries, especially those that host large numbers of refugees, need assistance in order to do development in those areas that will not only assist the refugees but also the host population. It has been observed that when the focus of assistance has been on development as well as relief, this has been successful. Creating large settlements in which the refugees cannot engage in gainful employment poses great danger both to the refugees and the host populations.[71] I will say more about this in the next chapter when we focus on the Kakuma refugee camp in Kenya.

The objectives and vision of ICARA I and II were along the lines of making it possible for refugees and the host countries to live in more amicable terms through development assistance. It is not clear how far the objectives of ICARA II have continued to be pursued in the following years. Immediately after ICARA II, there was a famine and drought in the countries of the Horn of Africa. The resources were diverted into meeting these emergency needs. The conveners of ICARA hoped that this would indeed bring home the idea that development needs had to be addressed in order to avert any forthcoming disasters. All these programs happened in the last two decades but it is not clear what is taking place with regard to the issues of development and aid in the recent years. In the 1990s and 2000, the refugee problem has reached even more acute levels and we need, more than ever, to

---

68. Ibid., 84.
69. Ibid., 162.
70. Kibreab, *African Refugees*, 100.
71. Ibid., 100.

look for viable solutions. What is evident, however, is that those responses that have integrated development with humanitarian aid were successful. It is even more effective when the host population is included so that it is not just restricted to the refugee population, because this builds good relations between the host country and the refugees.

Repatriation as soon as the situation in the sending countries has been alleviated has been another solution that has worked. The church should focus on this area by working toward facilitating reconciliation between the warring parties and also by preparing refugees to be ready to promote peace within their countries when they return.

Conclusion

The refugee problem in Africa is enormous. It has been proven as we have studied that the causes that fuel the problem are not just located within the continent of Africa. There has been a long history of external interference, especially because of relationships that have developed between Africa and the northern countries. I believe, therefore, in light of this history and the enormity of the refugee problem, that it will not be easily tackled by the international community alone or by the host countries in and of themselves. Because there has been cooperation in creating the problem, there must be a sense of working together toward just solutions. Much has been done in providing assistance and relief to the refugees who are caught up in the power web of their countries, but this has not resolved the problem. It seems these people have become even more dependent than ever. There needs to be serious attempts to address the development needs of the countries generating refugees, as well as those who host them. We can no longer afford to debate the social, political and economic causes in order to try isolate economic refugees from others. As long as there is an active divide caused by the economic imbalance between the Northern and Southern countries, we will continue to have refugees. Thus, a strong commitment is needed from the Northern countries not only to address the symptoms but also to look deeply into the root causes. I think the advice by UHNCR at the end of the recent volume sums it up best:

> Meeting the needs of the world's displaced people—both refugees and internally displaced—is more complex than simply providing short-term security assistance. It is about addressing the persecution and the violence and conflict which bring about recognizing the human rights of men, women and children to enjoy peace, security and dignity without having to flee

from their homes. This is the task ahead for governments, and international organizations and the people of the world in the new millennium.[72]

While UNHCR recognizes the importance of dealing with the refugee crisis, the weaknesses of the UNHCR in bringing about lasting change and just solutions to it have been noted by one reviewer: "It has failed to condemn the perpetrators of political persecution,"[73] for fear that they will "implicate or offend the governments in power."[74] UNHCR's efforts need to be supported by other interested groups. I suggest, therefore, that what we need to see is an active involvement by the church, not only through humanitarian assistance but also through mobilizing populations so that there is a turning away from war to the dynamic pursuit of reconciliation and peace. I strongly believe this can be done effectively by the church because it is the most grassroots institution. This should be implemented both regionally and in the individual countries where the problems are faced acutely.

In the next chapter, I focus in detail on how Kenya has handled the refugee problem, presenting the history, the challenges, the opportunities and the way forward, with a view to assessing how the church can be actively involved in this.

---

72. Cutts, *The State of the World's Refugees*, 287. Also, Oka, "Coping with the Refugee Wait," 23–37; Jones et al., "Lessons from Introducing," 239–45.

73. Hammond, review of *Losing Place*, 203–205.

74. Ibid., 205.

4

Kenya: A Refugee-hosting Country

Mgeni siku ya pili, siku ya tatu mpe jembe

A guest is a guest for two days;
   on the third day give him/her a hoe.

—KISWAHILI PROVERB

Introduction

KENYA HAD NOT HOSTED refugees in large numbers until the late 1980s and more in the 1990s. In 1990, Kenya's refugee population was 12,500 but, by 1992, it experienced the world's fastest growing refugee population, with 420,000 registered by the end of that year.[1] At this time, the refugee situation was particularly acute in the whole of Africa. It was also the time when Kenya faced the worst pressure socially, politically, and economically. First, there was drought, which resulted in an acute shortage of food, causing famine and starvation. Second, Kenya faced an economic recession due to debts owed to the IMF and the World Bank. As a single-party state, Kenya was forced to institute reforms so that foreign aid would be resumed. All these factors disrupted the already volatile ethnic relations, leading to ethnic clashes that reached a peak in 1992. Although Kenya had previously hosted refugees with an exemplary spirit of hospitality, this period was the worst time for the country to be called upon to be generous. There was pressure and strain experienced by both the Kenyan nationals and the refugees. On one hand, due to the stresses mentioned above, for the country and the people of Kenya, hosting large numbers of people was really an added strain on the flailing economy and the poor infrastructure

1. Okoro, "Africa's Refugee Problem," 219. I still want to retain the title Kenya as refugee-hosting country because I want to critique the fact that they have not done it well.

of the country. In general, Kenyans did not deal with the situation well and complained a lot.[2] More specifically, refugees have testified that they were not given the best treatment, and some say they were blatantly harassed, especially by security personnel.[3]

In this chapter, I give the background of the refugee problem in Kenya and the various responses to it. First, I give a short history of the social, economic and political situation of the country before and after independence. Then, I document the history of the response to the refugee problem: when, how, where, why, and how long this has happened. I focus on the main agencies responding to the refugee problem internally, such as the government, the host community, and the churches. Then, I examine the external agencies, such as UNHCR and the NGOS, both local and international. The story would not be complete if we did not hear how the refugees themselves have responded to this experience, so that we can sense what happens in the refugee camp and how it feels to be a refugee.[4] Throughout this section, we ask ourselves whether we have acted according to the wisdom of the Kiswahili proverb, "*Mgeni siku ya kwanza, siku ya pili mpe jembe*": A guest is a guest for two days; on the third day give him/her a hoe. This means that guests should not be considered a burden but instead should be allowed to participate in their own general wellbeing and that of the home in which they are welcomed. We have had refugees in our country in large numbers for the last ten years. Have we provided them with the skills necessary for their livelihood?

---

2. The above research done by Okoro, in "Africa's Refugee Problem," shows that the reception and treatment of Somali refugees was not good. This is supported by the research done by Veney, "The Politics of Refugee Relief Operations." She also shows that refugees have faced numerous hostilities in Kenya because they are perceived mainly as an economic liability and security risk rather than an asset.

3. It was interesting to note that most refugees I talked to told me they were treated well by individual Kenyans and especially within the churches. One lady in particular told me she was given great care through the ministry of the PEFA church in Gikomba, Nairobi. However, they do not have much good to say about the police and other security personnel. But there has been a change in the present government. In the *Daily Nation* (May 6, 2003) letters to the editor, a refugee thanked the government for removing road barriers along the road between Kitale and Lokichoggio, because these are the places where the police took the opportunity to extort money from the refugees.

4. See Rawlence, *City of Thorns*, 9–358 for the nine refugee narratives in Dadaab refugee camp.

Background

A British colony until 1963 when it attained independence, Kenya has had relative peace and stability in comparison to its neighbors. Geographically, Kenya lies across the equator on the East Coast of Africa. The country has a total area of 224,960 square miles and is surrounded by five countries with a long history of political instability. It is bounded in the east by Somalia, the north by Ethiopia, the northwest by Sudan, the west by Uganda and the south by Tanzania. All these countries except Tanzania have experienced political instability, causing large movements and displacement of peoples, most of whom have been hosted in Kenya as refugees.

The population of Kenya is over 30 million, with a high growth rate of 3.4 percent.[5] This consists of diverse people who speak about 40 different languages. The two main languages of communication are Kiswahili and English. There are three main linguistic groupings. The Nilotic group consists of the Luo, Kalenjin, and the Maasai. These people inhabit the Rift Valley province and the Lake Victoria Region. The other main group, the Bantu speakers, occupy the rest of the country from the coastal region to the central highlands, while the Luhyia occupy the western highlands. The third and smallest group are the Cushitic speakers such as the Somali, the Boran, and other related groups that occupy the northeastern part of Kenya. These peoples shared no history or common culture until their boundaries forcefully brought them together by the common legacy of colonialism. One author describes the arbitrary nature of this division:

> This partition made it virtually impossible for African communities ever to follow the path of similar medieval European societies by developing into nations . . . Every frontier is drawn across at least one, and often several tribal communities.[6]

This same author appreciates how this motley crew of people put together under the reign of colonialism found it hard to think of themselves as one nation; no wonder there have been many secessionist wars all over the continent.

There was no place called Kenya until 1920. It was left to the new political leaders to bring a semblance of unity to this new creation. Thankfully, Kenya had a man named Jomo Kenyatta, whose reputation and charisma united the country right through its struggle for independence. He became the first president of the newly independent nation and continued in power until his death in 1978. After this, his former vice president, Daniel T. Moi,

---

5. See the statistical survey given in "Kenya" in *Regional Surveys of the World*, 566.
6. Brooks and El-Ayouty, *Refugees South of the Sahara*, 8.

who hailed from one of the smallest tribal groups, came to power. President Moi maintained power by keeping the allegiance of the smaller tribes and pitting the larger groups against one another. He also managed to stifle almost all opposition by slowly eradicating his opponents and then by declaring the nation a one-party state. The only group that seemed to advocate and speak for the minority was the church, mainly the Anglican and the Catholic Church. But in the late 1980s, opposition began to escalate and so did the clamor for political change. External donor bodies like the IMF and the World Bank, who also demanded political reform, strengthened these internal voices' cries for change.[7] This was also the time when the refugee influx from Somalia, Sudan, and Ethiopia was at its highest. It is little wonder that Kenya was accused of not treating refugees well at this time; there was extreme pressure from all sides. Kenya was sensitive about issues of sovereignty and national security, with the tendency to blame all the political woes on the outsiders. Moi also took this opportunity to divert the opposition from himself by blaming the internal malfunctions of the state on those who had foreign masters, and especially those who were foreigners.[8]

Factors that Influenced Kenya's Response to Refugees

Kenya's response to the refugees has been influenced mainly by three factors namely: availability of land, economic conditions, and the boundary issues especially in relation with Somalia. We will now look at how of these affected the reception of refugees.

The Land Factor

Kenya's land is not at all fertile. Only seven percent is arable, one percent can be used for crops, seven percent is meadows and pastures and four percent consists of forests. Ownership of land is very crucial in Kenya, so that many people have a city residence, while also owning one in the farm or village where most of the members of their family live. Land ownership

---

7. See Veney, "The Politics of Refugee Relief Operations," 79.

8. Opala, "US Keeps Eye on Moi Exit," *Daily Nation*, April 13, 2001. In this article, Moi, who was the former president of Kenya, is recorded to have blamed the refugees for the wave of crime that engulfed the nation in the final years of his rule. Other politicians also blamed the refugees for Kenya's problems. See other previous articles: *The Standard Newspaper* (Nairobi, Kenya) "Refugees in Arms Trade: Put foreigners in Camps," July 23,1993; *Daily Nation* (Nairobi, Kenya) "Refugees Have Kenyan Jobs–COTU," December 11, 1992; Grace Gachie, "The Price of Hospitality," *Daily Nation* (Nairobi, Kenya) September 12, 1992.

was communal before the colonial days and land was allocated to different ethnic groups. This meant that individuals or families could not dispose of the land as they saw fit. The land issue has been a volatile one in Kenya ever since the colonial days when the foreign settlers took the best land and designated it as the "White Highlands." Following the First and the Second World War, this land was offered to the returning war veterans who came to settle on it. The indigenous inhabitants of these lands were pushed out into the margins where they lived as squatters, providing cheap labor for the European plantation farms that grew coffee, tea and sisal.[9] After independence, the longing of many Kenyans was to get a piece of the ancestral land back or to buy a piece of land in any part of the country. The government set up settlement schemes in order to give the land to those who had lost it during the colonial days. However, only a few people could afford the cost of the land; these were mainly bureaucrats, politicians and wealthy business owners.[10] This meant that the majority of the people were landless. This became a heated issue that would produce an explosive situation later.

In 1991 to 1992, as a precursor to the multiparty elections, the land issue came to a head. Ethnic groups such as the Luo, Kikuyu and Luhyia who had bought land from the white settlers in the Rift Valley found themselves in land clashes that were beyond their control. Because the main support of the ruling party, KANU, was from the Rift Valley this was used as a political motivation to declare opposition against any other upcoming parties. The non-Kalenjin groups were labeled as enemies to the ruling party, so they were forced to vacate the land within the Rift Valley that was seen as belonging to the Kalenjin people. In truth, these land clashes disrupted both the Kalenjin[11] community as well as the rest of the Kenyan population. These clashes also occurred in the coastal provinces where

---

9. Kibreab, *African Refugees*, 17–18. See also Veney, "The Politics of Refugee Relief Operations," 68; Ndungu, "Land and Violence in Kenya," 59.

10. See Veney, "The Politics of Refugee Relief Operations," 68.

11. This is the time when, for the first time, I started thinking about the plight of strangers and foreigners. I was a lecturer at Moi University in the heart of Kalenjin land, but people from all over the country come to this school and some even teach there. Those foreigners who had bought farms in the area felt that their lives were in danger. It was a tense period. I woke up several nights to see houses burning where several foreigners had bought land. I was really concerned and disturbed, but I did not know how to respond. I knew there were Christians among both groups, and I wondered how we should make a difference in that situation. My fellowship group on the campus decided to have a twenty-four-hour prayer chain. That was our response. Fortunately, other Christians responded by giving refuge to those who were being harassed in their homes. The churches, thankfully, also were used as sanctuaries for those who were displaced from their homes. See also the IDP resettlement and peacebuilding in the Rift Valley in Nzau, *Transitional Justice*, 116–74.

many other upcountry people had settled; it was land that was supposedly free. Thus, one can see why land issues become very sensitive, especially if land is being allocated to refugees.

Economic Factors

Economic issues have also determined Kenya's response to the refugees. Prior to 1980 Kenya had been doing well economically, mainly based on tourism and agriculture. With the world economic recession, the agricultural sector was the first to feel the pinch. It was based mainly on a cash crop economy with the main cash crops being coffee, tea, sugar and corn. These suffered first with the fall of coffee and tea prices in the world market as well as the rise of oil prices. Following this Kenya faced severe drought in 1984 and 1992, which moved the country from being an exporter of food into an importer. Kenya then borrowed large amounts from the IMF and the World Bank. But in 1989, these financial institutions demanded changes in the political, economic and human rights records. When Kenya did not respond to these demands positively, these donor communities withheld aid, worsening the economic situation. Some of the demands made by the economic community were that the government should stop corruption, scale down the civil service, and liberalize and privatize most of the parastatal[12] companies. The government decided to accept the donor demands by holding multiparty elections. The ethnic clashes that ensued at that time did not help the tourist industry, and this meant that this sector of the economy felt the hardship. The devaluation of the Kenya shilling and structural reforms that the IMF imposed, including the high rate of inflation and the high price of agricultural products, hurt many of the farmers and prevented them from recovering from the economic downfall.

The result of these economic woes was that the unemployment of many of the youth, and the early retirement of people, caused general dissatisfaction in the country. Added to this was the large influx of refugees from the neighboring countries, especially Somalia. The general tendency was to blame the economic and political woes on these newcomers.[13] The truth is that they did put a strain on what was already an ailing economy, but they were not the cause of all the problems.

---

12. Parastatals are government-owned corporations that set and control the prices of commodities that can range from wheat to milk. See Veney, "The Politics of Refugee Relief Operations," 79.

13. Ibid., 199.

Boundary Factors

Once the colonial masters in Berlin without African participation defined the borders, they were inherited by the independent African nations who, although they saw the arbitrary nature of the boundaries, could not make any changes because this would create more problems. The Organization for African Unity (OAU) decided to ratify the integrity of these boundaries. For this reason, many African nations have fought to keep the boundaries intact. One such border issue that has fueled the refugee crisis in Kenya is the Northern Frontier District (NFD).[14] The main population in this region has always been made up of people of Somali descent. The Somali have been divided into five different nations in the Horn of Africa but they have never ceased to agitate for a greater Somaliland. During colonial days this northern region of Kenya was given a measure of autonomy. It was closed to outsiders and one required a special license in order to go in there. When Kenya became independent and wanted to assert control over this area, a secessionist group known as Northern Frontier District Liberation Front posed a challenge. This movement lasted from 1963 to 1967 with Somalia providing assistance. This did not put Somalia in favorable working relations with Kenya, who wanted to guard its boundaries jealously. The Kenya government reacted very harshly and declared a state of emergency which lasted until 1993. At one time, President Jomo Kenyatta told Somalia that Kenya would not surrender any part of its territory to them. In 1981, President Moi of Kenya and President Siad Barre of Somalia signed an agreement to end cross-border fighting. When Barre's regime fell in 1991, the flow of refugees naturally came to Kenya because this is where their relatives have lived, but on the other hand, this is where many of them have had problems because they were identified as not being genuinely Kenyan. This is the background that informs Kenya's relations with Somali refugees.

A History of Kenya Hosting Refugees

Though Kenya did not host refugees in large numbers until the decade of the 90s, her history of hosting goes back to the colonial days. From 1936 to 1938, for example, three types of refugees were believed to have entered or attempted to enter into the country's Northern Frontier District, "a vast dry area containing nearly half of Kenya's total land, but only a small fraction of her population. These refugees were mainly pastoralist conscripts trying to

---

14. See Okoro, "Africa's Refugee Problem," 131, on Kenya's relationship with Somalia. See also Veney, "The Politics of Refugee Relief Operations," 198.

escape from the armies of Ethiopia."[15] Other reports say that Kenya's earlier experience goes to 1969, when a large number of refugees arrived in Kenya after a civil war broke out in Ethiopia.[16] Other refugees who came from the neighboring countries such as Burundi, Rwanda, Congo, Ethiopia and Somalia joined these. Several others also came from South Africa, Yemen and Mozambique. I remember in the 1970s, there were a large number of Ugandan refugees in Kenya because of the dictatorship of Idi Amin. Most of these were professionals who were employed in many Kenya institutions such as hospitals and schools. When Idi Amin expelled the Indians from Uganda, most of them also found refuge in Kenyan towns. But these numbers were still small compared to today's numbers. One report says that prior to 1990, the government's official overall refugee population was estimated to be 15,000. By 1992, the population was about 1 million with Somalis accounting for 384,910.[17]

The two categories of refugees that Kenya hosts are from urban and rural areas. Like the rest of Africa, the majority are the rural population. They usually occupy the remotest parts of the host country. One author has described them thus:

> They command little or no attention, lack media coverage, and at times their plight is ignored. Hence, they are best called the invisible Africans . . . They are poor, have little or no education, no personal belongings and most important of all command little or no national or international media attention.[18]

Most of these are mainly women and children. During the height of the refugee problem in Kenya the majority of the camps were in Northern Kenya, i.e., in Kakuma, the northeastern and the coastal province. There were about twelve camps in total. In the coastal province were Utange, Jomvu, Hatim, Swale Nguru and Marafa. In the northeastern province, there were mainly Hagadera, Dadaab, Ifo, Dagahaley, Liboi, Elwak and Mandera. Kakuma is the only one in the northwestern part that is near the border of Uganda, Sudan and Ethiopia. By the year 2002, the only refugee camps still in operation were Kakuma and Dadaab. Kakuma houses many refugees from Sudan,

---

15. Okoro, "Africa's Refugee Problem," 98. I recently saw a film, "Where in Africa," in which a Jewish German family took refuge in Kenya in 1938 before the Second World War, when the Jews were being persecuted by Hitler. If the movie is right, there seem to have been a number of Jewish families who took refuge in Kenya at that time.

16. Okoro, "Africa's Refugee Problem," 98.

17. Ibid., 99.

18. Ibid., 100.

while Dadaab predominantly hosts those of Somali origin. I will discuss this further when I describe life in these camps.

A small number of refugees are also in the urban areas. Their population is uncertain because many of them settle among their relatives. In 1992, when Kenya faced a huge influx, the government issued a policy that all the refugees were to be hosted in camps. This was an attempt to curb the strain of resources in the city. Despite this, some refugees decided to stay in the city but they did so at their own risk and volition. Okoro describes urban refugees as:

> ... educated, very articulate, positively active, and demand and receive more attention than the rural refugees. They come from the group of lawyers, parliamentarians, nurses, doctors, engineers and other professions. Their unique sophistication and skills make their flights to neighboring countries very organized and most times deliberate.[19]

In addition, their sophisticated backgrounds coupled with their educational advantage make them highly competitive, and in most cases, very successful in the job market. Their easy assimilation infuriates the locals and increases the level of resentment. The cause for hostility is that they share the meager social services and amenities and infrastructure like water, food, medical services, transportation and others. Those who seem to have an advantage are the most visible members of the refugee population that people from the host country usually encounter on a daily basis. They are not exposed to the desperate and needy populations that are usually in the rural areas. The perception of many Kenyans of these people is that they are successful and compete for the few jobs that are available to the local population. These are the ones who run the *Matatu*[20] business in Nairobi, Eastleigh area. Most of the local population complain that when these refugees came the rent of the houses went up because the refugees had a lot of money to pay. The *Daily Nation* reported that since the refugee influx, housing cost had increased from Sh. 1000 to Sh. 2000 per month.[21] In other areas the prices had risen from Sh. 7,500 to Sh. 10,000.[22] They also run a thriving shopping complex that is called Garissa Lodge in Nairobi.

It is also a known fact that some of these refugees do not get the kind of employment that they are expecting and therefore many of them turn

---

19. Okoro, "Africa's Refugee Problem," 101.

20. This is a form of public transportation run by individuals in the city of Nairobi.

21. *Daily Nation* (Nairobi, Kenya), "Refugees Have Taken Kenyan Jobs–COTU," December 11, 1992.

22. Okoro, "Africa's Refugee Problem," 126.

to crime and illicit businesses in drugs and prostitution. One researcher interviewed a customer of the Florida nightclub in Nairobi, who claims that their business in prostitution has declined because there are many available Somali girls who are preferred by their clients.[23] They are usually the ones who suffer the brunt from the host country. A recent report by Amnesty International shows that urban refugees are the most neglected since the government policy mandates that all refugees be confined to the camps. Due to this the security personnel who demand bribes from them harass them so that they will not be repatriated into the camps.

Kenya's urban refugee population was scattered in many urban areas, but a large number was housed in an organized camp in Thika. This camp became a security problem to the government because it was close to a military base. So, it was closed in January 1994 by the Kenya government. Refugees from this camp were transferred to Ruiru Transit center, a temporary facility that was opened in 1993. This has also closed and the two main centers that receive refugees are now Kakuma and Dadaab.

Before I can describe the condition of life for the refugees in the camps and settlements, we should know who actually responds to them once they enter the country of asylum.

Respondents to Refugees

The Kenya government and UNHCR are major respondents to the refugees. In this section, I assess how these bodies have responded to the influx of refugees. My concern is to gauge how effectively they have applied the wisdom of the African proverb, *Mgeni siku ya pili siku ya tatu mpe jembe*.

The Kenya Government

The first group that the refugees encounter upon their entrance is the border authority of the country of asylum that they are fleeing to. Trends have shown that refugees usually flee to those areas where they know they will find favorable reception, most likely among their relatives across the borders. We have already shown how the boundaries of African states are so fluid and arbitrary, dividing communities across different states. So, in this case we can understand why the Somali people would flee and live among their Somali relatives across the border. Sometimes it has been difficult to tell the difference between the Kenyan Somali and those from Somalia. In

---

23. Ibid., 120.

the same way those in the northern border from Sudan have found refuge among the Turkana in Northern Kenya. The same thing happened with Sudan on the Uganda border. When the Sudanese were fleeing the civil war, they found refuge among their people in the northern part of Uganda, and likewise, when the people from Uganda were fleeing from the atrocities of Amin, they fled to Sudan.

The African countries granting asylum to populations from neighboring countries are guided by the 1969 *OAU Convention Governing the Specific Aspects of Refugee Problems in Africa*. Among those guidelines is that these populations should not be settled too close to the border because they might be targets of those from whom they have fled. The other guideline is that no one should be refused entry unless it can be proven that they are a security risk. The UN convention also was strong on this clause of *non-refoulement* and on forceful repatriation. Of course, the right for asylum is still the prerogative of the receiving country.

Thus, we will examine how Kenya has fared in this initial reception of refugees. We will use the case of the Somali and Sudanese for many examples because they are the ones who have come in huge numbers across the Kenyan borders. Much research has been done in the area of Kenyan reception and treatment of Somali refugees.[24] What seems to be the overall tone is that, during the initial entry of the Somali refugees into Kenya, they were not received well. The first group of refugees came as early as 1988 but the largest influx came in 1991 as the fighting intensified in Mogadishu. Most of these refugees were refused entry and others were forcefully repatriated. It is not difficult to understand why these Somali refugees were repatriated because of the previous relations between Kenya and Somalia with regard to the ongoing unstable situation of the northeastern province. The Kenya government also reasoned that they did not want to encourage an ongoing influx of refugees so they had to delay the construction of refugee camps. It must be mentioned that the Kenyan government, of course, felt that the country could not handle such a large influx of population, especially when the country was going through its own political and economic hardships.

But the Kenyan government found itself being criticized by the donors from abroad and they were forced to improve refugee policy or suffer the consequences. And as the numbers increased the camps were built in Dagahaley and Hagadera. Veney records that health and sanitary conditions in these newly constructed camps were poor.[25] She continues to say that the government refused to improve the conditions in these camps because

---

24. See, Okoro, "Africa's Refugee Problem."
25. Veney, "The Politics of Refugee Relief Operations," 95.

they did not want to encourage the ongoing influx of refugees from these countries.²⁶ They also viewed the situation as temporary. Though the government refused entry to these early refugees, this did not deter the influx, so they resorted to closing the border with Somalia. This did not work either and the country had to acquiesce to building more refugee camps all over the eastern part of the country. The countries that had handled large numbers of refugees, such as Tanzania, stepped in to provide help and guidance. Despite this change of policy, the government still subjected the Somali to harassing conditions as they hunted for illegal aliens. One person describes it thus: "People are requested to provide birth certificates, identity papers or a passport to determine their eligibility to remain in Kenya."²⁷

Although this shows a negative picture of the Kenyan government's response to the refugees, certain positive elements within the policy and practice balance the picture. For example, under Kenya's immigration Act chapter 172 (classes of Entry permits, M) a refugee is a person who:

> Owing to well-founded fear of being persecuted for reasons of race, religion, nationality, membership of a particular social group or political opinion, unwilling to avail himself of the protection of the country of his nationality or who, not having a nationality and being outside the country of his habitual residence for any particular reason, is unable, or owing to such fear, is unwilling to return to such country; and his wife or child over the age of thirteen years of such a refugee.²⁸

This shows that the Kenya government indeed recognizes in its statutes the existence of such persons in need. The country shows further commitment to the refugee issue by being a signatory to the international and regional conventions dealing with the refugee issue. On February 4 1993, Kenya ratified the 1969 OAU "Convention Governing the Specific Aspects of Refugee Problems in Africa." The government is also in the process of establishing a comprehensive national refugee law. This has already been proposed in Parliament under what is known as "The Refugee Bill 1990."²⁹

In September 1992, the government established the National Refugee Secretariat, which plays the leading role in refugee affairs within the government. The Secretariat is under the ministry of Home Affairs and the National

---

26. Okoro, "Africa's Refugee Problem," 145.
27. Veney, "The Politics of Refugee Relief Operations," 98.
28. Republic of Kenya, *The Laws of Kenya*, 20.
29. Okoro, "Africa's Refugee Problem," 141. Every time this bill has come up for discussion, it has not found much support because the government is not ready for the full implications of giving the refugees their full status. The Refugee Bill was finally signed into law in Kenya in 2019.

Heritage and Office of the Vice President. Veney notes that this is a commendable act on the part of the Kenya government because few African countries have the capacity and personnel to recruit and adequately train personnel to administer refugee affairs alone.[30] She further states that "very often refugee matters are subsumed under the military, security, or other departments that are not trained to handle issues of asylum and protection."[31] Furthermore, in Kenya, the Ministry of Health also permits the use of district and provincial government hospitals by refugees.

However, the major contribution is from the Kenya government that donates the land used for camps and settlement sites. At the peak of the refugee crisis, there were thirteen camps, mostly in the northeastern province, and six border sites. These sites are located in the remote parts of the country where there is no danger of incurring the anger of the host population when the land is given away. Most of these areas are in the arid or semi-arid parts of the country. The government is supposed to ensure security in these camps once they are established. This has been a difficult aspect to maintain because of the banditry that goes on in these parts of the country. Most of the times these camps, especially those on the border, are targets of both the bandits from Kenya or the Somali soldiers who view these settlements as sources for cars, food and easy money. Many refugees have been harassed and it has been a constant complaint that women have been raped in these areas.

It is the policy of the government that all refugees should reside in the camps. On some occasions the government allows the refugees to leave the camps for school or medical treatment. But above all, the government does not want the refugees in the urban areas where the unemployment rate is high and the social services are stretched to the limits.[32] Veney records a recent strategy of the government to keep all the refugees in the camps. Previously, those who were seeking resettlement in a third country could be interviewed in Nairobi, but the government has decreed that this process has to be done in the refugee camps. This ensures that the refugees reside within the camp and thereby do not get into the cities to take advantage of the available social services. In this case, the "urban constituency is less likely to feel threatened by the refugees because they can no longer be viewed as competitors for the scarce resources."[33] Of course this puts at a disadvantage those refugees who have been granted full refugee status and who usually

---

30. Veney, "The Politics of Refugee Relief Operations," 188.
31. Ibid., 189.
32. Ibid., 97.
33. Ibid., 194.

prefer to stay in urban centers where they can get jobs or go to school as they await resettlement in a third country.

Another policy that the government has instituted in order to protect its few educational resources from being consumed by the refugees is to put forward a new educational policy. Refugees who want to remain outside the camps to attend school have to obtain a full scholarship that includes subsistence fees. Before the new policy was adopted, refugees only had to provide a guarantee that their school fees would be paid.[34] Those who would be hardest hit by this would be those refugees who have been granted asylum status. If one cannot provide proof for full funding he or she would have to go back to the camp. But even with the guarantee, it will not be automatic to attend school.

Above all, what seems the most constraining factor for the refugees in Kenya has been the refusal by the government to grant refugee status. This usually determines the kind of assistance that a refugee gets. The granting of this status by UNCHR and the government entitles the refugee the same rights and privileges as any citizen of the host country. These rights include the right to remain in Kenya, to attend school, to obtain a work permit and a business license and to have access to hospitals and social services. This is not usually the first thing that happens when refugees enter a country, but they are encouraged to do this after the emergency phase has passed. As Veney reports, "Refugees in Kenya have found it difficult to obtain full refugee status even after they have been recognized by UNHCR. These individuals are classified as mandate refugees, but they are not entitled to the same rights and privileges as full status refugees."[35] Though one can criticize these policies for being hard on the refugees, it must be understood that Kenya is doing what it can under the circumstances. Their own citizens cannot even obtain a decent education and they are struggling to make ends meet, so this becomes a difficult balancing act. When I visited Kakuma refugee camp in August 2001, I was impressed by the education system that has been set up within the camp.[36] This is, of course, is funded by the NGOs, but most of the personnel are Kenyan-trained and they are able to bring their expertise to this context. It was also noted that the children from the local Turkana community were allowed to enter and to benefit from the school system.

34. Ibid., 102.

35. Veney, "The Politics of Refugee Relief Operations," 190. As mentioned earlier, Kenya has put off passing the Refugee Act because this might create a huge demand for the meager resources.

36. See also Monaghan and King, "How Theories of Change," 365–84; Bellino, "Youth Aspirations in Kakuma Refugee Camp," 541–56.

United Nations High Commission for Refugees (UNHCR)

UNHCR as a body that deals with refugees worldwide has been addressed in other sections. However, now we will look at the specific work that UNHCR does within Kenya in response to the refugee problem within these borders.

In order to fulfill its objectives, the UNHCR works in cooperation with the Kenya government and the operating partners. The services they all provide include legal and physical protection, resettlement, repatriation, provision of material support mainly to the refugees but also to the local communities living near the refugee camps, building roads, schools, transportation, sanitation, water systems, social services, food and shelter.[37]

We will look at the work of UNHCR in the three areas where it is supposed to function. In the case of protection, UNHCR does it in two ways: by providing physical safety and also legal support. UNHCR has done this work in conjunction with the Kenya government. This area has been fraught with disagreements because of the presence of many factors that affect the insecurity. UNHCR has accused the government of not providing enough security in the areas surrounding the refugee camp. It is difficult to ensure security on an ongoing basis. So, this is an area that needs continuous attention.

Camps are always a target for bandit activity. UNHCR also provides legal protection to refugees who may be caught up in some illegal and criminal activities. They pay attention to special need groups by providing social service programs to target the most vulnerable groups such as women, the handicapped, children, unaccompanied minors and single-headed households.[38] Social service workers visit homes, collect data and identify unmet needs in the camp.[39] In 1993, they assisted women by implementing the Women Victims of Violence. Women who were victims of violence were able to find help materially and legally through female counselors who assisted them in recovering both physically and psychologically. They provided them with the practical skills and material resources to help them become self-reliant. The report is that approximately 19,000 women from Sudan and Somalia have been assisted.[40]

Resettlement is another function of UNHCR. It is the process whereby refugees are removed and resettled from the first country of asylum to a third country. In order to solve the problem of refugees in Kenya, UNHCR has used this process. This is usually for a limited number of people and for

---

37. Okoro, "Africa's Refugee Problem," 222.
38. Veney, "The Politics of Refugee Relief Operations," 105.
39. Ibid.
40. Ibid., 106.

special cases, for example, medical needs, raped women, reunion of children and families. This is fraught with difficulties because it is usually up to the third countries to give the quota for admission and the Western countries have not really admitted many refugees from Africa. These countries of asylum are imposing restrictions and many conditions as to who should be admitted and when. But it seems that this situation has improved because in 1992, 3,550 people were resettled to various countries of the world, and in 1993, 5,972 were accepted. Lately, there was a special group of minors known as the "lost boys" from Sudan who were resettled in America. A group of about 10,000 Somali Bantu were also accepted for resettlement in the US in 2002.[41] Okoro shows in his research that the refugees who were interviewed in Liboi camp preferred to be resettled in a third country. The danger of this is that those who are not resettled immediately decide to remain in the refugee camps rather than accept being repatriated.

Repatriation is usually seen as the most durable solution to the refugee problem. Those who intend to return to their countries are usually encouraged to register with UNHCR officials in their respective camps. Many have done so without the assistance of the UNHCR. It is commendable to note that by September 1993 about 230,000 from Somalia had registered for voluntary repatriation.[42] This shows that there is relative political stability after the signing of the Addis Ababa Peace Agreement in March 1993. This meant that several refugee camps were closed in Kenya. By 2001, there were only two refugee camps in Kenya: Dadaab in the Eastern border, and Kakuma toward the northwestern region. This kind of picture is encouraging because there is evidence that this work can actually come to an end someday.

In addition, the UNHCR has done some commendable work especially on the Kenya-Somali border by implementing the cross-border program. They realized that they could not assist all the victims of the war, especially if they waited for them to move into Kenya as refugees, so they implemented what is known as the cross-border program. It is an attempt to help people before they cross the Kenya-Somali border. This provides relief and assistance to people within 150 kilometers of the border of Kenya, in Somalia. The program provides agricultural materials such as seeds and tools, health clinic rehabilitation, food, water, and sanitation facilities.[43]

With regard to those settled in camps, UNHCR has also helped meet the physical needs of the refugees by establishing eleven hospitals and clinics

---

41. Juma Kwayera, "US to Resettle Thousands of Somalis," *East African Standard*, January 21, 2002.

42. See *Kenya and Somali Cross-border Operation*, 4. See also Okoro, "Africa's Refugee Problem," 229.

43. Ibid., 10. See also Veney, "The Politics of Refugee Relief Operations," 105.

that provide both preventative and curative care in each of the camps. At the peak of the refugee problem there were about 300 health workers, many of whom were themselves refugees and provided care and services to several members of the refugee families.[44] This has helped to decrease the mortality rate and reduce the infections from the common ailments such as malaria, respiratory infections and diarrhea. Children under the age of 5 years are usually the most affected.[45] During the rainy seasons when there is the high likelihood of infection, the UNHCR helps by distributing mosquito nets. Also, insecticides and larvicides are sprayed, but an immunization program is yet to be implemented and improvement of the sanitation and environmental protection is being worked on.[46]

In addition to helping the refugees in the camps, UNHCR has assisted Kenyans living near the refugee camps. For example, they have improved water supplies by sinking additional wells in Mandera town.[47] Similar amenities were given to local communities elsewhere. UNHCR has also helped to provide additional medical equipment to the local hospitals in such areas as Mandera, Malindi, Elwak, Garissa and Kakuma. They have also improved road and airstrip maintenance.[48] The UNHCR has erected new schools and improved the existing ones. At the peak of the crisis there was a good sign of 35,000 children in the camps who were attending the schools.[49] This included children from the local population as well. Extension of help to the local community has helped to improve the relations between the host community and the refugees because the locals realize they can benefit from the refugees' presence. It has also helped the Kenya government in meeting those needs for its own population.

Though it appears that the UNHCR has done good work, there have been criticisms about some of its shortcomings, especially in its two main functions of protection and providing durable solutions. The main criticism mentioned by Okoro is that it has failed, along with the international community, to provide adequate protection for the Somali refugees in the various camps scattered all over Kenya. Many of these refugees have suffered rape, violence, robbery and many other violent crimes that the UNHCR consistently ignores.[50] The UNHCR also has failed in coming to the

44. Veney, "The Politics of Refugee Relief Operations," 106.
45. Ibid.
46. Ibid.
47. Okoro, "Africa's Refugee Problem," 231.
48. Ibid.
49. Ibid., 231.
50. Okoro, "Africa's Refugee Problem," 219.

aid of the host countries such as Kenya when they attempt to respond to the problems. For example, it is said that when the Somali problem started, Kenya responded by giving aid even before the international community came in. This criticism was also received from the Refugee Policy Group based in Washington:

> The UNHCR was to provide legal protection to these individuals and some assistance to help them pay for shelter and food. When mass movements began in 1991, UNHCR was ill prepared to respond to the growing crisis. With personnel that were primarily concerned with legal representation, UNHCR-Kenya did not have the staff, resources or experience to mount an emergency operation. Faced with mounting crises in many parts of the world, UNHCR'S Geneva headquarters ignored the growing problems in Kenya. It was not until May 1992, when the world's attention was shifting to Somalia, that the UNHCR recognized the severity of the problem in Kenya and sent Kenya the team that had been running UNHCR'S Kurdish emergency operation.[51]

The US Committee for Refugees also criticized the UNCHR for using a "conscious policy of neglect." This is also known as the policy of "light intervention" or "intentional neglect." Unfortunately, this led to the deaths of about 2,000 to 4,000 refugees in the Northeastern province of Kenya.[52] However, the situation changed once the international media focused on the plight of Somali refugees in Kenya. This focus resulted in better organization by the UNHCR in Kenya and better provision of services and caring for the needs of the refugees.[53]

The UNHCR does its work with several assisting partners, who are the NGOs. These are different types of organizations; some are secular, while others are religious. Some are international and some are local. The international organizations usually have more clout and finances than the local ones. Okoro commends the local ones that work among the refugees because the people are able to see Africans helping them and not just foreigners. They specialize in different types of relief services for which they have expertise and personnel. In different camps UNHCR gives different services to different NGOs. For example, the organization in charge of camp management in Kakuma is the Lutheran World Federation (LWF). World Vision is in charge of housing construction.

51. Ibid., 221.
52. Ibid.
53. Ibid.

NGOs in Kakuma Camp

NGOs work closely with UNHCR and are known as Implementing Partners. Among those that I will focus on will be the Lutheran World Federation, NCCK (National Christian Council of Kenya), World Vision and Jesuit Refugee Services (JRS).

Lutheran World Federation

The Lutheran World Federation (LWF) is a global communion of Christian churches in the Lutheran tradition. It was founded in 1947 in Lund (Sweden) and now has 131 member churches in seventy-two countries representing over 60.2 million of the nearly 64 million Lutherans worldwide. The Lutheran World Federation/Department of World Service operates programs in relief rehabilitation and development in twenty-four countries. Its mandate is the expression of Christian care to people in need irrespective of race, sex, creed, nationality, religious or political conviction.[54]

LWF is the partner that has been working the longest in Kakuma. In mid-1992, UNHCR invited LWF/DWS to establish a refugee camp at Kakuma, in response to the influx of about 20,000 Sudanese who were fleeing fighting in Sudan. Most of these were boys who ranged between the ages of ten and seventeen, and had fled on foot to Ethiopia, and with the overthrow of Mengistu, they again fled to Kenya.[55] LWF/DWS then took charge of the camp and have had several responsibilities which have changed over time. When the camp was established, they were in charge of distributing food, social services and security. Presently, they are in charge of education, community services, water and sports activities in the camp. In line with UNHCR's objective to improve access to quality education they have worked closely toward that end. Right now, there are six pre-schools, twenty-three primary schools and three secondary schools under the management of LWF. As of December 2002, 21,307 pupils (6,356 girls) attended primary schools, a total of 2,332 (302 girls) attended secondary school, and 6,455 (3,189 girls) attended pre-school.[56] Those girls and women who drop out of school because of forced early marriages and pregnancy attend afternoon classes especially prepared for them.

---

54. *Refugee Insights*, 4.
55. Ibid.
56. UNHCR, *Community Services Brochure*, 3.

The special component of the educational service that is offered by LWF is the peace education program.[57] This was established in the two camps, Kakuma and Dadaab, after a number of consultative meetings and participatory Action Research groups that involved a number of communities. The objective of this peace education is to promote knowledge, values and attitudes that will lead to behaviors that encourage peace by preventing and minimizing conflict.[58] To facilitate this process, concepts such as cooperation, communication, perception etc., are gradually reinforced through the school grade. Half-day community workshops also encourage adults to develop skills and attitudes that are conducive to peaceful behavior and tolerance. The program has three components: structured school system, structured community workshops, which includes the host community, and semi-structured public awareness.[59] This is a significant project in view of the fact that what the refugees are suffering from has come as a result of lack of peace in their own countries. I talked to the director of this program in Kakuma and he said that there was an improvement on how disputes were handled.[60]

Other educational and recreational activities done by LWF are focused on the youth and children who make up fifty percent of the population in Kakuma.[61] Such programs include the development of arts and crafts, drama, theatre, and sports. The programs which focus on children and adolescents take into consideration that this is a group that is especially vulnerable, with special needs. They help to promote public awareness for the needs of this special group, including foster care for those who have no parents, and the need to protect them against exploitation, abuse and sexually transmitted diseases such as HIV/AIDS.[62] Their needs are enormous and one group cannot hope to meet them all; so other groups give various services that will help increase the dignity and humanity of the refugee situation.

Jesuit Refugee Service (JRS)

Jesuit Refugee Service is another support program geared toward the educational needs of the refugees and offered under the auspices of LWF at

---

57. Ibid.
58. Ibid.
59. Ibid.
60. Kankuri, interview; Onyango, interview.
61. UNHCR, *Community Services Brochure*, 4. See also Lutheran World Federation, *Community Service Handout*.
62. Ibid. Kamau, interview.

Kakuma. Father Pedro Arrupe SJ, then the superior General of the Society of Jesus, in order to respond to the plight of refugees and to coordinate Jesuit services to them founded JRS in 1980.[63] JRS in Kakuma runs three programs. One is the JRS scholarship, established in 1997 to offer promising refugee students the opportunity to study in Kenyan secondary schools. It provides the possibility of studying four years alongside the local population away from the stresses of the camp, enabling these gifted students to reach their full potential. JRS also coordinates a Distance Learning Program for the University of Southern Africa (UNISA); thirty-two refugee students are attending this program. They also offer generalized counseling services in conjunction with UNHCR for individuals and groups in Safe Haven who are survivors of abuse. In collaboration with LWF, peace building, conflict resolution, and the gender programs provide counseling services and material support to vulnerable individuals and refer cases dealing with protection and special assistance to UNHCR protection and the community services unit.[64]

Don Bosco is another body that works under LWF in providing vocational training courses that include, masonry, carpentry, metal work, plumbing, electrical installation, motor vehicle mechanics, agriculture, tailoring/dress making and typing in three centers within the camp. By 2002, 568 students (115 females) attended the training program. Computer courses are also offered by Don Bosco.[65] Windell Charitable Trust is another scholarship program associated with the University Service of Canada for refugee students. It also runs English language training for adults. Attendance of women is high compared to other programs. The program was initiated with a sensitivity to enabling women to communicate their social problems to aid workers.[66]

NCCK (National Christian Council of Kenya)

The NCCK works with all the collaborating partners, and especially with IRC (International Rescue Committee), which is in charge of community health, both curative and preventative, in the Kakuma camp, while they work with CARE in the Dadaab camp. Their understanding is that the health of the individual is the ultimate goal, so that all other services such as food provision, water and sanitation are geared toward supporting and

63. Jesuit Refugee Service, *Scholarship Programme Brochure*.
64. UNHCR, *Community Services Brochure*, 4.
65. Ibid.
66. Ibid.

motivating health. That is why NCCK collaborates with all the partners in the camp as well as in the refugee community, in promoting and selling the Reproductive Health Component of the program. Before NCCK came to the scene this Reproductive Health component was not being attended to. The issues of sexually transmitted diseases, HIV/AIDS, child spacing, sexual and gender-based violence and the dangers of female circumcision were not considered as important. But after the Cairo meeting of 1994 and through the work of NCCK in the camps, Reproductive Health awareness was incorporated into most of the refugee programs.

The main component of this program is information awareness to all the implementing partners, allowing for all these elements to be incorporated into their programs. Reproductive Health is defined as a complete state of well-being, physically, mentally, and socially—not merely the absence of disease or infirmity—in all matters relating to the reproductive system, its functions, and processes.[67] Thus, the main contents of this information education include: raising the awareness of the normal anatomy and functions of the female and male reproductive organs to help the refugees understand their bodies; raising awareness on the dangers of female genital mutilation, mainly the complications both in the short and the long-term, prevention and management of STDS and HIV/AIDS. It also encompasses family planning and family planning methods, child spacing, counseling and service provision for needy cases, and provision of drugs.[68] These are provided with the understanding that the woman is the major stakeholder in this matter so that the particular health service should pay special attention to the woman.[69] The African culture does not allow for free discussion of sexual matters. In the last seven years they have focused on these areas that affect women's health: safe motherhood, sexual and gender-based violence, family planning and child spacing, STD and HIV infection, economic standards of women and environmental factors that may cause infertility.[70]

They have noted success in most of these areas; for example, in the area of safe motherhood, child spacing methods and drugs for sexually

67. NCCK and Ruingu, *Reproductive Health Training Manual*, 1.

68. Ibid., 5.

69. The United Nations Fund for Population Activities' representative urged that providing refugee women with reproductive health was a basic human right. This is particularly urgent because the report says that women, adolescent girls, and children make up 75 percent of the total population of refugees and internally displaced people. They also run the risk of infection from sexually transmitted diseases and death through pregnancy-related complications such as unsafe abortion and inadequate care in pregnancy and childbirth. See *Daily Nation*, November 23, 1999. Also, Jones et al., "Lessons from Introducing," 239–45.

70. NCCK and Ruingu, *Reproductive Health Training Manual*, 7.

transmitted diseases, including education on safe condom use, are shared by refugees. IRC, NCCK and MSF-B in Dadaab, UNHCR, and CARE support all the activities against sexual and gender-based violence; for example, female lawyers are now called to hear cases for victims of rape.[71] GTZ is involved in provision of firewood for the refugees to reduce the time women spend in dark and dangerous areas. It has been noted that most of the rapes occurred when the women were collecting firewood in the bushes. Above all, there is an Inter-agency Reproductive Health Coordination Committee that has been formed in both camps that holds monthly meetings to monitor and review what each agency is doing to promote reproductive health. The goal of the program is that reproductive health becomes everybody's business.[72] Refugees are more open to discussing issues such as female genital mutilation, sexually transmitted diseases and increasingly, many are receptive to the technique of child spacing.[73]

World Vision

World Vision came to Kakuma in June 2000 under a specific memorandum of understanding with UNHCR. Their main duty is the construction of shelters and other infrastructure in the refugee camp. World Vision is also responsible for maintenance of the roads in the camp, the construction of mini-stores within the camp, and the erection of security barriers and the police post. They also maintain the airstrip that is close to the camp.

As regards to the shelters for refugees, the previous structures were temporary houses constructed of timber poles, mud walls and grass-thatched roofs. This kind of shelter was unsuitable for the termite-ridden soil of Kakuma. They required more frequent repairs, at least once a year, to prevent their collapse. A pilot project has recently started that is attempting to replace timber walling with mud-bricks and it has been successful. A full-scale shift to mud-bricks for walling, and corrugated galvanized iron sheets for roofing, is underway.

A new way of promoting this change among the refugees is to allow them to participate in the process right from the beginning. Each community has a construction committee that looks into the needs of the community as regards to shelter. These are the ones that report the issues for maintenance and new construction needs to the World Vision officials. Previously, the refugees were given the materials and it was their responsibility

---

71. Riungu, interview.
72. Ibid.
73. UNHCR, *Kenya and Somali Cross-border Operation*, 9.

to construct the shelters. Now because of the emphasis on capacity building, World Vision participates with the refugees in the process so that they can transfer the skills to them.[74] They provide the water to make the bricks and they show them how to make the bricks. The refugees can also participate in the roofing if they are able to do so. The project manager says that because of this kind of emphasis they have a good problem, that of having more shelters than they can roof because people are really motivated to construct their houses. World Vision extends their reach to the local community. In 2001, they constructed a classroom for a primary school that is thirty-one kilometers from the camp and they have a committee that assesses the needs of the host community in the coming years. They plan to construct a boarding primary school for girls of the host community.

The Host Community

The immediate host community of the Kakuma refugee camp are the Turkana people. The land they live in is semi-desert. This has forced them to live a nomadic existence mainly depending on pastoralism as a source of livelihood. They supplement their diet with fish from the fresh water of Lake Turkana. The government authorities have neglected this section of Kenya, and not much attention has been paid to the development of infrastructure.[75] When land was needed to host the refugees this was chosen because of the availability of the large open ground that was not being used by the local population. Since the land is not that productive the government knew that they would not run the risk of annoying the local inhabitants. But this has not been exactly true; it has resulted in friction, mainly on two fronts. The first has been centered on the ownership of cattle. Because of the pastoralist livelihood, the Turkana hold cattle dearly as their source of wealth. This explains why the residents in this area experience much insecurity due to continuous cattle theft. Cattle are a valuable commodity, not only to the Turkana but also to their immediate neighbors in Kenya, the Pokot, and their next of kin, the Karamojong of Uganda. To make the situation worse, because of the prevailing war conditions in the surrounding nations of Sudan and Uganda there has been a proliferation of weapons in the area.[76] This

---

74. Nyamai, interview.

75. See Aukot, "'It is Better to be A Refugee than a Turkana,'" 73–83. He provides an insightful assessment of the situation between the refugees and the Turkana from an insider's perspective. He shows that the missionaries have provided both education and health services to these people.

76. A recent report in the *Daily Nation* said that almost every adult in Pokot and Turkana district owned a gun. It further said there were about 7,000 guns in the area.

situation is extremely critical, such that vehicles require a security escort or they have to travel in a convoy to guard against bandit attacks, as they move between Lodwar through Kakuma to Lokichokio, the town on the border of Kenya and Sudan. The value of cattle also explains why the Turkana do not tolerate any competition from the refugees who would also want to keep cattle. If the refugees defy this, the local people come and forcefully take the cattle that the refugees might have. This sometimes results in bloodshed between the Turkana and the refugees.[77]

Secondly, many hostilities occur because of land issues. The camp occupies much of the land that used to be pastureland for Turkana cattle. So, the Turkana feel they have been deprived of much of their precious land. Furthermore, the refugees have also contributed to environmental degradation because they have cut down many trees for use as firewood, which has also been a cause of much friction.[78]

But the presence of the refugees among the Turkana has not been entirely a negative factor. Ironically, the camp in Kakuma has revealed that the Turkana are very needy people who have been neglected by the Kenya government for a long time. The extent of their neediness is manifested by the fact that they are employed by the refugees as "house-helps, dishwashers and baby-sitters."[79] So, in a sense, it is a good thing that services are now being extended to them through the presence of the refugees. Such services include water-bored holes that provide water for their cattle. They have also benefited from the health services and educational system within the camp. Recently World Vision put up shelter for a *baraza* at Kakuma Divisional Headquarters. They have fenced the area and improved on the local airstrip. The road between Lodwar to Lokichoggio has been repaired because it is used for regular transportation by the UNHCR. This has helped to connect the area with the rest of the country. Montlcos and Kagwanja[80] say that the camp has become like a city with direct transportation to Nairobi, and refugees are the main customers. Through the establishment of the camp in this part of the country, some Turkana who have acquired some formal education have also been employed by UNHCR and other NGOs. There is,

---

Daily Nation, May 20, 2003.

77. In my last night at Kakuma during my visit in January, I heard many gunshots and much commotion in the UNHCR compound. When I inquired about the commotion in the morning, I was told that some bandits came and robbed eight cows from a butcher in the refugee community.

78. See Aukot, "'It is Better to Be a Refugee Than a Turkana,'" 78.

79. Ibid., 81.

80. Montclos and Kagwanja, "Refugee Camps or Cities?" 212.

however, a feeling that other Kenyans from outside the district come to take jobs that should belong to the Turkana.[81]

Still, good informal relationships exist between the refugees and their neighbors, the Turkana, facilitating such activities as the exchange of food items on the barter market. The famine that occurred in 2000 benefited the Turkana indirectly because their plight was brought to the attention of most Kenyans because of the presence of the refugees. Unfortunately, starving Turkana could only stand and watch, as huge trucks passed by to deliver food to the refugees. When the *Daily Nation* brought this to the attention of the Kenyans the response to the situation was commendable.

Unfortunately, since the camp was started, morality in the society has broken down, resulting in the increase in prostitution. One pastor noted that this is because the Turkana are very needy and desperate to exchange their daughters for food.[82] But fortunately, honest intermarriages also happen between the refugees and the local people. The Turkana, however, have expressed the need to see a balance in this marriage exchange. They feel that the Sudanese are quick to take Turkana girls but they are very protective about allowing their own girls to marry outside their community.[83]

Despite some of the unhappy stories about refugee interactions with the local people, there are examples of good neighborly relations. One is the story of Pastor Simon Ekai Narogoi. He is a Turkana from the local area. After he completed high school, he started working for an NGO in the refugee camp. He had a negative attitude toward the refugees because he felt that they had intruded into his community. He also had a personal grudge because the Turkana girl he wanted to marry instead married a Congolese at the camp and he never saw her again. He attended church regularly but did not have a personal relationship with God, so he lived a reckless life of drinking, smoking and sexual immorality. One Sunday morning, as he was taking a walk through the camp, he heard beautiful music emanating from

---

81. Montclos and Kagwanja, "Refugee Camps or Cities?" 218. They report that, among the approximately two hundred Kenyans employed by humanitarian organizations, the Turkana are a minority. They also say that NGOs generally tend to hire refugees rather than Kenyans because they work for less money.

82. Namuya, interview. See also Aukot, "'It is Better to Be a Refugee Than a Turkana,'" 79.

83. Ekai, Abong, Akolong and Natapar, interview. These are four Turkana young ladies who have positive views about the refugees' interaction with the Turkana. Three of them have married outside their community. They also noted areas where the relationship could be improved, especially in the area of marriage. See also Aukot, "'It is Better to Be a Refugee Than a Turkana,'" 78. He discusses the cultural misunderstandings between the refugees and the Turkana on marriage negotiations, such as the need to pay dowry.

one of the church buildings. He entered the building and it was the Congolese Fellowship. The music was very impressive. He says that he was touched by the fact that these people who had lost everything were able to praise God with such joy and abandon. This was the beginning of his conversion experience. From then on, he continued attending the church and he also joined the choir. He was invited to a leadership role within the church and now he is one of the pastors in the Congolese community. This is an ideal example of reversal and reconciliation, showing the great benefits that have come to the Turkana community through the presence of refugees. There are also other stories in which refugees have become pastors in the local Turkana community. This all demonstrates how the barriers that have divided people are being broken down.

Response from Local Churches

There is not one uniform response from the local churches to the refugee crisis. It varies from those who are close to the camp to those as far away as Nairobi. I interviewed pastors and lay people from three locations: the nearby Kakuma area, The Anglican Church Diocese of Eldoret and Nairobi. Among all of these, Pastor Namuya of the Full Gospel Church, Kakuma was in the most unique situation. He is a Turkana from the local community, so he is able to assess honestly the effect that the presence of the refugees has had on his people. He interacts with the refugees on a daily basis. Refugees and NGO workers from the refugee camp are members of his congregation. He also participates actively with the refugee pastors in the camp to arrange for open-air outreach ministry and the training of pastors. He is a board member of the Kakuma Interdenominational School of Mission (KISOM).[84] This is a training program for refugee pastors, founded through the initiative of one refugee, Pastor Tito Mayaribu from Burundi. No doubt, Pastor Namuya has a key role in this area in influencing both the refugees and the local community. He is well respected among the refugees and his church is doing admirable projects to alleviate the dire conditions of his people.

As I moved further away from the refugee camp into Eldoret, I was still impressed that the people I interviewed had some knowledge about the refugees mainly through the local media, radio, TV, and the daily

84. This is a wonderful cooperative effort between the refugees and the Kenyan Christians. The refugee churches are in dire need of trained pastor and leaders, and the Kenyans provide the resources—both the personnel and materials. I will talk more about this in chapter 5 when I discuss what the church in Kenya should be doing in response to the refugee problem.

newspapers. However, it was evident that those who had a personal interaction with refugees had concrete information about their plight. Reverend Omusundi, the archdeacon of St. Matthews Anglican Church, Eldoret, told me some poignant stories about the living conditions of some refugees in the city of Eldoret.[85] He said that most of them lived in congested households such that a house that should have one family accommodated as many as ten large families. He also reported that those who live in the city are of relatively higher status in their home country; that is why they choose to live in the city rather than in the camp. But as it appears, they still bear the burden of their unfortunate relatives. Rev. Omusundi also told me how St. Matthew's Church has tried to help the refugees with the basic provisions of food and clothes, but the numbers are too great for them. One of their greatest needs is school fees for their children, both in secondary and primary school. He has advised some to go back to the camp to take advantage of the free educational system there. The church has also provided them with the facility to worship at their own service, using their own language. However, due to lack of trained leadership,[86] they no longer meet in the church sanctuary but in the homes. Rev. Omusundi visits various households periodically, so that he can pray with them.

While I was within the Diocese of Eldoret, I also interviewed members of my local church in the village, St. John's Anglican Church, Cheptingting. I was really impressed by what they knew about the refugee problem. They did not have full details about the dismal conditions that the refugees live in and when I gave them a full report, they were overwhelmed. They decided that within that week they could collect food (maize and beans) and clothes to take to the refugees. I informed the Bishop about this so that he could encourage other donations from the diocese but I have not been home since to know the outcome of these efforts. Still, this just showed me that people in the village are generous. Their immediate response indicated that they felt a sense of affinity with the refugees and they wanted to share in their plight.

In Nairobi, I collected data and interviewed members of two congregations, St. Francis Church, Karen, and St. Luke's Church, Kenyatta. The data collected from the two churches proved that St. Luke's Church had a closer affinity with the refugees than St. Francis, Karen.[87] The reason for

---

85. Omusundi, interview.

86. Rev. Omusundi said that every time he had trained one young person to lead, they would leave immediately after acquiring the skills in order to serve as pastors in Kakuma.

87. The discrepancy also might be explained by the fact that I did not have time to talk to the members of the church at Karen. Due to lack of time, I asked them to complete a written survey.

this might be that St. Luke has offered their building to be used by two refugee congregations,[88] the Oromo Fellowship, which meets on Wednesday evenings, and the Sudanese congregation, which meets on Sunday afternoons. However, it was still interesting to note that there were no interactions between the refugee congregations and the local people. One factor that can partly explain this is the language barrier, but it was still surprising that the pastors did not even visit these fellowships. One exception to this was the youth service at St. Luke's. The young Sudanese and the Kenyans mingled freely at the youth service. The Kenyans I talked to who attend this service said they had learned a lot about dedication and commitment to God through the lives of the Sudanese by being in fellowship with them. Some members of this group had even made friends with these refugees and had gone as far as visiting their homes and even the refugee camp. I found this group to be really well informed about the refugees. In fact, they even knew the particular areas in Nairobi where the refugees resided. However, I discovered that they still held the stereotypical notion that some refugees were quite affluent because of the areas in which they lived in Nairobi. One important point is that the pastors confessed to me that they had not preached a sermon regarding refugees.

In summary, one can say that people from all three regions had general information about the refugee problem because of the local media, mainly the newspaper, TV and the radio. But it is only those who had personal contact with the refugees who had a more sympathetic attitude and were able to articulate their problems much more concretely.

The Rest of the Kenyan Population's Attitude toward Refugees

Okoro[89] did his research to assess the attitude of the Kenyan population toward the Somali refugees. His findings show that the response is multifaceted and it is mainly determined by ethnicity, religion and locality. He also found out that those Kenyans who were of Somali origin were closer in proximity to the refugees, and those of the Islamic religion had a positive attitude toward the refugees and felt that the government was not doing enough to help them. Those who lived in the urban areas and were of the Christian religion felt that the government was doing enough and that the

---

88. Another Anglican Church, Christ the King, Ngando has allowed their compound to be used by Hope international School, a French-Speaking school started for refugee children who come from the Great Lakes Region: Rwanda, Burundi and Congo. The members of the congregation do not have any interaction with this school.

89. Okoro, "Africa's Refugee Problem," 237–70.

refugees should not be resettled close to them. In my own findings, it was clear that those who lived close to Kakuma or had personal encounters with the refugees, through going to school, or work, church, etc. had a more positive attitude toward them. However, many felt it was the responsibility of the government to handle the situation and the refugee plight really did not have much to do with them.

A Refugee Camp Experience: Kakuma

Living in a camp is an important experience in the lives of the refugees in Kenya. Each camp has its own peculiar characteristics and features. We will now look at what Kakuma is and what place it holds in the lives of the refugees who live there.

Basic Facts

Kakuma camp was founded in July 1992 in response to the entry of some 23,000 Sudanese refugees into Kenya, of whom 13,000 were unaccompanied boys. It has grown in size and diversity and currently hosts in three locations over 80,000 refugees, originating from eight different countries in Africa, namely, Sudan, Somalia, Ethiopia, Eritrea, Democratic Republic of Congo, Rwanda, Burundi and Uganda. The majority of this population is from Southern Sudan, followed by those of Somali origin. Recently however, the "lost boys" from Sudan have been resettled in the US and UNHCR is presently working toward the resettlement of about 10,000 Somali Bantu people. Due to the war that is still ensuing in Southern Sudan the refugee influx continues unabated.

Kakuma camp is located in the northwestern part of Rift Valley province in Turkana District. It is very dry and faces harsh climatic conditions. The poor climatic conditions mean that the camp is almost entirely dependent upon outside assistance provided principally by the UN and some international and Kenyan NGOs.

The Lives and Aspirations of Refugees

The lives of the refugees at Kakuma are often fraught with a mixture of frustration and hope in light of their physical surroundings. The dismal and dry conditions at the camp are graphically described by one author:

First there is the sun, cracking up like a siren at dawn, blazing down all day, making any plan or activity seem futile or [sic] absurd. Afternoons are so hot you don't want to talk. Then there is the dust; lift up a glass and you'll find a ring of dust beneath it. When you walk on the unpaved pathways of the camp you keep your mouth closed. Even so, the dust grinds between your teeth. And worst of all, there is the wind. A dry insistent wind that steals the very moisture from your mouth. It blows all day and night, as if longing to tear down this fragile human settlement staked out of a dry riverbed.[90]

This means that life for a refugee in the camp is not really a pleasant experience. The longing and desire is to be able to go back to their countries in order for them to contribute effectively to their communities. Their hindrances are the lack of resources and the lack of peace in their country. Yilma depicts this in his poem "If only I could":[91]

> Please don't ask me
> Why don't you go back
> Do you think I like staying for 12 beans,
> Or two weeks of rationing
> Wishing to stay without soap
> Suffering malaria, typhoid
> Here in the bush
> Where
> Wind dust-blowing trumpet
> Do you think I like staying?
> Seeking for second hand clothes
> While I can help myself
> While I can build my homeland
> Do you think my shoulder has carried
> Rather than a fountain, a head, a human brain
> Which can't think far.

Here are some snapshots of some of the activities: In Kakuma refugee camp life goes on with its normal rhythms, despite the intrusive reminders

90. Andrea Useem writes a foreword for Yilma Tafere Tasew's book of poems, *Agonizing Wounds*, that commemorates his life as a refugee in Kakuma before he moved to New Zealand.

91. See the complete poem, "If Only I Could" in Tasew, *Agonizing Wound*, 39–41.

of the alien status into their existence.[92] They celebrate with joy the miracle of new birth.[93] They go to school, prepare meals and have wedding celebrations.[94] The sad reality is that even while they are in the refugee camp, they lose loved ones in death.[95] Though these normal activities take place as they would anywhere in the world, in the refugee camp they take on a new sense of purpose and meaning. As portrayed in the poem above, the refugees do not forget that they are in a foreign country and will one day return home. So, they are able to endure the present difficulties because they are looking forward to a better time someday. The following are a few stories that will depict that kind of anticipation and preparation for the future.

She is 23 years old. Every day, she goes through the regular routine of life at the camp. She wakes up at 6:00 A.M. She prepares breakfast for her four brothers. At 6:30 A.M., she goes to school. At school, she learns the following subjects: English, Mathematics, Geography, History and Civics. She goes home at 12:30 P.M. to prepare something for her brothers to eat. Then she goes to fetch water from the tap far away. She and her siblings do not go back to school in the afternoon because it is too hot. The older women go for adult education. She goes to teach them how to handle the word of God. She knows that she is preparing to go back to Sudan where she will be used by God to touch the lives of many women.

---

92. Oka, "Coping with the Refugee Wait," 23–37.

93. It was at Kakuma maternity ward that I witnessed for the first time the birth of a baby. I joined my friends on their rounds through the maternity ward that day. They have a medical background but I do not. I curiously inquired from the sister-in-charge if there was anyone about to give birth that day. To my surprise, she told me there was a Somali lady who had an extended labor and they were going to assist her, and they kindly allowed me to watch the process. It was the most beautiful process I have ever watched. She did not scream and she was totally calm and relaxed. There was not even much loss of blood, something I had feared would happen. The baby was clean and healthy. As one could guess from her calm composure, this was not her first child, but her eighth. I consider it a privilege to have experienced this. It just showed me that God continues to give life regardless of the circumstances.

94. In January 2003, I was privileged to attend the coffee-making ceremony of a newly-wed Ethiopian bride. It was an elaborate ritual. What was interesting for me to see was how customs and rituals from the motherland were rigorously observed and maintained. These traditions gave them a sense of belonging even while they were in a foreign land.

95. When I visited the camp in 2001, I met with Pastor Endolo from Congo. During this last visit in January 2003, I learned that he had passed away during my absence. He is one of the pastors I interviewed during my visit, so his voice takes on a new sense of significance now that he is not alive. Another young man also told me his sad story of losing his beloved wife in the camp. This caused him such distress that he almost lost his mind. But for his faith in God, he had lost all desire to continue living.

Twenty-six-year-old Jean Pierre Gathera is from Burundi. His wife's name is Riziki Appoline and she is from Rwanda. He came to the Kakuma camp in 1997. His original home is Burundi but he was born in Rwanda in 1973 because his parents were refugees. They later returned to Burundi, but when the war began, he left his parents in 1994 and went to Congo. The conditions in the Congo were so unbearable that he left and went alone to Ngara Camp in Tanzania. He came to Christ at this camp through the help of some Rwandan refugees. In 1997 he came to Kenya. He faced many difficulties when he came to Kakuma camp. First, he did not have a ration card, so he could not get a share of the food. Secondly, the Burundi community rejected him because he did not speak Kirundi well since he had grown up in Rwanda. But he says that these difficulties helped him to grow in his faith. Pastor Tito had known his father in Rwanda a long time ago, so he came to Gathera's rescue by helping him settle into the community. He also helped to counsel and instruct him so that he could grow in the word of God. Gathera became a man of prayer. He had been prayerful to God to provide a wife who could help him in the work of God. He met Riziki at the church in the camp. They had gone to the same secondary school, and had sung together in the choir. Though he was attracted to her and felt that God was leading them together, he felt that she needed to get the confirmation herself. When she gave him a positive response, he still continued to pray about it because he did not know how this could come together seeing that he was in a refugee camp. God gave another additional word of guidance and confirmation through Kenyan evangelist Kariuki. Also, God instructed him to talk to Pastor Tito. And the young woman was also told to do the same without Gathera's intervention. God promised to provide for his wedding which took place on June 2001. Gathera and Riziki hope to return to Rwanda as missionaries to help others learn the word of God and hopefully to stop the wars. For them the Christian community became a family in a way that they had not experienced before. This is because the ties with home had been cut off; they were now free to live an existence where those barriers from home no longer confined them.

Refugee life is a life of suffering, not only for the individual but also for the entire family. This next story is about a family that fled together to Kenya. They have experienced one hardship after another but they have exhibited tremendous courage in the face of despair.

This Burundian family hesitated to share their story because they have suffered so immensely. Previous to my talking to them the wife had experienced an extremely difficult pregnancy for most of her term. But they testified that God had healed her miraculously, and she was able to give birth to a healthy baby boy. Their flight from Burundi followed the political upheavals that led to the overthrow of Melchior Ndadaye in 1993 by the army. Civilian rule continued until 1996, when the army took over again. The military forces began killing both the Hutu and Tutsi who were educated. At first, they fled to Tanzania, but were not comfortable in the refugee camp. Then they moved to Nairobi and lived in Satellite Estate for one year until they got a protection letter from the UNHCR. During the 1997 Kenyan elections, they were harassed by the police. The husband and father spent nine days in jail, and although he had a legitimate letter to attend school in Nairobi, he was not allowed to remain because they wanted all the refugees to go to Kakuma. On September 18, 1997 they came to Kakuma camp. They were surprised to experience such a dry and dusty land—very different from their homeland. They suffered much illness during the adjustment period. In 1998, they experienced some relief when it finally rained for three months, and they were able to plant some crops.

From the stories above, one can see that refugees experience various types of hardships in the camp. One of the greatest of these is the separation from family members, especially children, wives and husbands. Also painful is division and conflict in the community and loss of their homeland. Though they make new relations in a new land, nothing can replace this longing for home. It does not wane no matter how long they stay away from their land. This is clearly demonstrated by the Rwandan refugee experience in Uganda. They had been away for about thirty years but they waited patiently to return. When this was denied to them, they fought for it. Many refugees are also plagued with suspicion and fear as to whom they can trust because they have been previously betrayed and disappointed. However, through it all, those who were Christians testified that the trials had helped them to grow in their faith. They also gave stories of individual Kenyans who helped them in their plight and they were very grateful for even the smallest help they received.

Conclusion

It is evident that Kenya has been given a unique experience by hosting these many nations within her borders. It is also clear that response to the refugees was favorable in the decades of the 1970s[96] and the1980s when the numbers were still small and the socio-economic climate of Kenya was good. However, in the era of the 1990s to the present, when Kenya has

---

96. In May, 2003, I met an Ethiopian in the Palo Alto area who had been a refugee in Kenya in the 70s. He spoke favorably about his time there and he also said he considered Kenya his second home. He even went back to visit Kenya in 2002.

had too much to bear on its shoulders, the refugees have been seen as an added liability and sometimes they have been used as a scapegoat for the country's problems. But is also important to note that despite the overall negative picture, there are encouraging stories of individuals who have stood with the refugees in their time of need.

If we assess ourselves according to the Kiswahili proverb, "*Mgeni siku ya kwanza siku ya pili mpe jembe,*" we can say that looking at the big picture, UNHCR and the NGOS are trying to provide the skills for the refugees to make a living, but their biggest constraint is that they cannot exercise this since they are confined to the restrictive conditions of camp life. The government of Kenya needs to work out a way for the lives of these people to be sustainable while they are in this country. This will be the topic of the coming chapters. Individuals in Kenya, especially Christians, can learn a lot from the refugees about the experience of living an alien/pilgrim existence. The Bible does not just describe that experience, it commands the Christians to live as such. In the next chapter, I look at what the Bible and, more specifically, the epistle to the Hebrews, says about pilgrim existence.

5

The Pilgrim Motif in the Book of Hebrews

> These all died in faith, not having received the promises, but having seen them afar off, and were persuaded of *them*, and embraced *them*, and confessed that they were strangers and pilgrims on the earth. (Heb 11:13, KJV)

Introduction

THE PILGRIM[1] MOTIF IS central to the Christian life.[2] It plays a key role in the identity and the life of the people of God in both the Old and the New Testament. The pioneers of the faith Abraham, Isaac, Jacob, and their

---

1. I use the word "pilgrim" both in the classic usage, meaning one who makes a journey to a sacred place and also in the general sense, suggesting that life on earth is a pilgrimage toward some destination. The understanding, therefore, is that life on earth is temporary but it also has a dimension of purpose. Thus, all strangers, aliens, resident aliens, sojourners, migrants, exiles or refugees share the element of strangeness or unsettledness, but they are not pilgrims unless there is the added dimension of goal or purpose in their lives. This is what sets out a pilgrim from an ordinary stranger. See the Introduction for more on the meaning of pilgrim and pilgrimage.

2. This theme is evident throughout much of modern Christian devotional material, whether novels, plays, songs and more recently, movies. Some of the popular Christian songs that incorporate this theme are: "Guide me O thou great Jehovah, Pilgrim through this barren land" and "This world is not my home, I am just a passing through." Novels also employ this theme extensively. The most popular Christian classic, translated into several languages (I read it in my own language, Nandi) is John Bunyan's *Pilgrim's Progress*. Also, from C. S. Lewis's Narnia series, *The Voyage of the Dawn Treader* depicts life as a voyage. In my own African tradition, life is understood to be a journey. This journey motif is incorporated into many stories and proverbs that are meant to instill morals and values in the society. Some such sayings and proverbs include the following; *Safari ni taabu*, literally, "travel is full of danger" and *Safiri uone mengi*, literally "travel and you will see much." Another saying, "*Asiye safiri uthani mamaye anaye chakula kitamu*," means "He who has not traveled thinks his mother's cooking is the best."

wives lived as "strangers and pilgrims" even in the land of Canaan, the land of promise. The book of Hebrews tells us that they were looking for the "city that has foundations, whose architect and builder is God" (Heb 11:10).[3] In the Old Testament, the Israelite journey to and from Egypt, and later to exile in Babylon, continues this theme in the life of the people of God. We also note this kind of existence in the life of Jesus as "he set his face to go to Jerusalem," he had "nowhere to lay his head."[4] The life of the early Christians is also one of movement as is depicted by the life of the apostle Paul, who made several missionary journeys to establish churches around the region of the Mediterranean sea, and later in Rome. It is important to note that in both the Old and the New Testament the emphasis is placed on the practice of hospitality or love for the aliens and strangers, as an appropriate response to pilgrim existence.[5] The idea is that people who understand what it means to be a stranger should treat strangers better than those who do not. This was expected of the people of God in the Old Testament, but no less for those in the early church and in the present.[6]

The book of Hebrews focuses on the pilgrim motif and also on the response of hospitality to those who are experiencing various kinds of trials, especially Christians living in a hostile environment. My work in this chapter will be to examine how the author of Hebrews uses the pilgrim motif to speak to the situation of the early listeners.[7] The key questions will be: Why

---

3. Unless otherwise noted, biblical quotations are from the New Revised Standard Version (NRSV).

4. See Luke 9:51 and 9:58.

5. See Tzoref, "Knowing the Heart of the Stranger," 119–31.

6 Pohl, "Biblical issues in Mission and Migration," 3, 5. She suggests that these two important motifs are in Scripture. She says, "The first is the continuing experience of the people of God as aliens and exiles; being a stranger is normatively central to the Christian identity. The second is the expectation that as strangers themselves, the people of God will welcome strangers and will embody hospitality as a way of life." These two motifs are key to my work, and hospitality will feature as an important practice that should accompany the pilgrim way of life. I will expand the discussion however, to show how Christians in Kenya should respond to the pressing needs of refugees. See also Small, *The Characterization of Jesus*, 307–13; Mitchell, *Hebrews*, 249–51.

7. I use the term "listeners" here rather than "readers" because many scholars argue that the book of Hebrews is more of a sermon than a letter. Attridge says that Hebrews is "a masterpiece of early Christian rhetorical homiletics or in its own terms a 'word of exhortation'" (Attridge, *Epistle to the Hebrews*, 1). DeSilva also notes that the author of Hebrews uses verbs of speaking when referring to his communication (2:5; 6:9; 8:1; 9:5; 11:32), "he also voices his concern for the addressees' attentive hearing (not reading) of the message" (5:11). See deSilva, *Perseverance in Gratitude*, 36. The excellent rhetorical features lend themselves more to the ear than to the eye. See also Lane, "Standing Before the Moral Claims of God," 204. He says that the writer of Hebrews "crafted the written text for the ear, not the eye, to convey a sense of structure and development. By

does the author use this motif? How does the use of this motif communicate something about the life of the early listeners? What ethical values, principles and practices does the author of Hebrews promote in order for one to persevere in the pilgrimage? Are these values, principles and practices applicable to the church today? My thesis is that the use of the pilgrim motif sets the tone for radical faith and hope in the face of adverse circumstances. That kind of hope should characterize the body of Christ anywhere in the world, but more specifically in Africa where wars, famines and diseases have caused huge displacements of peoples who live scattered in various lands as refugees, aliens and strangers. Most importantly, Hebrews provides us with the key principle of pilgrimage, namely, the necessity of entering into God's presence, the true goal of all pilgrimage. Therefore, this is not a theoretical or an abstract reflection but an urgent call to Christians everywhere to reflect on our true identity as "pilgrims and strangers" and on how this will change the way we live and view the world.

In order to do this work, I first look briefly at how the pilgrim motif is portrayed in and lived out in the life of the people of God in ancient Israel, at the time of Jesus, and in the early church. Then I will examine what various authors say about the use of the pilgrim motif in Hebrews. This will set the stage for examining what Hebrews says about this theme, as I do both a comprehensive overview of the whole book, as well as an exegetical analysis of a key passage, Hebrews 11:13–16. I will then discuss the ethical implications that result from the pilgrim motif with a view to applying them to the church in Africa, more specifically the church in Kenya. In the final analysis, I hope that these principles and practices can be carried on by the church worldwide because this calling for Christian to live as "pilgrims and aliens" is for the whole body of Christ regardless of time and place.

Background: The Pilgrim Motif in Ancient Israel

The central understanding of the people of God both in the old and the new covenant is that of a people always on the move. They are those who have set their eyes on the city "whose maker and founder is God" (Heb 11:10, 16). Here on earth, they have no fixed residence. They live as resident aliens, strangers and foreigners, or pilgrims on a journey to the heavenly city. This identity that embodies movement was brought into place with the calling of the father of faith, Abraham, who was told to move out of the land of the Chaldeans to the land that God would show him. At first, we think that the

---

appealing to the dynamic relationship of speaking and listening, he is able to establish a sense of presence with his audience."

land that he was to inhabit is the land of Canaan, but Hebrews reinterprets this by saying; "By faith he stayed for a time in that land he had been promised, as in a foreign land, living in tents, as did Isaac and Jacob, who were heirs with him of the same promise. For he looked for a city that has foundations, whose architect and builder is God" (Heb 11:9–10). This shows that from the beginning the heirs of faith were aware that their goal was the eternal or heavenly city; the unshakable realm (Heb 12:22, 26–28).[8]

This pilgrim existence was also embodied by Abraham's descendants, the Israelites, who had been promised that kind of life even before they came to be: "Then the Lord said to Abram, "know this for certain, that your offspring shall be aliens in a land that is not theirs, and shall be slaves there, and they shall be oppressed for four hundred years" (Gen 15:13). Even when they had been removed from the bondage of Egypt the people of God were to embrace their alien and pilgrim existence in the key institutions of their life in the land, the temple and the Law.[9]

First, we see how their pilgrim existence influenced their relationship to the land. They were clearly instructed not to forget that they were aliens in the land because the land of Canaan belonged to God. So, they could not treat the land in any way they wanted. Every seven years the land was to be left fallow so that the poor and the aliens could eat from it. At every harvest they showed their concern for the aliens by not harvesting to the edges of the field so that the poor and the alien could glean from those areas (Lev 19:9–10, Deut 14:28–29). The land was also not to be sold in perpetuity. They had to observe the Jubilee principle, which meant that after fifty years the land could be restored to those who had lost it through any means, especially through poverty. Those who fell into hard times were to live among their brothers and sisters as resident aliens until the Jubilee year when they could reclaim their land. The reason is stated here: "The land shall not be sold in perpetuity, for the land is mine; with me you are but aliens and tenants" (Lev 25:23).

We can note the centrality of the pilgrim existence, which was also embodied in their worship life. They included the resident aliens when they worshipped at the tabernacle, during the wilderness experience and also later at the temple in Jerusalem (Deut 16:1–8) The weekly Sabbath was meant to

---

8. See deSilva, *Perseverance in Gratitude*, 381, and Ellingworth, *Epistle to the Hebrews*, 587.

9. There were several words for strangers in Israel. The word "Rg" is translated "sojourner/pilgrim" (KJV), "alien" (NIV), or "resident alien" (NRSV). This is the one who is given full legal rights in Mosaic Law. "Bovt" is also used almost in the same way. The Hebrew: "Rkn" or Hebrew: "Nkn nb" was a foreigner. It covers anything foreign, regardless of residence. Hebrew: "rz" means "stranger" and takes its coloring from the context.

be a time of rest for those who were hired servants and aliens (Exod 20:8–10; 23:12). When they offered their annual tithes they made the confession, "A wandering Aramean was my ancestor; he went down to Egypt and lived there as an alien . . ." (Deut 26:5).[10] They were to celebrate the harvest of these first fruits with the Levites and the aliens. Every third year they had tithes dedicated to aliens and Levites (Deut 14: 28–29; 26:12). One of the annual festivals was the feast of booths (Deut 16:13–15) in which they reenacted their pilgrim and wilderness existence. Three times a year also, they set out on a pilgrimage to the house of worship in Jerusalem when the temple was built. Later, when they were scattered in the Diaspora, they still made these pilgrimages to the temple and also to the city of Jerusalem.

Due to their experience as aliens in the land of Egypt, the Israelites paid special attention to the treatment of the aliens, especially as it was stipulated within the law.[11] They recognized that such a sacred responsibility could not be confined to the level of charitable feelings, so it was enshrined within their legislation. The seriousness of violating this legislation can be seen from the consequences that would befall such offenders: "You shall not wrong or oppress a resident alien, for you were aliens in the land of Egypt, You shall not abuse any widow or orphan, If you do abuse them, when they cry to me, I will surely heed their cry and my wrath will burn and I will kill you with the sword, and your wives shall become widows and your children orphans" (Exod 22:21–23). The severity of the punishment is expressed in the fact that the consequences would not just befall individual offenders but the nation as a whole. The prophets view the Israelites' exile in Babylon as a result of not heeding this warning; they did not remember their own alien existence and did not treat the poor, the orphans, the widows and the aliens well, so they literally became aliens in a foreign land.

In the exile period, the people of God were called to live a pilgrim existence. Yoder offers an important dimension of what the exile meant to the Jews.[12] He argues that the Diaspora or *galuth*, which had been earlier prefig-

---

10. Von Rad argues that these verses contain the earliest digest of Israel's faith. He also suggests that they summarized the core of Israel's salvation history, and he claims that the outline of events contained in the creed formed the basic historical outline of what came to be called "Genesis to Joshua." See von Rad, *The Problem of the Hexateuch and Other Essays*, 1–2. In his commentary to Deuteronomy, he says that the creed is the most important item in the ceremony offering the first fruits of the land. See von Rad, *Deuteronomy*, 158.

11. Van Houten, *The Alien in Israelite Law*, 67, 108, 155–78. She has traced the development of Israelite laws with regard to the aliens, showing how they are progressively given an equal status in the community.

12. See Yoder, *For the Nations*, 53–54. We will use this in the next chapter to develop an ethic for those who are scattered as pilgrims and refugees.

ured in the life in Egypt, was a normal part of Jewish existence and this should also be the case for Christians. He says, "To be scattered is not a hiatus, after which normalcy will resume. From Jeremiah's time on . . . dispersion shall be the calling of the Jewish faith community." He shows further that this was the reason that Jeremiah had to write to the exiles in Babylon to "seek the welfare of the city where I have sent you, and to pray to the LORD on its behalf, for in its welfare you will find your welfare" (Jer 29:7).

During the time of Jesus and the early church, this motif of living a pilgrim and alien existence was part and parcel of life. Caring for those who were marginalized in this way is clearly continued. Jesus was born while his parents were on a journey because of a census that had been imposed, and there was no room for them in the inn. As a baby, he and his family escaped the wrath of a wicked king by fleeing as refugees into Egypt. This shows that from the start of Jesus' life he had to depend on others for his safety and sustenance, and this no doubt shaped his ministry. He welcomed those who were strangers to the community, the sinners, tax collectors and women. When he sent his disciples on a mission, he also urged them to depend on the hospitality of those to whom they ministered. In one of his key teachings on the final judgment, he shows that our eternal destiny was determined by how they treated strangers. He says, "Come, you that are blessed by my father, inherit the kingdom prepared for you from the foundation of the world; for I was . . . a stranger and you welcomed me . . ." (Matt 25:31–46).

The life of the early Christians was also a life of movement. Due to the persecution that came upon the believers that were in Jerusalem most of them had to move to several places all over the Roman Empire where they learned to live as aliens and pilgrims. First Peter is especially addressed to such, "to the exiles of Dispersion . . ." They are specifically urged to live an exemplary existence, "Beloved, I urge you as aliens and exiles to abstain from the desires of the flesh that wage war against the soul" (1 Pet 2:11). In his missionary journeys, Paul lived out the pilgrim existence. This is the reason that one of the practices the early church emphasized was hospitality (Rom 12:9–13; 15:1; 1 Tim 3:2; Titus 1:2; 2 John 10–12; Heb 13:2).

The Book of Hebrews

The book of Hebrews has exerted great influence over the Christian church throughout the centuries despite the fact that much about its authorship[13]

---

13. About the authorship of Hebrews, Origen said, "But who wrote the epistle in truth God knows." See Attridge, *Epistle to the Hebrews*, 1. But this summary statement by Origen has not prevented commentators from speculating about various authors.

and composition are unknown. It has appealed to many people for various reasons. For some, the attraction has been the beautiful and artistic literary and rhetorical features[14] which the author has used to craft and blend the expository and exhortation parts together. For others it has been the great themes, such as the completed and superior work of Christ in comparison to the Old Testament religious systems,[15] the exhortation to follow the heroes of faith by moving toward that eternal home, as well as the call to be faithful even in difficult times in their particular contexts.

There is no doubt that this book has been a source of inspiration and encouragement to believers for all times,[16] though the author is unknown,[17] the date[18] of writing is unclear and the original recipients are not identified.

Names that have been proposed include Apollo, Luke, Silas, Priscilla and Aquila, or Mary the mother of Jesus. See Attridge, *Epistle to the Hebrews*, 1–5, Koester, *Hebrews*, 42–46, Ellingworth, *Epistle to the Hebrews*, 3–21.

14. Attridge, *Epistle to the Hebrews*, 1. He says "The document known as the Epistle to the Hebrews is the most elegant and sophisticated, perhaps the most enigmatic, text of first-century Christianity. Its author is unknown and the circumstances of its composition remain mysterious. Its argumentation is subtle; its language refined; its imagery rich and evocative." See also Heil, *Hebrews*; Martin and Whitlark, *Inventing Hebrews*; Cockerill, *Hebrews*, 60–81; O'Brien, *Hebrews*, 24–34.

15. Donald Guthrie (*Hebrews*, 36–39) and Richard Hays do not think the book of Hebrews contains supersessionist theology. Hays writes, "the Letter to the Hebrews nowhere speaks of Jews and Gentiles, nowhere gives evidence of controversies over circumcision or food laws, criticizes nothing in the Mosaic Torah except for the Levitical sacrificial cult, and contains no polemic against Jews or Jewish leaders." Hays, "'Here We Have No Lasting City,'" 154. Cf. Mitchell, *Hebrews*, 25–28.

16. After the events of September 11, 2001, I listened to several sermons from the book of Hebrews to encourage the believers in their situation. See also Laansma, *The Letter to the Hebrews*, 1–48; Laansma, "Hebrews: Yesterday, Today, and Future," 1–32; Lee, *Today When You Hear His Voice*, 218–25; Koester, "'In Many and Various Ways,'" 299–315; O'Brien, *God Has Spoken in His Son*, 15–20; Mitchell, *Hebrews*, 13–16.

17. Though the name of the author is not known, there are clues from the book that tell us what kind of a person he was. He was not an eyewitness of the events of the life of Jesus (2:3). He was probably in the traveling band with Paul because he mentions Timothy (13:23). He was most likely a Jew who used the LXX because he takes his Old Testament quotations from it. He is well educated in the rhetorical features of his day (See Attridge, *Epistle to the Hebrews*, 20–21; and deSilva, *Perseverance in Gratitude*, 35–71, on the author's knowledge of rhetoric). He is also aware of the philosophical applications of the Scripture during his day. Some people think he was a converted Philonist.

18. Two dates have been suggested, pre-70 ce and post-70 ce. One of the arguments for the pre-70 ce date is that, if the destruction of the Temple had already taken place, this would have been his proof to show that the sacrifices in the Temple were obsolete. However, this is not considered conclusive because the author uses language that refers to the tabernacle rather than the Temple so it might have been a theological rather than physical matter. Allison says that the fact the author used "tabernacle" instead of "Temple" was that the author was careful in the choice of words, especially

What is clear, however, is that the author, who is well known to his audience, is aware of the fact that they are facing a twofold danger, as Attridge tells us: "external pressure or persecution (10:36–12:13) and a waning commitment to the community's confessed faith."[19] So his response to the first danger is "stern warnings and exhortations to faithful discipleship."[20] For the second danger he "proposes a renewed and deepened understanding of the community's confession that will inspire covenant fidelity."[21] My argument is that the author uses the pilgrim motif to call his audience to an awareness of themselves as a covenant people: a reminder that theirs was a pilgrim faith right from the beginning. This would inspire them to persevere through the external trials while giving them a proper perspective on the eternal treasures that they were to hold on to.

Literature on the Pilgrim Motif in Hebrews

A number of scholars have recognized the importance of the pilgrim motif in Hebrews. As a "cloud of witnesses," in this area of study, their work has provided me with the theological framework and inspiration necessary to show that this theme has special relevance to the African situation. Those who have focused on the pilgrim motif as a central theme say that it helps us to understand the message of Hebrews, especially with regard to the situation of the original hearers. However, because time and space will not permit more, I will only mention a few who have focused on the pilgrim motif specifically in their work.

These include Käsemann,[22] who shows that pilgrimage is the central motif that explains the existence of the people of God both in the Old Testament and the New Testament. However, he argues that the Gnostic-Redeemer myth provides the motif of the wandering people of God "in its most conceivably pronounced form."[23] Though the Gnostic origins of the book of Hebrews have been disproved,[24] it does not discount the fact that

---

since this was in a very explosive time just before 70 ce. See Allison, *The End of the Times Has Come*, 230.

19. Attridge, *Epistle to the Hebrews*, 13.
20. Ibid.
21. Ibid.
22. Käsemann, *The Wandering People of God*.
23. Käsemann, *The Wandering People of God*. 87. In this, many commentators have questioned him.
24. See Thompson, *The Beginnings of Christian Philosophy*, 3. He shows that the themes that Käsemann attributed to the Gnostic background have been widely found

Käsemann convincingly demonstrates that the pilgrim motif ties together the cultic and the parenetic sections of the letter to the Hebrews. As he says, the picture that is set before the Hebrews is that of Israel wandering through the wilderness (Heb 3:7—4:13). This journey is set in motion by the word of God, which is also described as the promise: "It calls to a way, the goal of which it points out by way of promise and which can only be reached in union with the Logos and on its promise."[25] Israel failed to appropriate [the word] because she "failed to recognize the character of the Logos as a promise hastening one on the way. Only obedience that achieves this wandering beneath and together with the Word to the end is evidence that the acceptance of the Word has actually occurred."[26] Käsemann's understanding is that one possesses the gospel only as promise:[27] "the logos grants no final revelation."[28] And this, therefore, calls for a unique lifestyle. He argues that the "form of existence in time appropriate to the recipient of revelation can only be that of wandering."[29] But this wandering is not done on an individual basis. He says, "the existence of the bearer of revelation is not only determined by wandering under the sign of promise but also by incorporation into the fellowship of the people of God."[30] He puts it even more emphatically: "Apart from the people of God there is neither revelation nor a bearer of the revelation, nor is there a wandering that is oriented to a goal, but only the solitude of existence left to itself and the hopeless and aimless erring of world becoming wilderness."[31] Thus in Hebrews there is no "private Christianity."[32]

This journey is waged through suffering, and the staying power that keeps the pilgrim on his or her way is the promise that is appropriated by faith. "The *epaggelia* (promise) is more than an expression of the divine good will. That is, it is a statute of the future order of salvation and thus establishes

---

in other contexts. He notes that themes like pilgrimage still remain relevant. See also Ellingworth, *Epistle to the Hebrews*, 42. He says that the discoveries of Nag Hammadi show that Gnosticism was prevalent from the second to the fourth centuries so there was possibly no literary influence on Hebrews. He does not rule out oral tradition material.

25. Käsemann, *The Wandering People of God*, 19.
26. Ibid.
27. Ibid.
28. Ibid.
29. Ibid.
30. Ibid.
31. Ibid., 22.
32. Ibid. The communal element of faith will be one of the key practices that will characterize an ethic for refugees. I will focus on this when we look at the ethical implications of the pilgrim motif.

the way of faith on unshakable ground, anchored, as it were, by divine right."[33] This faith he argues, is not the same as in Paul's writings;[34] it carries with it the idea of hope and endurance. "The concept contains both aspects: Assent to the divine promise and the persistence with which this assent is maintained in assurance of the future."[35] He also says, "In Hebrews the obedience of faith is fulfilled when, in trusting the divine promise, one is willing to be led patiently through the present time of suffering into the heavenly future."[36] This promise is made sure by the covenant or the word of God. The goal of this wandering is the heavenly city.[37] This theme is tied together because of Christ who is seen as the example who has gone before and is also seen as the high priest who has made certain the way to God. Thus, Christology in Hebrews is linked to the journey motif. He concludes:

> For the Christian community itself, the message of the high priestly activity of the exalted one spells the certainty of salvation even in the face of *asthenēs*. It is in need of *parrēsia*, to complete the wandering begun in faith. A new *paraklēsis* should restore to this community, shaken by various concrete temptations, this original confidence.[38]

Käsemann has brought into the foreground three key elements that are related to the pilgrim motif: the example and the work of Christ who is the pioneer who has set the way, the importance of the community of faith, and the component of endurance and hope in the midst of suffering. These will be explored later as we look into the practices and values that are expected of the pilgrim community.

Jewett acknowledges the centrality of the pilgrim motif in Hebrews by entitling his commentary *Letter to the Pilgrims: A Commentary on the Epistle to the Hebrews*.[39] He says that the commentary is the culmination of several decades of his reflection on the epistle to the Hebrews and on the pilgrim

---

33. Käsemann, *The Wandering People of God*, 31; cf. Guthrie, *Hebrews*, 61.

34. Ibid., 37–38. Though Käsemann is quick to note that Hebrews and Paul share the understanding of faith as obedience to the word of God, there is a departure between the two when the believers in Hebrews are told to hold fast their confidence to the end. This brings in the idea of endurance and hope. Käsemann also says that while faith in Paul is preserved despite the scandal of the cross, faith in Hebrews is held on in view of the delay of the consummation (Käsemann, *The Wandering People of God*, 39).

35. Käsemann, *The Wandering People of God*, 38.

36. Ibid., 39.

37. Ibid., 37, 48.

38. Ibid., 239.

39. Jewett, *Letter to the Pilgrims*.

theme in American culture.[40] He says further, "We are convinced that Hebrews' acceptance of adversity and rapid change, its conception of faith as pilgrimage through insecurity and its sense of dialogical fulfillment along the pilgrim path correspond with some of the most profound treatments in the American experience . . ."[41] Therefore Jewett says that he sets out to write his commentary in agreement with the statement by William G. Johnson that "the recognition of the pilgrimage motif in Hebrews opens a wholistic view of the document."[42] He notes, "My goal is to set forth the relevance of the pilgrim faith for the original audience of the letter to the Hebrews, and thereby to suggest its possible bearing on the present situation."[43]

Jewett's argument that the letter of Hebrews was written at the same time to the inhabitants of the Lycius Valley like the letter to the Colossians is on shaky ground. This is mainly because he bases his argument on Käsemann's Gnostic-redeemer myth. However, his recognition of the central theme of pilgrimage is very valuable. "The meaning of the pilgrim journey is not in arrival, he argues, but rather in the encounter with God and God's word moment for moment along the pilgrim path. "Today when you hear his voice" is when the heavenly city is reached and that occurs not in the realm of manipulation, but "outside the camp," in the secular realm of daily life.[44] He also shows that part of the pilgrim existence is the acceptance of suffering and adversity as the way of life. He says, "Hebrews interprets adversity as an inevitable and unresolvable aspect of the created order as designed by God."[45] The comfort through this suffering and adversity is that there is one who has gone ahead, so Jewett argues that Hebrews places Christ as head of the band of the pilgrims. He says:

> The Christ of Hebrews is daringly reinterpreted as the one who redeems his pilgrim community by sharing the conditions of pilgrimage: insecurity, temptation, and death. He is the "pioneer" and the "leader" of the band, striding before them through the secular realm of Golgotha, outside the wall of the holy city. His death is viewed as sharing the element of vulnerability to the final degree, taking away its threat, and bringing a troubled band of pilgrims with him to the very throne of God. He is the great

---

40. Ibid., 1.
41. Ibid., 1.
42. Ibid., 2.
43. Ibid., 2. This is one of the chief contributions of Jewett's commentary. He reinterprets the themes in Hebrews to fit into the technological age that America faces. He answers the question, "what does it mean to be a pilgrim people in America today?"
44. Ibid., 12.
45. Ibid.

high priest whose activity eliminates the need for other cultic ceremonies, because he achieves what the best of the cult intend but always fail to provide: atonement with God and transformation of humans into genuinely mature and humane persons.[46]

But Christ is not the only one who comforts the believers on the way; the believers also encourage one another along the way. He says, "Rather than devoting their lives to gaining security through religious rituals, seeking to raise themselves above the plight of humankind, the followers of the great high priest find fellowship with fellow humans along the pilgrim way, serving and helping and exhorting one another to keep the pilgrim faith."[47] The result of such a lifestyle, Jewett argues, is "A secular ethic with particular concern for the outsiders, the strangers, and the prisoners . . . integrating worship and service in the realm that Jesus made his own by suffering outside the gate."[48] He says that the proper application to the American context is to shatter any illusion that America is the chosen nation protected from adversity, but on the contrary to call the nation to embark on a pilgrimage that "accepts insecurity as the norm and that assumes the meaning of the journey is to be found along the way."[49] This also means that one is called to live in midst of the tension of "sacred discontent": a tension between the promises and the performance, between what has already been achieved and what is yet to be accomplished.[50]

Lane also recognizes that pilgrimage and promise is the one most distinctive note in the book of Hebrews. He sees this especially in Hebrews 3:7–4:13, "when attention is focused upon the wilderness experience of Israel who failed to enter God's promised rest because of unbelief and disobedience."[51] In the same way, the community of faith lives in terms of the promise of God, and this brings into broad daylight the peril awaiting them, if they disobey as the Israelites did. He also shows that the emphasis in Hebrews 11 is "the pilgrimage of the Patriarchs who were attested by God as faithful . . . as the model for obedience."[52] Indeed, he notes:

46. Ibid., 13.
47. Ibid.
48. Ibid.
49. Ibid., 15.
50. Ibid. See Martin and Whitlark, *Inventing Hebrews*, 259: "We suggest that throughout Hebrews the promises of God are held out as the goal of God's actions and the motivation for ongoing perseverance on the part of the faithful (cf. 2:3, 5, 10; 4:1; 6:12; 10:34; 11:13–16; 12:28." Cf. Cockerill, *Hebrews*, 535–63.
51. Lane, *Hebrews 1–8*, cxlvii; see also Yeo, "'Rest' in Hebrews and the Yin-Yang Worldview," in *What Has Jerusalem to Do with Beijing*, 80–111.
52. Ibid.

> In this life the Christians have no enduring city; they seek intently the city that is to come (13:14). Only in this perspective do they emulate faithful men and women of God like Abraham and his family who lived in tents, seeking a city or a home (11:10, 14, 16). Pilgrimage is the characteristic of the obedient people of God under both the old and new covenants, and it cannot be in vain since God has prepared for them a city (11:10, 16). The new people of God must remain a pilgrim generation, continually open to the call of God upon their lives.[53]

This brings into focus what he calls, "Pilgrim ecclesiology," which "is a survival ecclesiology, it implies separation from–a place–it entails hardship."[54] He also reiterates a fact that had earlier been mentioned by Käsemann that what God has spoken is only in the form of a promise. Therefore, he underscores the issue by saying:

> The fact that the revelation of God is possessed on earth only as promise explains why one form of existence appropriate to the community of faith is pilgrimage. Christians must pursue the promise and lay hold of it. Reference to the wandering of Abraham, or of Israel through the wilderness, becomes a useful vehicle for the calling of the Christian community to a life of faith and obedience shaped and sustained by the promise of God.[55]

Lane also argues that because of the pilgrim motif the definition of faith in Hebrews is distinct from that of Paul. He differentiates it in this way:

> For Paul faith is essentially firm commitment to God's accomplished redemptive action through Jesus; it entails a retrospective turn especially to the cross and resurrection. The theological perspective of Hebrews is profoundly different. Faith is both an openness to the future, which is given expression in obedient trust in God who has promised, and a present grasp upon truth now invisible but certain because it is grounded in the word of promise.[56]

This he sees as an eschatological understanding of faith, which is closely linked to the pilgrim motif in the book of Hebrews.[57]

---

53. Ibid.
54. Ibid.
55. Ibid.
56. Ibid., cxlvix.
57. Ibid., cxlix.

K. K. Yeo suggests a four-fold definition of rest in the book of Hebrews. First, Yeo points to the author's, who is a homilist, usage of *katapausis* (rest) relating to resting in a physical locale with the presence of God. The "Canaan" rest, where the Israelites entered the land of Canaan after their exodus from Egypt as an example of this type of rest. This sense of rest can be understood as being location specific and bodily and physical.[58] Secondly, Yeo argues for an active form of rest, based on the theology that God is active and being present with God is dynamically relational and interactive.[59] Third, Yeo points to the eschatological nature of rest in Hebrews where this rest "is heavenly rest because heaven (which, according to the author is not just a future reality but a present one; see 12:22) is the eternal place where God dwells and reigns with his people forever."[60] In this case, rest is a future reality and inevitability, as well as a present activity. Finally, Yeo points to a cognate of "rest" as *sabbatismos* meaning as "creation rest", where all of creation including humanity will be in final sabbath rest in God.[61]

William Johnsson reviews the studies that have been done on Hebrews. He focuses on the works of Buchanan and Dey. Johnsson shows that Buchanan's contribution is the "Utter Jewishness"[62] of Hebrews. This is a Qumran-type community that awaits the promise to Abraham in Jerusalem. To him Jesus is an exemplary figure but not God. Dey on the other hand, says Johnsson, seeks to show that Hebrews can only be understood in the thought world of the Hellenistic Judaism of Philo: "The letter to the Hebrews endeavors to establish the superiority of Jesus to readers steeped in such ideas."[63] He also notes that both Dey and Buchanan cannot accommodate the pilgrim motif in their work. He commends Käsemann who put this motif forward as significant for the interpretation of Hebrews, though he agrees that the Gnostic-redeemer myth needs to be discarded. Johnsson says Käsemann "has succeeded in isolating the poignant note of Hebrews. As pilgrims, God's people are on the move; they have not yet arrived, although great privileges are theirs, the possibility of failure to attain the goal is ever present; the great need is for faithfulness."[64]

---

58. Yeo, *What Has Jerusalem to Do with Beijing*, 87–90, 93–94. See also Laansma, *The Letter to the Hebrews*, 109–11; Healy, *Hebrews*, 91.

59. Yeo, *What Has Jerusalem to Do with Beijing*, 94.

60. Ibid., 95.

61. Ibid., 95–96.

62. Johnsson, "Issues in the Interpretation of Hebrews," 170.

63. Ibid., 174.

64. Ibid., 180.

In his article, "The Pilgrimage Motif in the Book of Hebrews," Johnsson[65] expounds further this motif in Hebrews. He investigates the evidences from the text that point toward the centrality of the theme of pilgrimage. Chapters 3 and 4 are the first candidates he examines. Though these chapters do not use the word pilgrimage, the backdrop is the exodus and the wilderness wanderings. Johnsson also says they at least portray "a movement toward a goal."[66] In chapter 11 the thrust is "God's people in the OT look beyond the present life to a heavenly reward. They sighted the better country, the city of God, but did not attain it. This world was not their true home: here they were merely sojourners and foreigners, passing through, as it were to a heavenly goal and the world treated them harshly."[67] Thus faith is more than just "a belief and trust in the unseen, it suggests a marked element of faithfulness deriving from a belief and trust."[68] The ideas that are implicit in chapter 3 and 4 reach their full expression in chapter 11.[69] Johnsson notes two ideas about pilgrimage in Hebrews chapter 13: "here we seek no lasting city" and ill treatment of God's people "outside the camp."[70]

In his review of the literature on pilgrimage, he discusses both the devotional and the scholarly articles. For the devotional, he shows how Hebrews has influenced many hymns and sermons with the idea of pilgrimage, but he does not focus on this. On the scholarly works, he shows that the main work is that by E. Käsemann especially as translated by Barrett, though he seems to show that maybe Barrett has read more into Käsemann's idea. Spicq's work also does not expound the idea of pilgrimage.

Johnsson chooses the phenomenological model of H. B. Partin, who structures the idea of pilgrimage according to the Muslim *Hajj*.[71] He shows that Partin identifies four key elements of pilgrimage: separation which is equivalent to a leaving home, journey to a sacred place, specific purpose, and

---

65. Johnsson laments the fact this idea is lacking in Western thought. It only seems to be supplied by such works as *Pilgrim Fathers*, *Canterbury Tales* and *Pilgrims Progress*. Jewett however says this motif is dominant in the American scene in the 1970s. See Johnsson, "The Pilgrim Motif in the Book of Hebrews."

66. Johnsson, "The Pilgrim Motif in the Book of Hebrews," 240.

67. Ibid., 240.

68. Ibid., 241.

69. Though Johnsson says that chapter 12 does not contain any allusions to pilgrimage, the idea of running the race that is set before us brings in the idea of movement. This also points to Jesus as the one who has gone ahead of us. See Johnsson, "The Pilgrim Motif in the Book of Hebrews."

70. Ibid., 241.

71. Ibid., 244.

hardship.[72] He argues that all these points are satisfied in the book of Hebrews. The people of God are on a journey to a new land; they seek a better country whose builder and maker is God. They seek this journey in order to find the rest that can come only from God. The way is difficult because they will even experience martyrdom. But Johnsson also notes that the book of Hebrews goes beyond the structure of pilgrimage that Partin gives in terms of "the figure of Jesus, the nature of the goal, and the concern with an event in the past . . . The shadow of Jesus looms large over the Hebrew pilgrims. He is the *archēgon* the pioneer or pathfinder (2:10; 12:2) and the *prodromos* forerunner (6:20)."[73] The goal also is not to an earthly city; in Hebrews, "It belongs to the realm of the invisible."[74] But this is not just future; it is shaped by an event in the past, the "purification of sins," so "the past colors the present." However, he also shows that the motif for pilgrimage occurs in the pareneses, while the separation occurs in the cultic section. This allows Johnsson to argue that the two dominant motifs in Hebrews are cult and pilgrimage. In fact, he describes the Christians in Hebrews as a "cultic community on the move."[75] Thus the two motifs are unified. The cultic motif explains the past and separation including the temptation of defilement, while the pilgrim motif looks forward to the future with the problems of "unbelief and unfaithfulness with particular perils in the present which may cause the goal to be lost." The cultic takes care of the already and now, and the pareneses, the not yet.[76] Thus, the pilgrimage motif of Hebrews opens up a holistic view of the document. This enables us to understand the alternation of the cultic argumentation and the pareneses of the document.[77]

P. J. Arowele's[78] point of departure is Käsemann's book.[79] He uses this to show that the understanding of the pilgrim motif has been key to unraveling the ecclesiology and the eschatology in the book of Hebrews. His main argument is that the pilgrimage and sojourning are the character of the church today and are as relevant today as they were at the turn of the first century.[80] He says, "Today the church formally acknowledges being an

72. Ibid.
73. Ibid., 247; cf. Guthrie, *Hebrews*, 117.
74. Johnsson, "The Pilgrim Motif in the Book of Hebrews," 248.
75. Ibid., 249; Yeo, *What Has Jerusalem to Do with Beijing*, 105.
76. Ibid., 250.
77. Ibid.
78. Arowele, "Pilgrim People of God," 238–455.
79. He agrees with Käsemann's thesis that the pilgrim motif is what ties the strands of *pareneses* and exhortation in Hebrews together, but he does not support the idea of the origin of this motif in Gnosticism.
80. Arowele, "Pilgrim People of God," 438.

exile community on earth."[81] To my great delight, he also locates this theme in the African continent. He says:

> Nowhere is this more evident than in the church in Africa and in the third world at large. Here, sojourning and exile (caused by poverty, famine, political instability, tribal and racial discrimination, and so on) are the realities of daily life. This situation in which the church finds itself in Africa is not without relevance for theology, especially when cognizance is taken of the traditional conception that earthly existence is the sojourn away from the real home.[82]

Arowele discusses the passages in Hebrews that bring out the theme clearly. First, he notes that the similarities the author of Hebrews draws between Israel and the church is "wandering and sojourning" in chapter 3:7—4:13. He says, "the church as the eschatological community is on pilgrimage to God's rest just as Israel once was 'en route' to the promised land."[83] Salvation is described as eschatological rest[84] and the readers are invited to come into this rest. Then he features chapter 11, in which faith is seen as a "force that summons the believer beyond the visible realities (cf. 11:1)."[85] In this way, "it makes him a sojourner and exile on earth. It does not only hold a promise of better things beyond the believer, but sustains him through the vicissitudes of his wandering existence on earth."[86] The one who exemplifies this is Abraham, whom he calls *paroikos* "par excellence,"[87] but Jesus is the example *par excellence* who has attained the full promise and the crown of faith.

The goal of this sojourn is the heavenly city into which paradoxically they are said to have already come (12:28). Arowele examines the sense in which they have already come: they have come through the participation in the cultic worship: "Whenever they are in the cultic get-together, the readers are said to have come to the heavenly city."[88] In this communion they get together with three groups of people; the innumerable angels, the assembly of the firstborn and the spirits of the just men made perfect. There is a reason for this participation and he says, "This 'communio sanctorum' means assurance of salvation for the pilgrims because they not only

81. Ibid.
82. Ibid.
83. Ibid., 440.
84. Ibid., 438.
85. Ibid., 441.
86. Ibid.
87. Ibid.
88. Ibid.

have examples to follow, but can as well count on their intercession."[89] The last passage he examines is 13:13–14, the call to exit "outside the gate." This again highlights the picture of the Christians on pilgrimage: "Their exit is not an escape from the world which is no more worthy of them (11:28). Rather, it means their existence is predominated by the aspiration and yearning to be with Jesus in the heavenly home."[90]

Arowele also notes that the eschatological overtones in the book of Hebrews point to the "disillusionment among the members at the non-realization of the Parousia expectation."[91] In order to revitalize the community's understanding of itself there was need for a redefinition: "Herein comes his concept of the pilgrim nature of the church."[92] He argues that this concept is very relevant to the church today that finds itself "strange and alien to the modern technological age. Therefore, in acknowledging today to be an exile body on earth, the church is just true to itself."[93] For the African situation he notes:

> The stark realities of life in Africa literally verify exile and pilgrimage. Here large-scale poverty and famine constantly force whole populations to migrate and wander far away from home. Further, political unrests in several countries create the permanent race of exiles and refugees.[94]

This is not just an existential condition, but it is within the African concept of the reality of life on earth, which is described as a sojourn. He says, "it pertains to the belief in life in the hereafter,"[95] and also to the belief in ancestors and the living dead. He also notes, "Some scholars have proposed African ancestrology as the basis for genuine African theology, especially in ecclesiology, and eschatology as also in Christology."[96] The perfect way to communicate this Christology and make the pilgrimage of the African to come to a close would be to acknowledge Christ as the "forerunner, pioneer, perfecter and therewith unique ancestor with God."[97]

---

89. Ibid., 445.
90. Ibid., 446.
91. Ibid., 447.
92. Ibid.
93. Ibid., 449.
94. Ibid.
95. Ibid., 451.
96. Ibid.
97. Ibid., 453.

Arowele's exposition that makes a link with African theology is very accurate and thorough, especially as it makes links between the African and the Christian pilgrimage. My aim is to draw some ethical guidelines that would be suited for those who have embarked on this pilgrimage as espoused in Hebrews. Arowele's main shortcoming is that though he mentions the warning on perseverance and the danger of the love of money as some of the ethical exhortations, he does not elaborate on these themes.

Key Components of the Pilgrim Motif

The previously mentioned authors have discussed some of the main themes that comprise the pilgrim motif. However, I would like to draw out and analyze both the thematic and grammatical components that I have found to be key in understanding the pilgrim motif in Hebrews.

The Use of Old Testament Examples

The book of Hebrews draws heavily on the Old Testament and God's dealings with the Israelites as a wandering people (Heb 3:7—4:13). It is rife with both negative and positive examples of their journey in the wilderness. This journey in which they failed to enter the Promised Land because of their disobedience was used as a negative example. Thus, the failure of Israel to reach the land serves as a grave warning[98] to his listeners. They are aware that if they do not heed God's voice and receive by faith what they have been promised, they will be like their foreparents who perished in the wilderness.

How does this experience in the wilderness portray the pilgrim existence? The book of Hebrews says that this wilderness generation did not enter God's rest. In a literal sense, the people of God were on the move to the land of promise. The only source of sustenance was God, but they were not willing to trust God to receive his provision for them. The truth is that they complained all the way, desiring to go back where they had come from. They questioned the wisdom of God in leading them. Though they had seen God's works in the past—the greatest event being the deliverance from the Egyptians—they were not willing to trust God to see them through into the land of Canaan. The sad consequence is that they were not able to enter the rest that God had promised them.

---

98. Commentators mention the interchange in Hebrews of negative and positive reinforcement for the people of faith to be encouraged along the way. See deSilva, *Perseverance in Gratitude*, 58–71 on the use of socio-rhetorical strategy. See also Attridge, *Epistle to the Hebrews*, 20; Martin and Whitlark, *Inventing Hebrews*, 52–70.

On the other hand, the author later brings out positive examples in chapter 11 when he articulates the victories of the heroes and heroines of the faith. I will deal later with this in depth.

Verbs of Motion[99]

The author of Hebrews also uses the verbs of movement[100] to illustrate the pilgrim motif graphically. Attridge argues that the writer employs the hortatory subjunctives[101] to encourage "dynamic virtue and movement in various directions"[102] and to exhort the hearers to make progress in their walk of faith. The writer identifies with his audience when he urges them, "let us come, or go to, or approach"[103] (*proserchōmetha*) to the throne of grace (*tō thronō tēs charitos*) in order to obtain mercy and grace in time of need (4:16). Their assurance and boldness in approaching the throne of grace rests on the fact that Christ has a permanent priesthood, and therefore acts as the perfect mediator. Their former priests were limited by death but Christ ever lives to make intercession for them (7:25). He has also opened the way by his blood so they are cleansed (10:22). Faith and trust in God are the keys to this approach (11:6). The writer of Hebrews also makes this bold assertion that the believers have already come into that heavenly sanctuary (12:18, 22).[104] It shows that they already enjoy the benefits of the eternal kingdom even now on earth, and these benefits can be appropriated on their pilgrim journey.

---

99. Käsemann, 23. He discusses the verbs of motion on footnote 10. Thanks also to my friend and colleague Scott Mackie, who brought this element to my attention by letting me read his paper, "Entrance and Draw-near Terminology."

100. Attridge, *Epistle to the Hebrews*, 22–23. He notes that there are two types of hortatory subjunctives in the book of Hebrews. One group denotes movement, while the other encourages stability and steadiness or "holding fast" the faith.

101. See Attridge, *Epistle to the Hebrews*, 22. The usage of hortatory subjunctives in Hebrews. Examples are 4:1, 11, 14, and 16; 6:1; 10:22–24; 12:1, 28; 13:13,15.

102. Ibid.

103. BDAG, *Greek-English Lexicon*, 878.

104. This bold assertion portrays the "already" element of the eschatological tension that is characteristic of the pilgrim motif in Hebrews. See Wright, "A Christian Approach to Old Testament Prophecy," 18–19: "Hebrews' affirmations of what 'we have' is surprisingly comprehensive. We have the land, described as 'rest' into which we have entered through Christ, in a way that Joshua did not achieve for Israel (3:12–4:11); We have a High Priest (4:14; 8:1; 10:21) and altar (13:10); we enter into the Holy Place, so receiving the kingdom, in line with Haggai 2:6 (12:28). Indeed, according to Hebrews (13:14) the only thing we do not have is an earthly, territorial city."

The verb *eiselthein* to go or enter in, to come (4:1, 3, 6, 10–11) is used to call the believers to enter into the rest that God has given them. The context is Israel's sojourn in the wilderness. The warning comes out of the fact that because of disobedience they perished in the wilderness and failed to enter God's rest. The next set of verses, 6:19–20; 9:12, 24–25; 10:5, refer to Christ as the one who has entered into the heavenly sanctuary, in order to mediate on behalf of the believers.

The verb *eggizomen* (7:19), to approach or come near,[105] continues to highlight the insufficiency of the law and its ineffectiveness in bringing people close to God. On the contrary, the hope that saves is that which is based on the eternal priesthood of Christ. However, the writer of Hebrews shows that the movement is not just in one direction. He reverses direction when emphasizing God's call to move outside, *exerchōmetha pros auton exō tēs parembolēs* (13:13), meaning to "go out, come out,"[106] to join with Christ outside the camp.[107] This call is not unique. It follows the example "of those who left Egypt under the leadership of Moses" (3:16), and Abraham who came out of his homeland to seek the city with foundations (11:8). But even then, the believers are cautioned to make sure that their moving out is to join with Christ and not *pararyōmen* (2:1) "to drift away"[108] from the message they have received. Instead, they are encouraged to "carry on," *pherōmetha* (6:1), to maturity so that they can enjoy what they have been promised.

Metaphor of Contest

Contest or *agōna* is another imagery that portrays the pilgrim motif. Like the verbs of motion, it runs through the whole book, but it is more specifically discussed in chapter 12. DeSilva argues that the author of Hebrews uses this metaphor strategically in order to turn an "experience of disgrace and marginalization into a competition for honor."[109] He also quotes Aristo-

---

105. BDAG, *Greek-English Lexicon*, 270.

106. Ibid., 347.

107. Attridge calls this the "drastic reversal of the imagery of movement," which leads to the realm of suffering and prayerful service. He also says this "dynamic" virtue of movement is not entry but exit. See Attridge, *Epistle to the Hebrews*, 22; also, McKelvey, *Pioneer and Priest*, 151–61, 202–5.

108. BDAG, *Greek-English Lexicon*, 612.

109. DeSilva, *Perseverance in Gratitude*, 360. He notes that the athletic imagery is a common one in the literature of minority cultures, which he says, resonates with Stoic and Cynic Literature as well as Jewish martyrological and philosophical writings. Thompson also argues that Philo uses this imagery to describe training in philosophy,

tle who finds this metaphor is one that dignifies the experience of suffering so that the hearers can view their hostility and shame as a competition that allows them to display honorable virtues such as courage and endurance.[110] Koester also acknowledges the importance of this metaphor, saying, "The striking imagery is designed to transform the listeners' perception of the situation from one in which they are beleaguered victims to one in which they are vigorous contestants who can hope to participate in the festival gathering in God's city.[111] Both Koester and deSilva show that this use of the metaphor transports the imagery into a public[112] place where several unseen witnesses are watching the believers. They are cheering them on with roars of approval so that they can complete the race. The implication is that these witnesses have already finished, so they are saying, "We have done it, so you are also able to do it." However, Koester and deSilva note that the metaphor is good as far as participation in the contest is concerned. But for the Christian, the goal is to complete the race and not to beat any other contestants. Their antagonist is not another contestant. It is sin that they are to conquer and shed so that they can run the race (12:1).

The supreme example who has gone ahead of them is Jesus, who is seen as the pioneer and perfecter of the faith, *ton tēs pisteōs archēgon kai teleiōtēn Iēsoun*. Koester tells us that in an ordinary stadium there was an honored guest who sat on a platform at the edge of the track, about midway on the course. In Hebrews, Jesus takes this honored position. The fact that Jesus despised the shame[113] of the cross is meant to encourage them. They must have been culturally aware of the shamefulness as well as the pain of death on a cross. They are reminded that since they have suffered only little

---

as well in the context of endurance and suffering. He also reiterates that this imagery comes from minority cultures, and Philo uses it in the same way as Hebrews does. Thompson, *The Beginnings of Christian Philosophy*, 64–65.

110. DeSilva, *Perseverance in Gratitude*, 430.

111. Koester, *Hebrews*, 534.

112. DeSilva has shown they had publicly suffered shame, so their place of honor is also in the public arena. He says, "The technique of conjuring in effect, a specific crowd of spectators in whose sight a decision must be rendered or an action carried out is a sufficiently common strategy used to motivate hearers to choose a particular course of action." DeSilva, *Perseverance in Gratitude*, 428.

113. Shame is what the audience was being threatened with in order to bring them to live in conformity with community standards. In close-knit communities, it was very important not to overstep the society's boundaries and bring shame to not just to oneself but to the community. DeSilva has argued extensively on the use of shame as a means of exercising society's control. See deSilva, *Perseverance in Gratitude*, 12–13; 359–61; 433–38. See also his detailed work, *Despising Shame*.

in comparison to Jesus, they should persevere to the end, despite what the present circumstances are.

The Goal of the Pilgrimage

Hebrews uses various images to describe the goal for the believers. Allison says there is a tripartite reference to the goal in the pilgrim's journey. In chapter 3 and 4, it is seen as rest, not just in the earthly Promised Land, but in the heavenly home, which the Old Testament people were looking for. In chapters 7 to 10, what is being sought is the entry into the holy of holies, the heavenly sanctuary that has been opened by the blood of the lamb. In chapter 11 to 13 there is reference to the city "which has foundations." In a literal sense, Jerusalem was the "city with foundations" (Ps 87:1–2). But ironically enough, the believers are also required to go outside the camp, outside the city. Traditionally, this was a place of shame but because Jesus had suffered there, it was now a place of blessing.

In all these three ways, the book of Hebrews reinterprets the hope of God's people. The land of Canaan was a land of promise, but we are told that the heroes of faith did not see Canaan as their homeland because they lived in it as strangers and pilgrims, seeking a better home (11:10). The author also reinterprets the hope of those who had depended on the cleansing system of the old covenant by saying, "Now we have a high priest over the house of God . . ." (10:21). Jesus has made possible an altar so that those who officiate in the tent have no right to eat there. The call is that those who follow him have to go outside the camp to identify with him; "Let us then go to him outside the camp and bear the abuse that he endured. For here, we have no lasting city, but we are looking for a city that is to come" (13:13–16). It was a radical step for the followers of Jesus to denounce that which was dear to them and to be identified with the Savior in all the shame and abuse that he had suffered. Not only were they to leave the altar that was securely situated in the holy of holies, but they were also being called to abandon the city of Jerusalem, the place that was central to their lives. Allison says Jerusalem was always the goal of the Jewish pilgrim.[114] But now, "The author of Hebrews has taken over this concept and applied it exclusively to the heavenly Jerusalem. Seen in this light, the practice of pilgrimage to the earthly Jerusalem was at best a picture of this important spiritual pilgrimage to the heavenly Jerusalem."[115] Those who lived far away and were seen to be at a disadvantage because they could not embark on the physical pilgrimage,

---

114. Allison, *The End of the Times Has Come*, 215.
115. Ibid.

did not need to do that because they had already "come to Mount Zion" (12:28). This shows that the believers had to abandon what was valuable to them in order to embark on joining with Christ in this heavenly journey. But the assurance they have is of a better homeland, a lasting altar at which to worship, and a city that will not be shaken.

The Importance of Faith along the Journey

The concept of faith is important in the study of Hebrews, seeing that the entire chapter 11 is dedicated to illustrating this key concept. Though there are varied views about what faith looks like, there is agreement that it is related to the overall message of the book. Rhee,[116] who gives it the central place, says that it holds together the various themes such as Christ's sonship, his high priesthood, and Sabbath rest. In his graphic description, Rhee sees faith as the thread or "string" that holds the precious themes of the book of Hebrews together so that it can shine like a beautiful "necklace made of pearls."[117] Those who affirm the centrality of the pilgrim motif see faith as an important virtue without which those who have embarked on the journey cannot survive.

The discussion of faith in Hebrews has been focused on what it really means. Does it have a Christological component or not? How does it relate to the concept of faith in Paul? What background does the author of Hebrews draw for his understanding of faith? Rhee in his extensive work sums up the various views of those authors who have written about faith in Hebrews. The three categories into which he groups these various authors are: the ethical view represented by Grässer,[118] Lindars, and Attridge; the eschatological, represented by Longenecker, Käsemann, Thompson, and Lindars; and the Christological represented by Hamm. While Rhee has probably worked too hard to isolate these views, he has also shown that there is an overlap in the understanding of faith. The views represented by all these perspectives of faith can enrich how we understand the importance of faith in relation to the pilgrim motif.

The point of contention has been on the origin of the understanding of faith in Hebrews. This is in view of the fact Hebrews seems to represent a different understanding from the rest of the New Testament, especially from

---

116. Rhee, *Faith in Hebrews*, xvi.

117. Rhee, *Faith in Hebrews*, 1.

118. Rhee is not the only one who says that Grässer is the one who has the extreme view that faith is purely ethical in Hebrews, it has no Christological element. See Rhee, *Faith in Hebrews*. Cf. Thompson, *The Beginnings of Christian Philosophy*, 69n71.

Paul. Thompson has argued that the source from which the author draws his understanding of faith is Philo. He says that in Philo faith is related to the understanding of life as pilgrimage, which he shows that the book of Hebrews supports.[119] Attridge agrees that there are similarities between the presentation of faith in Hebrews and Philo, especially with regard to the discussion in chapter 11. However, he locates the understanding of faith in Hebrews in the Old Testament, the same source that Philo drew from as well.[120]

There is an agreement among scholars that the author of Hebrews does not speak directly of faith in Christ or belief in Christ, but this does not mean that Christ is not the object of faith. The understanding of faith is different from Paul and the Gospels. Rhee has argued that faith in Hebrews is Christological; Christ is the object and also the model of faith. What then is the understanding of faith in Hebrews?

The word "faith" in Hebrews appears occurs 32 times throughout the epistle,[121] out of which 25 are in 11:1—12:29. There are also several faith-related words, which show the centrality of faith in the overall message of the epistle.

It is evident from the references that faith in Hebrews has to do with the finished work of Christ. Although there is no direct reference to faith in Christ, it is clear from the interchange between the doctrinal and the parenetic sections that this faith is understood as having its origin in Christ, that is faith in Christ.[122] This can be seen throughout all the major sections of the doctrinal as well as the parenetic sections. After he has given the emphasis on the supremacy of Christ in creation and over the angelic hosts (1:1—14), the author gives a call to his listeners to pay attention to this message. Then he gives a warning that if this salvation is neglected then there are dire consequences that would befall the hearers (2:1—2). When he has

---

119. Thompson, *The Beginnings of Christian Philosophy*, 75–77. He also shows that Philo parts ways with Hebrews when he presents the motif of pilgrimage with the dualism of body and soul.

120. See Attridge, *Epistle to the Hebrews*, 311–14.

121. See Swanson, Kohlenberger. Goodrick, *Exhaustive Concordance of the Greek New Testament*, 800–807, entry 4409–4413. See also Rhee, *Faith in Hebrews*, 2. He gives a summary of the occurrence of the word "faith" in the New Testament.

122. Rhee, *Faith in Hebrews*, 64. He has constructed his argument to prove that Christ is the object of faith in Hebrews. He says that the author employs both doctrine and exhortations to encourage the believers to remain in faith. The stylistic alternation between doctrines and pareneses implies that Jesus is to be considered the object of faith as in other books of the New Testament. Though his work is commendable, I think he has almost overworked the point. But the detail work he has done is good for an in-depth study.

shown that Jesus shared in our humanity,[123] he concludes this section by the appeal: "Therefore brothers and sisters, holy partners in the heavenly calling, consider Jesus, the apostle and high priest of our confession" (3:1). After this, he enters into a long discussion on Jesus as the high priest after the order of Melchizedek. His office of everlasting priesthood, and as well as his offering of himself as the perfect sacrifice on the cross, demonstrate the supremacy and completeness of his work.[124] Therefore, he says, "Let us approach with a true heart in full assurance of faith . . . Let us hold fast the confession of our hope" (10:22–23). A serious warning follows immediately that if one persists in sin, there is no more sacrifice for sin, and the punishment will be worse than that which Moses declared (10:26–29). The believers are exhorted to remain steadfast in their suffering as an appeal is made first to their previous exemplary behavior. They proved themselves in the past, and the writer reminds them of this to encourage them to continue in the same behavior (10:35–39). He also lists the Old Testament saints who stood firm in their faith (11:1–40). At the end of this long narration, he concludes this section by presenting Jesus as the *ton tēs pisteōs archēgon kai teleiōtēn* (12:1).[125] The believers are encouraged to look at his sufferings so that they are not discouraged (12:3–4). They are also encouraged to join him outside the city walls: "Let us then go to him outside the camp and bear the abuse he endured" (13:13). This shows that faith in Hebrews is linked to the life and work of Christ.

Faith in Hebrews is not only based in Christ but also it is a key component of the pilgrim's journey. Taking a warning from the wanderings of the people of God in the wilderness, the listeners of Hebrews are alerted that they should not have *apistia* (3:12, 19) lest they should also not enter into the rest that God has promised them. Faith is a necessary response to God for the work that he has done in Christ. It is manifested in trust, obedience, fidelity and faithfulness to the promise of God. That is why Christ is shown as the supreme example of faithfulness to God. Jesus was faithful (2:1). Moses was also faithful (3:5). The other saints in the hall of faith (11:1–39) demonstrated

---

123. See Easter, *Faith and the Faithfulness of Jesus in Hebrews*, 107–31 and 165–80 on shared destinies of Jesus and his followers, and how the pessimistic human story can be rewritten in Jesus Christ.

124. See excellent work on this topic by Jamieson, *Jesus' Death and Heavenly Offering in Hebrews,* especially 127–79.

125. Attridge, *Epistle to the Hebrews,* 314. He notes at the conclusion on his excursus on "Faith in Hebrews and Contemporary Literature, "Despite the absence of a christological referent, Hebrews' understanding of faith is clearly developed within a christological framework. The faith to which the addresses are here called is both made possible and exemplified by the 'perfecter of faith' (12:2), at whose exaltation hopes have begun to be realized and unseen things proved."

this element of faithfulness through obedience to God's promises regardless of the price that it demanded upon their lives.

Thus, faith in Hebrews also has the element of faithfulness, steadfastness, boldness, endurance and hope in the midst of suffering. Endurance is necessary on the pilgrim journey because as is demonstrated in the lives of those on the list of faith (11:1–40), there are difficulties on the journey. It is evident that the community has suffered (10:32–38), though not to the point of losing blood (12:4). A sense of premonition reveals that more persecution is expected, so there is an admonishment to the believers to endure in order to reach the goal of the journey (12:3). Jesus crowns this list as the one who has demonstrated ultimate steadfastness and endurance in his willingness to die shamefully on the cross. (12:1–4, 13:12–16). Earlier on it had been said that though he was a son, he learned obedience through what he suffered (5:8). The implication is that those who have accepted the role of a stranger or pilgrim have also accepted the indignities of being categorized as such. Thus, suffering is the fate of the pilgrim and that is why endurance, perseverance, and patience are necessary for the journey.

Faith in Hebrews also has a communal component to it. We get this from the negative example of the people of God in the wilderness. A few individuals disobeyed, but the consequences befell them all. A few of them did not obey, but they were all punished by having to wander in the desert for forty years. Those who left Egypt under Moses were unable to enter the promised rest because of their disobedience. The writer also gives the invitation to approach God in the plural, suggesting that the listeners might turn to God together. That is why the writer continually emphasizes the need to "encourage or exhort one another as long as it is called 'today'" (3:14) so that no one would miss entering because of the deceitfulness of sin (Jer 3:13). He also urges them not to neglect the habit of meeting together so that they "could provoke one another to love and good works" (10:24–25). He commends them for the partnership they had shown in sharing with those who had been persecuted (10:35). They identified with them to the extent that they even visited those who were in prison (10:34). Thus in order to urge them to be steadfast in this journey he points to the models, or exemplars of faith who have gone before them (11:1–39) and to the 'cloud of witnesses' who are watching and encouraging them along the way (12:1–2). At the conclusion of the letter, the writer encourages them to continue this mutual love through the practice of hospitality, to remember those who are in prison and to be generous in every good work (13:1–3, 16). Thus, this journey is not undertaken in isolation. They are in exemplary company in the past, the present and even in the future. As they look forward to the future, they are pointed to a great festive crowd of fellow believers gathered at Mount Zion (12:18–24).

Having looked at the way the pilgrim motif is demonstrated both thematically and grammatically in the book of Hebrews, we will now look at how this pilgrim faith is actualized by those who lived a life of faith. Our focus will be on Hebrews 11:13–16.

An Exegetical Analysis of Hebrews 11:13–16

This passage is located right in the middle of the chapter known as the encomium of faith. Attridge says that the writer uses the literary form, *exempla virtutis*, extolling the importance of the virtue in question.[126] Such example lists were a commonly used feature in contemporary Jewish[127] and early Christian literature, in order to inculcate virtues. It was a common parenetic device adapted to its own context and function. The uniqueness of Hebrews 11 is that it uses examples from the Scriptures. The rhetorical device that the author uses in order to highlight the examples of faith is called the anaphora. This means the repetition of the first element at the beginning of several successive periods. In this case, the words that are repeated are *kata pistei*. Cosby appreciates the use of this device by noting its effects. He says, "By beginning each example in 11:3–31 with *pistei*, the author conveys the impression of being able to go on giving more examples from salvation history to demonstrate the truth of what he said about faith in the introductory comments in 11:1–2."[128]

Chapter 11 is a self-contained passage that might be considered an aside or an "excursus between the remarks on the need for endurance in 10:36 and the explicit sermons to endure in 12:1,"[129] but it fits very well within the context. The theme of faith of 11:1–40 follows naturally from 10:32–39, where the author has reminded his listeners of the fact that their

---

126. Attridge, *Epistle to the Hebrews*, 306. He shows that Philo does something similar to Hebrews 11, when discussing hope. Both Hebrews and Philo begin with the definition of the virtue in question and proceed to use the figure of anaphora to list the examples. Like Hebrews, Philo concludes his reflection with athletic imagery. The only difference is that, while Hebrews uses examples from Scripture, Philo uses examples of general types of hopeful people, moneylenders, glory seekers, athletes and philosophers. Cf. O'Brien, *Hebrews*, 504–13.

127. Attridge cites an example similar to Hebrews 11 found in 4 Macc 16:16–23. It plays the same parenetic role, showing the need for endurance. Also, in this same category is Wis 11:10; 11:15—12:27. Attridge, *Epistle to the Hebrews*.

128. Cosby, *The Rhetorical Composition and Function of Hebrews 11*, 3.

129. Attridge, *Epistle to the Hebrews*, 306.

faith and endurance in a previous time had borne fruit for the community. They had stood in fellowship with those who had endured suffering; they had even gone to visit those in prison who had been persecuted; and they had also accepted cheerfully the plundering of their goods. The key element that explains their commendable behavior is faith, which is lived out in endurance. He seems to imply that this endurance in faith will be necessary in the future as shown in chapter 12:3–4, when harder times might befall them. But before he gives the exhortation on endurance in chapter 12, he concretely illustrates those who had in like manner demonstrated faith in God. Previously, in 10:38–39, he makes the remark, "but my righteous one will live by faith . . . but we are not among those who shrink back and so are lost, but among those who have faith and so are saved." This gives him the liberty to give the whole list of heroes in chapter 11 who endured hardships because they lived by "faith." At the tail end of the passage, he crowns his list by throwing his "trump" card, his example *par excellence*, Jesus Christ, "the pioneer and perfecter of our faith . . . who for the sake of the joy set before him endured the cross, disregarding its shame" (12:2). He does not forget to give them a sober reminder in case they thought their sufferings were unbearable. He says, "in your struggle against sin you have not resisted to the point of shedding your blood" (12:4). The believers were being encouraged to follow in the footsteps of Christ even if it meant persecution. I suggest the reason the heroes of faith had experienced persecution was because they had accepted the call of faith, which meant they lived a marginal existence of being "strangers and exiles" in their communities. DeSilva puts it this way, "Christian were subjected to prejudice, rumor, insult and slander and were even targets of pogroms and legal actions. It was thus both dishonoring and dangerous to be associated with the name of 'Christian.'"[130]

The immediate context of our passage is 11:8–22, which focuses on Abraham, Sarah, Jacob and Isaac. It stands out because the author interrupts the flow of the *anaphora*, which had been previously introduced by the dative *pistei* in the phrase *kata pistin*. This has caused some commentators to argue that this is a key passage.[131] Attridge notes that this interruption is "a

---

130. DeSilva, *Perseverance in Gratitude*, 12. I like the way deSilva further describes the marginalization of these heroes of faith. He says, "Abraham, Moses and Jesus (11:8–22, 24–26; 12:2) embraced marginalization and loss with regard to status and wealth in the society for the sake of faith. After living a liminal existence for decades, Abraham never went back to the city where he had status but kept his eyes on the heavenly city that God had prepared (11:13–16). Moses thought the loss of the throne and the endurance of reproach and maltreatment insignificant compared to the reward of God (11:26). Finally, the community's successful resistance to earlier attempts at social control becomes their own best example for their present situation." 18.

131. Rhee, *Faith in Hebrews*, 183–87. He has used a chiastic structure to map the

reflective comment on the condition exemplified by the patriarchs as wanderers in search of a homeland (vv. 9–10)."[132] He says further, "The situation of the patriarchs is, in important ways, analogous to that of the Christian addressees, whose commitment has alienated them from their "homeland" (10:32–34). These new sojourners will soon be summoned again to follow the ultimate example of faith by accepting the suffering that comes with their alien status (12:1–3; 13:13)."[133] The most commendable thing about all these people and especially those mentioned within our passage, Abraham, Sarah, Isaac and Jacob, is they proudly chose to live according to their identity as "strangers and exiles." The chiastic[134] structure that follows centers on the confession of these heroes of faith as "strangers and exiles."

The Structure of the Passage

    A: They all died by faith

        B: They greeted or welcomed from afar the promise

            C: They confessed

                D: Strangers and exiles (pilgrims)

            C': Those who say such things

        B': They were yearning for a better country

    A': Therefore God is not ashamed to be called their God

---

whole of chapter 11 and he puts vv. 13–16 as the center of the chiasm. His argument is that the phrase *"houtoi pantes"* refers not only to the immediate context of the patriarchs but also those from vv. 3–12 and vv. 17–40. I concur with him that this is a key passage but I don't think he has given a strong-enough reason for considering this passage as the center of the argument. The interruption of the rhythmic structure signifies that the author wants to make a key point. I think it is central because it exemplifies the pilgrim motif that characterized all those who are considered the heroes of faith in chapter 11. Ellingworth, *Epistle to the Hebrews*, 592, also notes the importance of this section, arguing that this is the author's interpretation of the history of salvation. He also says, "The central position of these verses is designed to give them prominence; they are not a mere parenthesis."

132. Attridge, *Epistle to the Hebrews*, 328.

133. Attridge, *Epistle to the Hebrews*, 329. Lane also notes the rhetorical purpose of putting this paragraph here. He says, "The writer placed at the center of the paragraph his most important affirmations in order to emphasize the eschatological perspective from which the entire unit (vv. 8–22) is to be understood. Lane, *Hebrews 9–13*, 355.

134. Rhee, *Faith in Hebrews*, 184. He also recognizes a chiastic structure but he does not put at the center the confession of these pioneers of faith who saw their designation as "strangers and exiles." Heil, *Hebrews*, 314, denotes 11:8–19 as having a chiastic structure.

Textual Analysis

A: "They all died without receiving the promise" (v. 13) is a solemn announcement that begins our passage. When we first ask ourselves who died, then it is not difficult to show that that section is set within the passage on Abraham (vv. 8–12). So, we know that this refers to Abraham and his immediate family.[135] It has been mentioned that Abraham had migrated to this land of promise. But even here he lived in tents as in a strange land, as did Isaac and Jacob. This then carries the implication that the land of promise that they were seeking was not an earthly place because they seemed to have attained it, but continued to live in it as strangers. But if it strikes us with some disappointment because they died without getting what they hoped for, we are propelled to a new level of understanding what the author is seeking to communicate here. What is it that turned the tide from defeat to overcoming? The clue is that the solemn announcement is introduced by the phrase *kata pistin,* which should provide us with a note of hope that their death was not an ordinary one. Lane says that *kata pistin* is emphatic because its position at the beginning of the sentence "signifies that their lives were regulated by faith."[136] Westcott even puts it more strongly, "Under the influence of and according to the spirit of faith, inspired, sustained and guided by faith. Faith was the rule of lives, the measure of their growth even to the end. They faced death as men who retained their hold on the invisible . . . so their departure was transformed into a 'going home.'"[137] This is the faith that has been introduced in 11:1 as grasping the unseen realities as if they were already there. This brings us to the unexpected pronouncement, which emphasizes that because they were willing to commit their cause to God even in the death, God stood by them. They had the kind of faith that went beyond life and the present realities, and God was pleased with them. Therefore, in line with their radical choice to live and die by faith, the parallel section in the chiasm makes the bold statement.

A': "Therefore God is not ashamed to be called their God" (v. 16b). This phrase rings with victory after what had seemed to be a tragic end. One wants to jump with joy with such an acclamation. Yes, they did make

---

135. Rhee, *Faith in Hebrews*, 185. He argues that "all these" refer to all the exemplars of faith in 11:1–38, so he sets this passage as the central chiasm of the whole passage. Lane, *Hebrews 9–13*, 356, argues that this refers to those who engaged in pilgrimage in response to God's mandate. Though they were promised a place as an inheritance, they continued to live in it as resident aliens. I agree with Lane that this refers to those mentioned in the immediate passage, but I also believe the idea of pilgrimage refers to all the exemplars of faith in this chapter.

136. Lane, *Hebrews 9–13*, 356.

137. Westcott, *Epistle to the Hebrews*, 362.

the right choice in the end. This means that God is eager to be identified with them. As Attridge says, "As the patriarchs confess themselves to be aliens, they recognize who their God is, and God recognizes them."[138] We are also reminded of the familiar self-designation of God in the Old Testament: "I am the God of Abraham, Isaac and Jacob." This gives us the assurance that these patriarchs really did not die. In Matthew 22:32 Jesus asserts that God best designates himself as God of Abraham, Isaac and Jacob, which in essence means he is a God of the living, not of the dead. That God is eager to be identified with these people, or their descendants, for that matter, is the ultimate test of his approval. This also parallels what the author of Hebrews says, who reminds his hearers that Jesus is not ashamed to call them his brothers or sisters (2:11).

But as if it is not enough that God has given them his coveted approval, we are further told that he has prepared a city for them. Earlier we had been told, "They looked for a city that has foundations, whose architect and builder was God" (11:10). It is as if all this has been confirmed and fulfilled. This city is actually prepared and waiting for them, showing that what they were longing for was legitimate. So, what had begun on a sad note ends in triumph because, although they died, it was not in vain because they had great things waiting for them. This leads to the next passage (vv. 17–22) that briefly recounts the story of Abraham who gave up Isaac, only to have God give him his son back. The writer of Hebrews reiterates that this is also a characteristic of some of the heroes of faith; they gave up their lives in order to experience "a better resurrection" (11:35). Attridge notes, "All this play on life and death is but preparatory to the ultimate example (12:1–3) of the one who in his glorification is saved from death."[139]

B: "They saw and welcomed from afar." This section continues to elaborate the reason the heroes of faith received such a high acclamation in the previous narration. They had the unusual capacity to grasp the promise with such clarity even when it was seen from a distance. This reminds us of Moses, who was happy to see the Promised Land from afar, when he had been forbidden to enter. Here the figurative use of the word *aspasamenoi*, meaning "greeted or welcome" is very interesting. Ellingworth notes, "Everywhere in the Greek Bible it is used with a person or a personalized object, generally, literally of greeting people . . . The unusual apparently impersonal object suggests for the author that the heavenly city is primarily a community."[140] From my African perspective, words of greeting and wel-

---

138. Attridge, *Epistle to the Hebrews*, 328.
139. Ibid., 329.
140. Ellingworth, *Epistle to the Hebrews*, 594.

come bring a sense of joy, excitement, anticipation and a positive outlook on life. *Aspasamenoi* communicates the message that though the pioneers did not receive the objects of the promise, they lived hopeful lives, which testifies to the fact that God had not let them down.

B': "They were yearning for a better country, a heavenly one" (11:16). This connects beautifully with the parallel section. The word from which 'yearning' is translated is *oregontai*, comes from the verb *oregō* in the middle voice. It means to "extend oneself, stretch oneself out" but with the genitive it means "to aim for, aspire to."[141] It is used to express intense inclination that "requires the sacrifice of other good things . . . a passionate desire."[142] This shows that for the heroes of faith, the realities of their situation did not dull their minds into focusing only on the present, but they had the tenacity to look into the future. This sense of longing for a future reality and being dissatisfied with the present is a characteristic of those who know of better things to come. So here we see the paradox of both having the assurance to welcome the promises as if they have already come, and yet experiencing the longing because it has not really come yet. It is clearly the interplay of the now and the not yet. Thus, the identity and existence of being "strangers and sojourners" best exemplifies the eschatological tension of the "already and not yet."

C: They confessed (*homologēsantes*) means they made a public acknowledgment[143] of who they were. It gives the picture that they were ready to make a public profession of their faith regardless of what the consequences of such a status meant. This should serve as an encouragement to the listeners of Hebrews who were also being encouraged by the author to "hold fast their confession" (4:11, 10:23) in the midst of the persecution. During such a time, the temptation was to be silent and not to reveal their identity, but the example of these pioneers of faith shows that they did not waver in their confession. When we look later at the content of their confession, it will reveal the reason they needed courage and boldness to make such a stand.

C': I have paralleled this with "those who say such things make it clear that they are seeking a homeland . . . (vv. 14–15)." Here it is as if the writer to the Hebrews wants to draw attention to the public confession of the pioneers and the implication of such a confession upon their lives. It shows that what they confessed with their mouths had a significant effect in their lives.

---

141. Ernest, *Theological Lexicon of New Testament*, 2:592.

142. Ibid.

143. BDAG, *Greek-English Lexicon*, 568. See also Lane, *Hebrews 9–13*, 35. He says the technical term means a public profession of faith.

It was plain to them and to those who observed them. This is reiterated by the use of the word *emphanizousin*, which suggests "an official report or declaration."[144] The intensity of their search for another land is also communicated by the word *epizētousin*. One of the meanings of this word is to "strive for."[145] This is an affirmation that the pioneers made an intentional and deliberate choice to seek another homeland.

This is further emphasized when the verse continues to say, "If they had been thinking of the land they left behind, they would have had an opportunity to return." They had ample opportunity to return to where they came from, but they rejected that option because they were looking for something better in the future. Lane says, "Their unsettled existence in Canaan offered them abundant "opportunity for returning." If they had not regulated their lives in accordance with faith, the experience of alienation in the Promised Land would have provided an incentive for turning back. That they showed no inclination to do so is indicative of the orientation of faith toward the promise."[146] DeSilva also describes their choice as preferring a lifetime of disenfranchisement in order to persevere in their quest for a "better heavenly homeland."[147] The use of the present tense in this section is very deliberate. The author wants to show that there is a close identity between the audience and the pioneers of faith. In other words, the listeners in their unsettled state were being encouraged to see that theirs was not an unusual experience. Their fathers and mothers in the faith had gone before them. If they persevered in the same way, they would be rewarded with the same honor in which God was not ashamed to be called their God. This brings us to the climax of the discussion.

D: They were "strangers and foreigners"[148] upon the earth: *xenoi kai parepidēmoi*. This is the center of the chiasm, which explores the identity of those who died by faith, those with whom God was not ashamed to be identified. These individuals, who looked from a distance to greet the promises, did not want to go back but desired a future heavenly home. They confessed boldly not only with their mouths but also with their lives that their identity was that of "strangers and foreigners" (NRSV) or aliens and pilgrims, who sought another home. This confession comes as a surprise because to be an alien or a stranger is not a position one is proud of, whether now or in the

---

144. Ellingworth, *Epistle to the Hebrews*, 595.
145. BDAG, *Greek-English Lexicon*, 292.
146. Lane, *Hebrews 9–13*, 359.
147. DeSilva, *Perseverance in Gratitude*, 402.
148. Lane, *Hebrews 9–13*, 357. Lane translates this as "strangers and sojourners," and he suggests that this is a hendiadys, which is equivalent to "sojourning strangers."

ancient world. The status of a stranger was a particularly precarious one in the ancient world, and that is why the Old Testament scriptures constantly remind the people that they should treat strangers well. DeSilva shows that in the Greaco-Roman world, lack of citizenship exposed one to disgrace and loss.[149] In fact, one preferred death rather than loss of citizenship. Describing the vulnerability of such a state, deSilva says, "Citizenship brought security, a 'mooring' within a society; lack of citizenship left one adrift, as it were, an easy prey to abuse and insult."[150] The author of Hebrews wants to express the transient and more precarious nature of the kind of existence that the pioneers of faith chose to live, by avoiding the term *paroikos* which meant resident alien. Instead he uses *xenoi kai parepidēmoi* which meant "transient foreigners,"[151] denoting their doubly marginal social status.[152] The enormity of choosing such a lifestyle is expressed by deSilva, who notes, "Astoundingly, they persisted in bearing the lower status of "foreigner" and "resident alien," embracing this status until their deaths rather than desisting from their search for the homeland God promised and seeking reenfranchise-ment in their native land."[153]

The expression *xenoi kai parepidēmoi* is an echo of Genesis 23:4 and Genesis 24:37, where Abraham describes himself as a temporary resident using *paroikos kai parepidēmoi*. The expression was later used to portray alienation from God (Ps. 38:13). Attridge also shows that in Hellenistic Judaism the imagery of the alien was used for the "fate of the soul in the world, an exile from his true heavenly home."[154] However, the writer of Hebrews uses this motif to show the alienation from their environment that his listeners faced.[155] He wants to call his listeners to their true identity so that like the heroes of faith they would not be sidetracked by the happenings in this life even if it meant being ostracized from their communities. Following the

---

149. DeSilva, *Perseverance in Gratitude*, 395.

150. DeSilva, *Perseverance in Gratitude*, 395. He also gives an extended note on the status of strangers and sojourners in the ancient world. One thing that stands out is that it was not an enviable position. If one were wise, they would avoid such a position. That the pioneers of faith were willing to take up this status as obedience to God's call is a great sign of faith. See the discussion in deSilva, "A Closer Look," 394–95. See also Spicq, *Theological Lexicon of the New Testament*, 2:592.

151. Koester, *Hebrews*, 488. A resident alien had few rights as compared to transient or temporary strangers.

152. Koester, *Hebrews*, 488. I have added the word "doubly" to emphasize the greater disadvantage the pioneers of faith faced as "transient foreigners." See also Ellingworth, *Epistle to the Hebrews*, 594.

153. DeSilva, *Perseverance in Gratitude*, 400.

154. Attridge, *Epistle to the Hebrews*, 330.

155. Ibid.

example of the pioneers of faith, they would not be ashamed of their lot, accepting their marginal status even with a sense of joy. Commenting on the choice by Abraham, deSilva notes:

> When the faith of Abraham and his family motivates them to embrace the life of "foreigners and resident aliens" (*xenoi kai parepidēmoi*, 11:13), this would be heard as a deliberate choice to live a life of lower status liable to dishonor and danger. Whether or not Abraham suffered any of these ills in his sojourning, the cultural context of the hearers suggests that both author and addressees of Hebrews would have understood Abraham's choice as embracing a loss of status for the sake of obedience to God's call. In effect, the patriarchs willingly embraced a lower status in terms of the world's estimation in order to attain at length an honored status in God's sight.[156]

This points to the fact that the pioneers of faith were not passive recipients; they made an active choice. The author makes this clear by saying that they knew they were looking for a homeland. They, in fact, had the opportunity to go back where they had come from but they did not because they were looking for something better. This "something better" is further described as something "heavenly." They had made a value judgment of what they considered lacking and that is why they went unswervingly to the promise ahead. They had a clear vision of what they were looking for. Later we are told that that Jesus, who is the pioneer of faith *par excellence*, demonstrated the same kind of attitude: "For the sake of the joy that was set before him he endured the cross" (12:2). The writer of the Epistle of Diognetus says the same of the Christians of his time: "[Christians] dwell in their own countries, but only as sojourners; they bear the responsibilities as citizens, and they endure hardships as strangers. Every foreign country is a homeland to them, and every homeland is foreign . . . Their existence is on earth, but their citizenship is in heaven" (Diogn. 5.5–9, cf 5.1–9).[157] Thus, we see why at the conclusion of our passage we are told that God was not ashamed to be called their God (v. 16). The pioneers had fully thrown their lot with the promises of God by choosing to obey God and by living the pilgrim existence. Despite the trials they faced they were rewarded with full honor and approval from God.

---

156. DeSilva, *Perseverance in Gratitude*, 394.
157. Cited in Lane, *Hebrews 9–13*, 360.

Some Ethical Implications of the Pilgrim Motif for the Church in Africa

From the above analysis, we note that the main components of the pilgrim motif in Hebrews include: the call to follow Jesus as the pilgrim *par excellence*, the community of faith as pilgrims who rally in support of one another in the journey, and the need to embody the virtues of courage, perseverance and hope in the midst of the vicissitudes of life. I will now examine how these will be played on in the specific Kenyan situation.

The Kenyan Situation

The conditions in Kenya, and this is true for most of Africa, are paradoxical: the dilapidating social, economic, and political climate has put people in the constant situation of exile, and yet it has resulted in the vibrant and enthusiastic reception to the gospel of Jesus Christ. This second factor has caused some contemporary theologians[158] to claim that Christianity in Africa has become a non-western religion. The statement is true not only with regard to demographics, but it is also the case concerning all other challenges and questions that the African situation brings to Christian theology: religious pluralism, theodicy, poverty, response to diseases such as AIDS, multinational corporations, church-state relations, and refugees.

First, I discuss the issue of suffering in Africa. Professor Ali Mazrui, a Kenyan historian and political scientist, has said that Africa has been the most racially humiliated continent in the world.[159] This suffering comes from the time of the slave trade, through colonialism, and presently, neo-colonialism. This does not mean that Africans did not suffer from ravages of war that they inflicted upon themselves, but it is to say that the sufferings that Africa has received from outsiders have been those that have done untold damage to the continent, the effects of which are still being felt. The recent wave of suffering that comes to the populations and nations of Africa is due to the economic debt that is owed to the West. Due to the structural adjustment programs, the countries cannot provide the basic social amenities such as water, health, education, and food security to the people.[160] These countries are so busy paying the debt to the World

---

158. See Bediako, *Christianity in Africa*, 3. See also Barrett, "AD 2000," 39–54. Walls, "Towards an Understanding of Africa's Place in Christian History," 180–89. Walls, "Africa and Christian Identity," 11–13.

159. Mazrui, *The African Condition*, 26.

160. See Acquah, "The African Economic Crisis," 54. See also Olofin, "The African Economic Crisis," 74–83; Monaghan and King, "How Theories of Change," 365–84.

Bank and the IMF that they cannot even meet the needs of their citizens. Those who suffer most because of this are the poor, which mainly consist of women and children. To make matters worse in Kenya, the country not only has to bear this burden of its internal problems but it also has to support the refugee populations that have come due to the relative stability of the country. Ever since the 1960s the countries that surround Kenya– Somalia, Ethiopia, Sudan, Uganda and more recently Rwanda, Burundi, and Congo–have suffered due to the ravages of war. Kenya has supported a huge refugee community in the northern part of the country and also in Nairobi. This is not to mention the economic burden and an acute sense of insecurity that has been put on the nation, because some of these people who declare themselves to be refugees come into the country illegally with firearms, and it is difficult to control them. No doubt, due to these unstable economic and social conditions this means that the crime rate has escalated, causing the general morale of the country to go down.

However, there is a ray of hope in this situation in that people are responding to the gospel in large numbers and the church is more vibrant in Africa than anywhere in the world. Due to this phenomenal growth David Barrett as early as 1970 asserted that Kenya had become a Christian nation.[161] He gave the following statistics to demonstrate this growth: "There were 4.6 million Christians in Kenya in 1962, there are 8.0 million in mid-1972."[162] Following this trend he predicted that by the year 2000 "there will be 28 million Christians in Kenya, of whom perhaps 15 million will be practicing Christians."[163]

Still, many have been critical of the growth of Christianity and have assessed that the kind of gospel that seems to appeal to the African is the so-called prosperity gospel that seems to promise material wealth because people lack the basic necessities of life. Arowele notes, "Some churches and evangelistic movements in Africa have been accused (not without justification) of materialism and commercialization of the gospel, that they make evangelization an avenue for the exploitation and acquisition of wealth at the expense of poor tithe-payers"[164] This is not the only problem. There is also the problem of false teachers and cults that are proliferating in the environment. Certainly every wind of doctrine that is passing by may be accepted because not only are Africans notoriously religious, they

---

161. Barrett, *Kenya Churches Handbook*, 168.
162. Ibid., 166.
163. Ibid., 177.
164. Arowele, "Pilgrim People of God," 450.

have a danger of "sacralizing the material."¹⁶⁵ Many Christians who are trying to practice an honest means of livelihood cannot make ends meet because of the poor economic conditions, and it seems that the only reasonable thing they can do is make shortcuts. They participate in cheating the system so that they can make ends meet. For example, those in the police force receive bribes in order to survive. No simple service is done without asking for or receiving a bribe. If one decides to be honest it takes a long time for a simple service to be done. If you do not adopt these social norms, you can suffer the consequences, so Christians are forced to be aliens and exiles even in their own homeland. Hebrews describes their situation aptly: "Here they do not have an abiding city."

This situation poses ethical questions to the church on how to minister to these people in a relevant way. How does the church minister to those who are literally aliens and exiles in their country—people who are living in a displaced and disoriented existence? How are we to treat them and make them live in a humane environment? And how can the Kenyan Christians who are really expended beyond their means practice the ethic of hospitality that affirms the dignity of those who live among them as pilgrims and exiles? What are some ethical principles and practices that the pilgrim motif in Hebrews prescribes to those on the journey?

Christ as the Pilgrim *Par Excellence*

Hebrews focuses on Christ as the leader of the band. Brown describes him as "the pilgrim *par excellence*, the victorious pioneer (2:10), the trail blazer, the pathfinder, who leads his fellow travelers to their eternal destiny, the forerunner (6:20) who, like a courageous military scout, goes ahead to make sure that the road is safe for all who follow him."¹⁶⁶ He is more superior than the angels. He is a high priest after the example of Melchizedek. We know from Hebrews that high Christology is not just demonstrated in the intellectual meditation of Christ for the people; it is directly linked to the adverse conditions of the hearers. As Käsemann puts it:

> Mere paraenesis [sic], as it preponderates in the close of the letter, does not suffice for this. Objective strengthening in hope

---

165. Bediako, "Africa in the New World Christian Order." Bediako argued that the danger Africa faced was not so much secularization of the spiritual as much as "sacralizeation of the material." He explained this as the tendency to call upon God in order to obtain material success. When religion is attached so much to the material, then there is the danger of using religious means for personal enrichment.

166. Brown, "Pilgrimage in Faith," 33.

is needed and is actually offered, first by showing the necessity of discipleship through the example of Christ as the *archēgos*, then by portraying the certainty of the goal through the vision of the heavenly high priest. Since Christ has broken through the power of death and accomplished the *aqethsis*, he is a guarantor of a new covenant and announces it through his unremitting intercession for his own before God. For God's wandering people on earth, this fact contains sufficient reason for *parrēsias*. Now it can continue and conclude its wandering confidently and certain of its goal.[167]

Therefore, Christ's priesthood and the fact of his actual accomplishment become an encouragement to his suffering brothers and sisters who are going through the same suffering. That is why the writer of Hebrews continually points to his readers the example of Jesus Christ who has gone before them. The believers need the assurance that they are with one who has suffered, thus making him able to identify with them. They also know that since he has overcome death, the most formidable enemy, then nothing can conquer them.

The African worldview gives great prominence to exemplary ancestors who have gone before. Jesus as leader and the ancestor *par excellence* would fit very well into African folklore. The fact that he not only lived an exemplary life, but he also offered himself as the perfect sacrifice to cleanse sin, will give him a supreme role in a society which understands what it means to offer sacrifices to cleanse sins. Thus, Jesus will play the role of ancestor, high priest and the perfect sacrifice for sin. All these roles have reconciling and mediating functions, necessary in a society that is torn by war, suffering and strife.

The writer of Hebrews pays attention to other heroes of faith referred to as the "cloud of witness." The believers are exhorted to model these great examples of faith who have gone before us. Our passage (11:13–16) mentions Abraham, Sarah, Isaac, and Jacob. The believers are also reminded of the leaders who spoke the word of God to them, and they are encouraged to imitate their faith and way of life (13:7, 13).

The African church has many examples of faith who have fought the good fight and have died doing so. In this group, we have the earlier martyrs who died in Uganda in the 1860s during the days of Kabaka Mutesa.[168] In more recent times, we are reminded of Archbishop Janani Luwum

---

167. Käsemann, *The Wandering People of God*, 239.

168. There is a shrine for the martyrs in the Kampala to remind the Christians of the work of these young ones during the inception of Christianity. "They did not cling to their lives in the face of death" (Rev. 12:11). Also refer to Ford, *Janani*.

of the Anglican Church of Uganda, who was killed because he dared to question the activities of the dictator Idi Amin Dada. Similarly, in Kenya, there is the Bishop of Eldoret, Alexander Muge, who also died in 1990 because he dared to speak against the injustices that the government was doing against his people. As in the African political and social system in which leaders are highly respected, Hebrews values obedience to leaders. This highlights the need to train leaders for the church in Africa who are worthy of integrity and respect.

Community

In the entire chapter 11, as well as the entire book of Hebrews, it is evident that this journey of faith is not undertaken individually. The communal element is emphasized in our passage (11:13–16) by the mention of the expression, "all died" (11:13). Recognizing this communal aspect Koester says, "Aware that without support people more easily give way to unbelief, the author urged listeners to exhort each other in order to maintain a high level of commitment to the faith (3:12–13)."[169] Koester also notes that in Hebrews, invitations to approach God are given in the plural (4:16; 10:22).[170] The Hebrews are also encouraged not to forsake the gathering together in order to encourage one another in these days of hardship (3:14; 6:10–12; 10:25; 13:1–2).

In the face of economic disintegration, the church in Kenya is threatened by the encroachment of individualism and a survival mentality that says, "Everyone for himself and God for us all." In Nairobi especially, insecurity has made people construct houses that are barricaded with barbed wire with signs on the gate, "ultimate security" or "*Mbwa kali.*"[171] Of course this goes against the injunction in Hebrews that we should practice hospitality because in doing so "some have entertained angels unawares" (13:2, KJV).[172] The church today needs to recover this ancient practice that is rooted within the scriptures and also within the traditions of the African peoples. As a result, this communal caring will touch those who are in prison, and others

---

169. Koester, *Hebrews*, 74. See also deSilva, *Perseverance in Gratitude*, 68–69, 78 on the importance of nurturing a supportive Christian community as a key element of discipleship.

170. Koester, *Hebrews*, 74.

171. The Kiswahili word literally means "fierce dog." This is placed at the gates of the rich residences to show that they are well guarded by dogs and that no stranger good or ill should show up at the door.

172. Backhaus, "How to Entertain Angels," 149–75.

who are needy (13:3, 16). This will ultimately lead to an ethic of caring for people rather than just material pursuit. As Arowele notes:

> We have noted that according to the NT in general and Heb in particular freedom from the love of money and wealth pertains to the rule of those on the Christian pilgrimage. Accordingly, inordinate pursuit and acquisition of wealth in the churches is a negation of the true followership [sic] of the One who has nowhere to lay his head (Luke 9.58), an obstacle to evangelization and contradiction of the heavenly inheritance. Besides the deplorable economies in Africa today call for a less materialistic attitude on the part of the churches, that attitude proper to the exile people of God . . . Expensive projects and costly establishments are an oddity in a pilgrim church in poverty-stricken Africa.[173]

There is no more important goal for the church in Africa than to be free from the love of money and to be content with what we have. It is comforting to note that these instructions to care for others are followed by the encouragement that Jesus Christ will never leave us nor forsake us (13:5–6).

Courage

The focus on the pilgrim existence in our passage shows that the examples of faith in Hebrews were willing to choose a marginal lifestyle for the sake of the promise of God. The author reiterated that they deliberately chose the pilgrim existence instead of going back to the comforts of a settled life in a familiar country. In the face of hardships, they are called to move with courage,[174] perseverance and faith. This is a central theme in the book of Hebrews and certainly in chapter 11. In the face of the hard times that have fallen and that are sure to come, the righteous will live by faith. This reminds me of a letter I received from a friend in Kenya telling me of the Christian response to the difficult times they were facing before the elections. She wrote:

> I am sure by now you have probably heard that Kenya faces a grim future. Well in my estimation, we are already in that grim future, but "the righteous (just) shall live by faith". For me as you know it is a case of the Lord drawing me from the miry clay. It

---

173. Arowele, "Pilgrim People of God," 450.

174. DeSilva, *Perseverance in Gratitude*, 430. He says that courage was one of the most important virtues in the Greco-Roman world. He quotes Aristotle, who spoke repeatedly of enduring hardships and terrible experiences because it was honorable to do so and dishonorable not to do so. Courage also was valued because it set moral obligation above physical safety and comfort.

> is right now very difficult for many families but the Lord has continued to sustain those who call upon his name. The exciting thing is that right now many are turning to the lord in repentance. Everyone right now realizes that unless we cry out to God and he aids us we are in real trouble . . . My steadfast testimony is that the Lord is Lord over Kenya and that he is good even in this apparent gloom.[175]

This kind of positive attitude in the midst of hardship is what we would like to inculcate in all believers. I believe that Hebrews calls for the kind of courage that can withstand hardships. As already mentioned above, in the African context, there have been those who have shown this courage even to the point of losing their lives; this can encourage Christians today not to give up hope. Those who have lost everything will be encouraged by the words that Jesus will never leave them nor forsake them (Heb 13:6). He is the same yesterday today and forever.

One of the traditional institutions that sought to inculcate courage to the African peoples was the rite of passage, which included circumcision. In this ceremony, both men and women[176] were tested in their ability to endure pain and harsh conditions. They underwent a painful operation without the aid of anesthesia and they were expected to live in tough situations, usually outdoors, for several months. Through this ceremony, young people learned that pain and suffering were a part of human existence. They also were made aware that in order to cope with life, they needed the virtue of courage and perseverance, as well as the support of others. They were also prepared to accept the responsibilities of adulthood with courage. In the same way, Christians can show that being a disciple of Jesus Christ does not demand less. There is need to demonstrate courage amidst the vicissitudes of life. Christians who are facing persecutions and trials in various parts of the world would be encouraged if they knew that their perseverance is a source of encouragement to other believers all over the world.

Conclusion

We have seen that the pilgrim motif ties the parenetic and expository sections of the book of Hebrews together. The writer used this method

---

175. Chungi, letter to the author.

176. I am aware that female circumcision or clitoridectomy has come under much attack. What I am endorsing here is not the practice but the values inculcated through it. I suggest that a relevant Christian alternative should be sought in order to replace the practice and continue the training of women in a wholesome way.

to encourage the Christians who are going through hard times and to highlight certain ethical principles necessary for this kind of existence. We have shown also the special significance that this has for the situation in the continent of Africa, and especially for the Kenyan situation. It is clear that certain themes come to bear upon the conditions in Kenya. Christ is the pioneer and finisher of the faith; thus, believers can hope in his deliverance and a successful completion of the pilgrim journey. The refugee believers as well as the Kenyan Christians are assured that they have the support of the community of faith, "the cloud of witnesses," who are encouraging them in this journey. They are reminded that they need to exercise faith, hope, courage and endurance in order to press on toward their destination. The goal of the journey is to reach that eternal city "with foundations" whose architect and maker is God.

The next chapter evaluates how the church in Africa, and more specifically in Kenya, has practically responded to the challenge of aliens and pilgrims, also called refugees. Our first aim will be to critique and assess the response so far and then we will examine how the study of the pilgrim motif in the book of Hebrews can guide us to formulating a workable and biblically-based response.

6

The Role of the Church in Kenya and the Refugee Problem

> The church is God's people gathered as a unit, as a people, gathered to do business in his name, to find what it means here and now to put into practice this different quality of life which is God's promise to them and to the world and their promise to God and service to the world.
>
> —JOHN HOWARD YODER[1]

Introduction

IT HAS BEEN AN ongoing debate as to whether the church should be involved in politics. The church leaders in Kenya have been specifically warned to keep out of politics because this is viewed as the sole realm of politicians. However, they have stood their ground in showing the politicians that they will not abdicate their role of speaking out God's truth and will, not only within the church but also the nation. This has brought them into direct conflict with the ruling powers, but they have been undaunted in their attempt to understand their prophetic role and how it benefits the community. A church that is clear about its role in the world and how it will practically carry out that role will be able to respond adequately to the refugee problem and conscientiously formulate an ethic of caring for refugees. They will also be able to articulate to the rest of the world what it means to be a pilgrim community.

This chapter seeks to answer these questions: What is the role of the church in socio-political issues in general? How does the pilgrim motif inform the church's participation in socio-political issues? My thesis is that because the church in Kenya has not understood her pilgrim identity, they have not been able to respond adequately to the problem of refugees. The

1. Yoder, *For the Nations*, 177.

pilgrim motif will provide us with the resources we will need to develop a community that will be caring to the stranger, the alien and the refugee. Such an ethic for refugees will include in its main components following Jesus as the pilgrim *par excellence*, a caring community that is characterized by hospitality and courage in the midst of adverse circumstances.

Though our main conversation partners in this reflection, with regard to the mission of the church in the world, will be two authors, John Howard Yoder[2] and the late outspoken Kenyan Anglican prelate, Bishop Henry John Okullu,[3] I will use themes derived from the pilgrim motif to sharpen their focus on what it means to execute our role in the world more faithfully. Both have not only written extensively on the role of the church in the society, but they have also lived exemplary lives of what it means for an individual to be a follower of Jesus Christ. They have demonstrated in their own lives that an ethic that cares for the outsider is not just what is spoken but also what is lived.[4]

Therefore, I will explore these two authors' understanding of what the mission of the church should be in the world. I will also assess whether the church in Kenya has fulfilled that role in their response to socio-political issues of the day, showing both the strengths and weaknesses. I will then discuss how much the church in Kenya has been involved in the refugee problem analyzing both the factors that have hindered and those that have enhanced this involvement. By using the four-dimensional Method of

---

2. John Howard Yoder (1927–1997) has reflected extensively on the role of the church in social issues. His well-known works include: *The Politics of Jesus, Vicit Agnus Noster*; *Body Politics: Five Practices of the Christian Community Before the Watching World*; *For the Nations: Essays Public and Evangelical*; *The Priestly Kingdom: Social Ethics as Gospel*; and *The Christian Witness to the State*.

3. Bishop Henry John Okullu (1929–1999). He has been an outspoken critic of governments. He began his attacks when he worked as an editor for *New Day*, in Uganda, and he spoke against the Obote government and, as a result, his life was in danger so he had to return to Kenya in 1967. In Kenya, he worked with the Christian newspaper *Target* or *Lengo* (Kiswahili), which he used to raise political issues like the tribal oathings and the death of Tom Mboya in 1969. He was the Anglican Bishop of Maseno Diocese from 1974 to 1994. In 1974, Virginia Theological Seminary awarded him an honorary doctoral degree for his "restless concern for freedom in Christ and his prophetic voice." His word and life reflect what it means to be a prophet of God in modern times. His written works include: *Church and Politics in East Africa*; *Church and State in Nation Building and Development*; and *A Quest for Justice: An Autobiography of Bishop Henry John Okullu*.

4. Yoder has done his ethics from the Anabaptist tradition, which is outside the mainstream church movement, and that is why his perspective is valuable. Okullu, on the other hand, also sharpened his understanding of the role of the church while working in Uganda, a foreign land for him, and also serving within a church that was racially dominated by whites immediately after Kenya's independence.

Concreteness in Christian Ethics developed by Glen Stassen and David Gushee,[5] informed by the pilgrim motif, I will introduce some guidelines toward developing a community ethic that will be caring toward strangers and refugees.

The Mission of the Church

The church is the concrete reality in the world that portrays God's purposes. Our understanding of that purpose with regard to socio-political involvement is important. Our focus in this section will be to show that the church that understands her identity as a pilgrim community will be better prepared to fulfill her purpose in the world: to proclaim the Lordship of Jesus Christ, the pilgrim *par excellence*, to be the community of God's people that transcends national, racial and ethnic boundaries, a paradigm for society, and to serve their communities in all areas. This is what a church guided by the pilgrim motif will look like.

To Proclaim the Lordship of Jesus Christ

Yoder and Okullu understand the church as the instrument that proclaims the supreme lordship of Jesus Christ over all creation. Jesus is not only Lord of the church but he is also Lord over all areas of life, including the state. That is why they were not afraid to proclaim his lordship in the political realm. The church in her relationship to the state should know that her ultimate loyalty is to Jesus Christ. Yoder, who has drawn extensively from the work of Berkhof[6] about powers, shows that human affairs are under superhuman entities known in biblical language as thrones, principalities, powers, authorities, archangels and dominions. These powers are in charge of ordering human institutions like the state, school, human traditions, economic systems, politics, etc. They are created by God and were good,[7] but they are now fallen and therefore in

---

5. I am indebted to my professor, Glen H. Stassen, for giving me this framework for approaching Christian Ethics, during the Fall Seminar of 1999 on Methods of Concreteness in Christian Ethics. He and David P. Gushee have developed the method further in their new book, *Kingdom Ethics*, 55–124. Its purpose is to point to what it means to follow Jesus, the Pioneer and Perfecter of the faith.

6. Berkhof, *Christ and the Powers*. The other recent author who has done much work on the powers is Walter Wink, in his trilogy: *Naming the Powers: The Language of Power in the New Testament*; *Unmasking the Powers: The Invisible Forces that Determine Human Existence*; and *Engaging the Powers: Discernment and Resistance in a World of Domination*.

7. Yoder, *The Politics of Jesus*, 142.

rebellion to God. They have subjected human beings to slavery and seek to separate them from the love of God. Nevertheless, even in their fallen condition they cannot fully escape the sovereignty of God who can still use them for ordering his good purpose.[8] Christ's coming was to expose these powers that have usurped the authority that really belongs to God. Through his death on the cross he triumphed over them and made a public spectacle of them (Col. 2:15). Christ broke their pretensions at divine sovereignty by showing that there is One who is Lord over all. Christ also disarmed the powers by unmasking their weapons of deception.

> Their weapon was the power of illusion, the ability to convince that they were the divine regents of the world, ultimate certainty and ultimate direction, ultimate happiness and the ultimate duty for small, dependent humanity. Since Christ we know that this is illusion. We are called to a higher destiny: we have higher orders to follow and we stand under a great protector. No powers can separate us from God's love in Christ. Unmasked, revealed in their true nature, they have lost a mighty grip on us. The cross has disarmed them: whenever it is preached, the unmasking and the disarming of the Powers takes place.[9]

The work of the church is therefore to proclaim the lordship of Christ over these powers. This is the mystery that the apostle Paul is called to proclaim to the Ephesians 3:10. Yoder puts it strongly this way:

> In spite of the visible dominion of the "powers" of this "present evil age," the triumph of Christ has already guaranteed that ultimate meaning in history will not be found in the course of earthly empires or the development of proud cultures, but in the calling together of the "chosen race, royal priesthood, holy nation," which is the church of Christ . . . The meaning of history—and therefore the significance of the state—lies in the creation and work of the church.[10]

Okullu does not speak explicitly in the language of powers but he talks about "challenging structures of alienating power which control economic and political"[11] systems. He says that the church lives under such historical reality and they cannot isolate themselves. The question is not whether to participate in the political life of the state but how. He argues that God's call

---

8. Ibid.
9. Yoder citing Berkhof in *The Politics of Jesus*, 147.
10. Yoder, *The Christian Witness to the State*, 13.
11. Okullu, *Church and State*, 4.

for the church is always to confront the unjust structures of the world that imprison God's children and hinder them from serving and enjoying him.[12] The clear call for the Christian is to know his or her distinct identity. He notes, "The authentic Christian is nevertheless one who affirms the reality and necessity of the world of politics, but demythologizes and relativizes its importance. The life of faith, hope, and love cannot be established by political powers."[13] He is also aware of the danger of the state assuming all power and moving on toward the brink of idolatry:

> The State assumes responsibility for its citizens in almost every department . . . Much as this national approach to the fight against poverty, disease, and illiteracy is appreciated, there is always the danger of the state absolutism leading to idolatry. Since the state has assumed all power, this absolutism and the idolization of leaders in Africa has in fact become demonic.[14]

Okullu was very brave in his denunciation of state power because during his time African countries had recently become independent and they believed that political power was the panacea for all evils. There was widespread euphoria because Africans had overthrown colonial rule and felt that there was nothing that could stand in the way. In fact, the slogan for most of the countries was "Seek first the political kingdom" and everything else will happen. Therefore, immediately after independence, the church in Kenya worked very closely with the government. This close cooperation prevented the church from speaking out against some of the social issues. These social ills include corruption, nepotism, tribalism and landlessness of the poor.[15]

Therefore, in standing against idolatry and declaring the lordship of Christ it is important not to work too closely with any form of government as if it has been blessed or endorsed by God. Yoder notes that no government is sacrosanct and those that are proclaimed as democracies should be watched even more closely because their view of themselves is often much higher. He notes, "The glorification of democracy as a new form of government categorically separate from the frailties of other forms is observable not only in the wars we fight in its name, but also in our peacetime missionary stance."[16] The realistic observation he makes is that democracies are only the least oppressive forms of government. He says:

12. Ibid., 5.
13. Ibid., 63.
14. Ibid., 66.
15. See Githiga, *Church as a Bulwark against Authoritarianism*, 51.
16. Yoder, *The Priestly Kingdom*, 151.

> Of all forms of oligarchy, democracy is the least oppressive, since it provides the strongest language of justification and therefore critique which the subjects may use to mitigate its oppressiveness. But it does not make of democracy, and especially it does not make of most regimes which claim to be democracies, a fundamentally new kind of sociological structure.[17]

Furthermore, any state has the capacity to perform both good administrative functions as well as tendencies to self-glorification. The Christian should be vigilant to prevent being sold into the system of any world power. In agreement with Yoder, Okullu says:

> One of the requirements for the church in order to bear such witness and render such service to society, is to adopt a position of critical detachment, in order to be free to be the watchdog in society. If church leaders allow themselves to be drafted into sycophantic political thinking and accept patronage from state officials, they will lose their prophetic freedom to correct whatever is wrong in society.[18]

Thus, Yoder and Okullu have demonstrated that loyalty to Jesus Christ and commitment to his Lordship work to keep the church true to her identity as pilgrim community always watching so that the state does not overstep its bounds. Furthermore, a church that understands itself as a pilgrim people always on the move, always seeing the land as belonging to God, and always seeking to be faithful to Christ, has grounds for an independent and prophetic relation to the state.

The Church as God's Instrument for Change across Ethnic and National Boundaries

The key to developing this critical stance against the state is to understand beyond any shadow of doubt that the instrument for bringing the change that God wants in the world is the church and not the state. Part of this prophetic function is to call the state to greater accountability and to warn against its idolatrous tendencies, especially in the form of nationalistic pursuits that ultimately exclude all other people. Yoder notes that just as the prophets denounced idolatry among the people of God in the Old Testament, the church today should expose the evils of nationalism. He says:

---

17. Ibid., 159.
18. Okullu, *Church and State*, 68.

> The prior choice of nationalism, preferring one people, one state absolutely above all others, is already idolatry. Nationalism sins against the first two commandments well before it infringes on the second table of the Law. Not only in the crude forms of Fascism and Nazism is nationalism idolatry; the same idolatrous claim is already made for a created value when it is thought that a given civilization or nation is the bearer of the meaning of history; when a given nation like the United States in the Cuba crisis, claims the right to be judge, jury and executioner in its own case.[19]

It is also interesting to note that Okullu was alert to call the church to the danger of nationalism and the glorification of one state over all others. Like the Old Testament prophets, who mainly prophesied to Israel but were able to call other nations to attention when they were not being obedient to God, Okullu was not hesitant to call attention to America's empire-building tendencies. He says:

> We are living in what some people have described as a 'global village' and this narrowly conceived nationalism whether in Africa or elsewhere, is not only impracticable but evil. That is why it is completely pitiable that Reagan's administration should have tried to drive the Americans back to the isolationist sense of nationalism at a time when they ought to realize more than ever before that they are everybody's brother, not *Big Daddy*. America could succeed in the world making true friendship with less naïve self-assertation and a little more diplomacy. No human being, however feeble, weak, hungry, primitive or ignorant, ought to be talked at by anybody, however rich or powerful.[20]

The antidote to this kind of nationalism is to show that the church is God's pilgrim community in the world that transcends all borders and languages. It goes beyond the narrow confines of one state. The blood of Jesus breaks the divisions that have kept people apart. Régis Burnet, Didier Luciani, and Geert van Oyen edited a volume titled *The Epistle to the Hebrews: Writing at the Borders,* composed of 11 essays of a conference held in Louvain-la-Neuve (Belgium) from April 7 to April 9, 2014. The contributors focused on the exegetical works of the Book of Hebrews and its reception history along the concepts of border, boundary, and frontier.[21] In addition both Yoder and Okullu affirm the trans-cultural and international nature of the church and claim that this should be preserved

---

19. Yoder, *A Christian Witness to the State*, 15–16.
20. Okullu, *Church and State*, 45.
21. Burnet et al., *The Epistle to the Hebrews*.

at all costs. Yoder notes that loyalty to state or national interests should not make a Christian consider the inhabitant of another nation an enemy. This narrow view even goes to the extent of equating the enemies of a state with the enemies of God, and therefore such a state will consider it their duty to God to go to war against these enemies. On the contrary, he says, "The God of the gospel loves His enemies."[22] He is also the God who tells his people in the Old Testament to take care of "the stranger at their gates." Yoder also exposes the limits of such a view that reveals a lack of the full grasp of what God has in store for his people. He says:

> The challenge is simple: if we accept the traditional territorial definition of the community under God, we deny the unity of the human race in creation, the cosmopolitan reality of the church in mission, and the eschatological vision of the world in redemption. The alternative is to accept the claim that this nation, any nation, every nation under God is called to multicultural reconciliation internally and to practical humanitarianism globally.[23]

Yoder also exposes the danger of nationalism that manifests itself in the form of military superiority and might. This is where he shows the fundamental difference between the church and the state. While the church is called to serve all people regardless of nation or tribe, the state's duty is to exercise its influence by wielding the sword. Yoder takes his guidelines from Jesus' description regarding the nature of earthly power in Luke 22:25–26: "The kings of the Gentiles lord it over them; and those in authority over them are called benefactors." Therefore, he notes that the state exists to exercise coercive power and violence. This is the reason he warns that the church should not be entangled in such domination schemes of the state but be free in order to serve all people.

Other forms of domination that he recognizes may also be in the form of exploitative economic interests over the populations of the less developed parts of the world. He warns about the danger of multinational corporations whose powers transcend national boundaries. Okullu, on the other hand, also laments the kind of development that is patterned according to Western standards and carried on by transnational corporations that do not take care for the human person but are concerned only about what they can produce. He says, "development has been falsely taken to mean the increase in gross national product, with human persons relegated to a secondary position to serve this material interest."[24] He also sadly notes that this kind of

22. Yoder, *A Priestly Kingdom*, 189.
23. Ibid., 190.
24. Okullu, *Church and State*, 118.

economic development has resulted in more poverty and a widening of the gap between the countries of the West and African countries, rather than the improvement in human life that was anticipated. He says, "There was to be a new international economic order, and the poorer nations pinned most of their hopes on a more equitable distribution of the world's wealth. At the moment the world's wealth is still in the hands of one-third of the world's people around the North Atlantic."[25]

Thus, the church is called to proclaim the lordship of Christ over all creation, and especially to the powers, as demonstrated by the power of the state. This means that the church has the role of maintaining her identity as a pilgrim people of God, while making known those evils within the nation that hinder people from experiencing the fullness of life that God wills for them. The pilgrim motif in Hebrews urges us to go outside the gate to meet with the stranger.

The Church as the Paradigm of What God Wants for Society

Not only is the church to announce the lordship of Christ over all creation by showing the church's transcendent nature over national and political boundaries, the church is also to reveal what the life of God looks like in concrete day-to-day terms. Okullu and Yoder are very clear that the church's witness in the society will be greatly enhanced by the demonstration in real life as to what such a community that is called by God should look like. The church is not able to denounce racism in the wider society if they are not living it in a concrete way in their own life. Yoder says:

> The witness of the church must be consistent with her behavior. Only if she herself is demonstrably and ethically working on a given problem does the church have a right to speak to others. A racially segregated church has nothing to say to the state about integration.[26]

Yoder also recognizes that the church does not have to struggle very hard in trying to provide a public witness because God had put within her life as an organism practices that she will naturally demonstrate just by being the church. These practices are not secret or esoteric but by their very public nature are easily accessible to the watching world. This is where Yoder introduces the five practices of the church that are translatable to secular observers. These practices can be emulated in the world using the

---

25. Ibid., 96.
26. Yoder, *A Christian Witness to the State*, 21.

language of the wider society. Yoder expounds these practices in his book, *Body Politics: Five Practices of the Christian Community Before the Watching World*.[27] Here, we will only mention them and give a brief explanation of their relevant meanings:

1. **Baptism:** This represents the breaking down of barriers of race, gender and class. In the early church baptism was the rite in which one participated in order to mark one's entry into the new people of God or the new humanity. By this practice, the church sends the message to the world that there is a "new interethnic reality into which people are called to belong." This is a reality that the world that is divided across nations, ethnic groups, race and gender cannot miss. In fact, Yoder points out this new humanity is what Paul says had been entrusted to him as the mystery which God had hidden in times past and he was now revealing through the preaching of the Gospel. "That is the Gentiles have become fellow heirs, members of the same body, and sharers in the promise in Christ Jesus through the Gospel" (Eph 3:6). There could not be a more powerful message that the church could preach to the world. The church in Kenya has missed the opportunity to learn this multiethnic community that is demonstrated before their eyes in the refugee community. By paying attention to the way refugees have learned to live together, to encourage and exhort one another as Hebrews says, the churches can learn a truer sense of their own mission from the refugees.

2. **Breaking of Bread:** This is a symbol of the concrete and tangible demonstration of economic concern for those who are the deprived members of the society. Yoder says that when the apostles shared in the breaking of bread in their homes, it was the fulfillment of God's will in Deut 15:4 that "there would be no more poor among you." Within the old covenant, there was the Jubilee principle, which if practiced periodically, would take care of the needs of members of the community. Yoder also notes that Jesus practiced it in his own ministry when he announced the acceptable year of the Lord's favor at his inaugural sermon in Nazareth in Luke 4:18ff. Jesus also demonstrated it practically when he fed the five thousand as well as the four thousand in his ministry. The message that this is sending to the world is that economic needs are to be shared within the body of Christ. An application of this in recent years has been the Jubilee 2000 Movement, which worked for the cancellation of debt of poor countries. This embodies the theme of Jubilee and the theme that the land belongs to God not to our own private profiteering,

---

27. Yoder, *Body Politics*.

and the theme of hospitality for the stranger, that we noticed in our study of the pilgrim motif in the biblical narrative.

3. **Binding and Loosing:** This is in the context of non-violent conflict resolution within the body of Christ. Yoder shows that Jesus draws from two rabbinic technical terms "to bind and to loose" which meant to be obligated or not to carry out a certain deed (Matt 18:15).[28] These two words were also used for ethical discernment. One was obligated if they were bound, but freed when loosed. Thus, these words have a twofold meaning, with regard to reconciliation and also moral discernment. The fact that there are three steps in the process before one gives up the process of reconciliation shows that the intention of the process is to win a brother or sister, and not to break harmony. The strength of this procedure for forgiveness is that it rests on the lay people the ability to extend forgiveness to one another. It does not depend on the pronouncement of clergy.[29] The beauty of this human process is that whatever the community has endorsed is also elevated to the level of a divine act that God has ratified.[30] Therefore God and the human community participate in this together. Yoder believes that if this were applied within the society, it would reduce the punitive and vengeful prison system.[31] There is also the acceptance that conflicts are normal within the body. " To be human is to have differences; to be human wholesomely is to process those differences, not by building them up but by reconciling dialogue . . . Therapy for guilt is forgiveness; the source of self-esteem is another person who takes seriously my restoration to community."[32] Practicing forgiveness and reconciling dialogue is crucial for maintaining the sense of community, and of serving and helping one another, that we saw in our study of Hebrews.

4. **The Open Meeting:** This is also called the rule of Paul. In 1 Corinthians 14:26, he instructs that whenever the body of believers is gathered everyone should be able to speak something as directed by the Holy Spirit and they should be listened to. This means that priority is not just given to those who are in the hierarchy of leadership. It underlines the fact that all the members are really valuable in the body. This is

---

28. Ibid., 2.
29. Ibid.
30. Ibid., 3.
31. See Yoder, *For the Nations*, 174. He argues that the prison system in the United States has become increasingly punitive. The principle of forgiveness would greatly transform the system.
32. Yoder, *Body Politics*, 8.

the principle that underlines the key freedoms in a democratic society, namely freedom of speech and freedom of assembly. It also sets the tone for a town meeting environment where the needs and contributions of all members of the community are given due consideration.

5. **The Multiplicity of Gifts:** This is based on the teaching of Paul in 1 Corinthians 12 where the church is compared to the human body which consists of different parts but each part is essential for the full functioning of the body. This practice affirms the fact that all the members of the body of Christ have been gifted and so they play a useful role in the body. It cuts against any form of hierarchism and the elevation of some at the expense of others. This shows the equality and the dignity of all people and is a better basis for human rights than any secular ideas. It also says that we should accord respect to those members of the community who are less visible because they are equally important to the function of the community.

Okullu does not specify five practices for the Christian community that he recommends, but he has recognized the importance of the community as a witnessing body. He says:

> Part of that total witness is for Christians to be a community—a loving, living, sharing, and serving community. This kind of witness is visible and effective where the churches are truly open to the poor, the despised and the handicapped for whom our modern societies have little care. The church as a worshipping community will have some minimum requirements for survival—opportunity for worship, eucharistic and other forms of fellowship, instruction and education.[33]

The Mission of the Church is to Serve the Community

The pilgrim motif gives the direction that the church should live its life not only by being a witness to the community, but also by rendering service to the community. The writer of Hebrews reminds the believers not only to be caring for the strangers but also for those who are needy and those in prison Hebrews 13:1–4. Yoder and Okullu also show that the church is given a role to be a leaven to the society by active service, like the building of schools, hospitals and offering other voluntary services. Both men actually urge the church to be proactive in entering new areas which have not

---

33. Okullu, *Church and State*, 66.

been ventured into even by the state so that they give the state an example of what it means to serve. Yoder says:

> The church has continued, in more specialized realms of education and medicine, and also in other areas of social concern, to be the pilot, creating experimentally new ways of meeting social needs, which when once their utility has been proved, can be institutionalized and generalized under the authority of secular powers.[34]

He further urges the church to do this because she can afford to experiment and fail, while those in control of the state cannot afford to do so.[35] He argues:

> Minority groups can also exercise pioneering creativity in places where none is threatened. They can do jobs nobody else is doing and thereby gradually draw attention to some realm of social need for which it would have been impossible to find an imposed solution.[36]

He also notes that the church provides a moral osmosis through their education of the young and also by exemplifying healthy social values like good neighborliness, honesty at work and in being active members of their communities. This is what he calls "conscientious participation"[37] in the community. Okullu expresses a similar view when he says:

> The church should be a factory of new ideas of development- agriculture, community health care, village technology, small size and rural industries. Our projects must be the innovative type. We must all the time be breaking new ground with courage; participating in God's continued work of creation.[38]

---

34. Yoder, *The Christian Witness to the State*, 20.

35. Yoder, *A Kingdom of Priests*, 92.

36. Ibid., 97. This is a true observation from my experience from the refugee community in Kenya as well as the migrant Kenyan community in the Bay area of California. They are creative in situations in which ordinary people would give up hope.

37. Yoder, *The Christian Witness of The State*, 20.

38. Okullu, *Church and State*, 116.

The Church in Kenya and Her Participation in Socio-Political Issues

Now we will look at how practically the Anglican Church in Kenya has fared in light of what the mission of the church should be in the world. The church has been present in Kenya for over 150 years but only in recent times has it began to play an active role in challenging the government about some of the evils that have beset the country. In his new book, Bishop Githiga has traced the involvement of the church in politics, highlighting key players and major events in which the church has played a significant role. He has done a good job at assessing how the Anglican church in Kenya has grown gradually in its understanding of the lordship of Jesus Christ over the political realm in order to play her role as a watchdog over the community. He has conveniently divided the history of the church into three periods: the colonial period, when the missionaries were in charge; the time of the first president Kenyatta; and the era of the second president, Moi.

In each of these times, the church has faced the temptation of siding with the ruling establishment and has been in danger of losing its prophetic role. But each time there were certain events that alerted the church that the government had overstepped its bounds. As a result, the church has risen up to be numbered with the faithful and played a prophetic role, and there have been individuals who have courageously spoken the word of God for the season. We have seen that a key component of faithfulness in the letter to the Hebrews is courage—courage in the face of threatened persecution, courage to follow Christ faithfully. It has taken great courage for some leaders of the church in Kenya to fulfill their Christian calling, and it will continue to take such courage. Thanks to those like Bishop Henry Okullu who constantly kept a vigilant eye, being conscious of when the state was stepping beyond its bounds, and calling attention to the church to denounce these evils. One needs to ask what has kept the church tempted to align with the ruling authorities to the point of losing its edge as salt and light for the society. We also want to find out what has made the church wake up to its call. First, we will look at the temptations that have led the church to support the status quo.

Racist, Tribal, or Ethnocentric Loyalties vs. Loyalty to the Body of Christ

There is the tendency to show loyalty to the ruling establishment because they share one's ethnic group rather than seeking unity with members of the body of Christ, regardless of tribal affiliations. In the colonial period, the missionary church aligned with the colonial regime because they felt they needed their protection. Because of the failure of the missionary church to speak against the evils of colonialism, a saying was coined in Kenya which asserts that there is no difference between the colonial administrator, the settler and the missionary: *"Gutiri ngurani ya Mubia na Muthungu."*[39] People resisted colonial rule so the missionaries felt they needed protection from their home country in order to pacify the natives. The missionaries were also co-opted into the system, by being appointed to the Legislative Council (LegCo) to represent the interests of the Africans. Some, however, could see through the colonial bias and spoke courageously for the interests of the Africans. One such person was the Archdeacon Owen, who spoke against land alienation and evils of forced labor in Western Kenya. He constantly complained to the colonial administrators about the humiliating nature of forced labor that was inflicted on both young and old, indiscriminately. He said that old women and girls were sent to work on the road reserves, far away from home, and were not allowed to go back home at night. The result was that young women were forced to immorality while the old were exhausted.[40] His unflinching stand against the colonial policies earned him the derogatory title of "archdemon" from fellow white people.[41]

In independent Kenya, the temptation to align with racial or tribal loyalties rather than to Christ did not cease. The first president of Kenya, Jomo Kenyatta, was a Kikuyu.[42] At the same time, the assistant Bishop of the Anglican Church, Obadiah Karuiki, was a brother-in-law of Kenyatta. Githiga also notes that the Kikuyu dominated the top leadership in the Presbyterian Church.[43] This should explain why the church was pro-establishment and could not speak against the evils of the Kenyatta regime until things came to a head. In 1969, Tom Mboya[44] was assassinated at the hands of a Kikuyu and many Kenyans saw this as a political assassination. This caused much unrest in the country. In order to consolidate the power of the government in the

---

39. Githiga, *Church as a Bulwark against Authoritarianism*, 3.

40. Ibid., 24.

41. Ibid., 56.

42. This is one of the largest tribes in Kenya. Most of their land was taken over by the settlers, so they were among the first to experience the evils of colonialism. They were also in the frontline in the fight for independence, so they felt justified to receive the good returns as a result of independence.

43. Githiga, *Church as a Bulwark against Authoritarianism*, 50.

44. He was a young upcoming popular politician from the Luo community. His leadership style and popularity became a threat to the ruling power at that time. He was shot down in the streets of Nairobi.

hands of the Kikuyu, tribal oaths to pledge loyalty to Kenyatta and his regime were administered to large numbers of Kikuyu people. This involved drinking raw goat blood and other secret tribal rituals. Christians who refused to participate in this were threatened by death. It took one who was a non-Kikuyu to see through the evils of the system. Bishop Okullu wrote against the killing of Mboya and also denounced the tribal oaths because they destroyed the unity of the body of Christ. Another group that also spoke against these oaths was the East African Revival Movement, a fellowship that transcended tribal boundaries. They argued that taking the blood of goats was tantamount to renouncing the oath of allegiance to Jesus Christ whose blood had paid the price for their salvation.[45] Many were ready to die rather than to renounce faith in Jesus Christ and the unity of the body of Christ.

Loyalty to the Political Leaders vs. Loyalty to Jesus Christ

The evils of colonialism and the courage needed to oust the system elevated the political leaders who stood against it to a position of super-human power. The British government accused Kenyatta of being involved with the Mau guerilla freedom movement and he was put in detention in 1952. As a result, he gained much sympathy and popularity. Many Kenyans began to see him as the embodiment of change and the rallying point for their freedom. He was viewed as a savior who would bring freedom upon his release. Christian songs were sung for him at political rallies. Githiga says, "At times Kenyatta was put in the place of Christ. One hymn for example said, "We see the love of Kenyatta in that book. He gave his life to save us."[46] Kenyatta was deified to the point that people thought he was immortal and shock waves went through the nation when he died in 1978.[47] In truth people could not even think of a Kenya without Kenyatta. The tumults of war and chaos that had racked our neighboring countries caused the Kenyans to desire a peaceful transition beyond anything else. So when Moi, who was his vice-president,

45. Githiga, *Church as a Bulwark against Authoritarianism*, 54.

46. Ibid., 41.

47. I remember that day vividly—August 22, 1978. People spoke in hushed whispers and walked on tip-toes. It was as if our world had come to an end. I was 18 years old, and my recollection of Kenyatta was of an old, powerful, almost mystical leader. In my elementary school days, I had the opportunity to go to the State House to sing for him. Such entertainment usually took place at night. School children and other choirs from all over the country came to sing to him every night. Then, at about midnight, he would come out of his shelter, wave his fly-whisk, say a few words, conclude with his characteristic call, *Harambee,* and then retire. To us, he seemed as unapproachable as a god. All the trappings of pomp and wealth dazzled us, who were from the village and had never in our lives seen such things.

took over power peacefully and promised to follow in the *nyayo* (footsteps) of Kenyatta, the loyalties and support of the church were transferred to him without question.[48] The church was also endeared to president Moi because he openly professed his Christian faith and he was seen in church every Sunday. He also formulated his ruling motto of *nyayo* with three Christian principles: love, peace and unity. At this time the church did not even see anything to denounce about the system. This humble, Bible-professing Christian blinded them, so they sang the praises to Moi. There was such a close connection between the church and state to the point that the church was almost a religious department of the state. When Kenya was declared a *dejure* one-party state without much of a debate in parliament (it took only forty-five minutes), the church leaders began to see the evils of the system. Then Moi began to consolidate power around himself and if you disagreed with him personally you were thrown out of the party, detained without trial or even killed. This caused division in the church between those who were personally loyal to president Moi and those who spoke out against the system. It was only after the introduction of multiparty rule in 1992 that people spoke openly against the president, but even so in a hushed manner. I have wondered about the reason for this excessive leadership cult in most African countries. I think it stems from the traditional system of authority in which leaders were both religious and political; they were almost given divine authority so that no one dared question for fear of being cursed.[49] When Kenyans also compared their leaders to those of neighboring countries like Uganda that was plunged into utter chaos under the military dictatorship of Idi Amin, Moi's ills appeared harmless.

The Temptation of Power and Wealth

The temptation to deify leadership was reinforced by the rewards and blessings that followed such allegiance. This is especially dangerous in situations where political power is also linked with wealth. We saw that in the colonial times, when missionaries were given positions in parliament to speak on behalf of Africans. Of course, their loyalty was to those who appointed them. In the same way, during Kenyatta's time, the church leaders who were

---

48. Bishop Githiga terms the early part of Moi's rule (1978–1985) as the "honeymoon period" between the church and state. The church and state worked very closely. They even helped the state to formulate the *nyayo* philosophy of love, peace, and unity.

49. One may compare this kind of superstitions and fears to those in ancient Greco-Roman society; out of such context the book of Hebrews speaks of "Godly fear" (5:7; 12:21, 28–29). See Gray, *Godly Fear*, 109–227.

closest to him were rewarded with wealth especially in the form of land that had belonged to settlers.

During the rule of Moi, those churches that supported him received parcels of land to build church structures, schools and hospitals. They were rewarded with positions as chaplains in the armed forces. The president contributed a lot of money in the form of *Harambee* contributions so that the church could build many church structures. As a result, they did not speak against him. Those who spoke against the government were considered as serving foreign masters or not submitting to the ruling authorities. As a result, they were denied the gifts and handouts from the government. The church that supported Moi was predominantly from his own community, the Kalenjin. Thus, in Moi's time ethnic affiliations were reinforced by religious loyalties.

Now we examine what has kept the church aware of its prophetic role in the community and prevented it from selling out wholesale. First, there was the recognition that Jesus is Lord over all creation and even other lords like the state, the presidency, or the tribe. This lordship of Jesus Christ was proclaimed by courageous church leaders who were committed to the cause of Christ more than to tribal loyalties. The commitment of these leaders was shown when they spoke the word of God through the sermon "in many and various ways",[50] during the worship that Hebrews indicates is present participation in the heavenly city. In their sermons, courageous church leaders knew their loyalty was to God in Christ, the Pioneer and Perfecter of our faith, and not to the status quo. These sermons were always disseminated through the newspapers, which unknowingly promoted the work of these people and the cause of Christ. Githiga says the press became the means of coordinating the church and the State debates.[51]

Second, there were believers in Kenya who have held to the unity of the body of Christ regardless of tribal or denominational divisions. This was not just a theoretical belief but it was concretely manifested in the group of committed believers who were drawn from various ethnic groups, known as the East Africa Revival movement.

> The East Africa Revival Movement (EARM), an indigenous Christian movement, brings together nearly every community in Kenya [and the whole of East Africa] for fellowships and conventions. The individual's experiences of Christ bring them together, to form a community that ignores past cultural and religious differences. The movement which is a "church" within

---

50. See Koester, "'In Many and Various Ways,'" 299–315.
51. Githiga, *Church as a Bulwark against Authoritarianism*, 92.

the church transcends not only denominational boundaries but ethnic boundaries as well.[52]

Third, the ecumenical bodies like National Christian Council of Kenya (NCCK) acted as a catalyst when the individual churches could not speak alone. They had a team of young dedicated leaders who were visionaries. This ecumenical vision of the church has been strengthened by the support of various churches abroad. The state in Kenya could not get past the fact that the body of Christ is a body of believers that transcends national boundaries. Those churches that felt that they had the support of their brothers and sisters outside risked the labeling that they had foreign masters. During the struggle toward multi-party democracy in Kenya, the Kenyan churches that had links with the greater body of Christ outside were provided support. Githiga notes that NCCK used 10 million Kenyan shillings (over 100,000 pounds sterling)[53] in preparations of the seminars and the booklets and seminar that were used to train Kenyans toward multi-party democracy. This funding came from brothers and sisters outside Kenya.

The Church's Response to the Refugee Problem in Kenya

The history of the refugee problem in Kenya can be divided into two eras, pre-1992 and post-1992. Before 1992, there was a small number of refugees hosted in Kenya and they lived among the people and were generally integrated. However, after 1992, there was a huge influx of refugees into the country due to the wars in Ethiopia, Somalia and Sudan. It was at this time that the government decided to build refugee camps to host this incoming population. Previously there had not been any planned settlements. Before 1992, the response of the churches toward refugees had been channeled through National Christian Council of Kenya (NCCK), All Africa Conference of Churches (AACC) and the Jesuit Refugee Services (JRS) on behalf of the Catholic Church. Individual churches responded as they were made aware of the problem but there has never been a coordinated program unifying all the churches except the work done by these organizations.

The response to the refugee problem was influenced by the internal problems that Kenya was facing in 1992. It should also be noted that the years leading to 1992 were very traumatic ones for the church in Kenya. The church was spearheading the call for multi-party democracy in Kenya. Many Kenyans at this time were internally displaced as a result of ethnic

52. Ibid, 180.
53. Ibid., 108.

clashes. The churches acted in an exemplary fashion by hosting internal refugees that were being chased from their homes. One such church is St. Matthews, Eldoret, which hosted thousands of people in their premises waiting for help to come to them.[54] The presence of internal displaced people might explain why there has not been a concerted response to the refugee problem by the individual Kenyan churches. They have had their own internal problems to deal with and their hands have been full. They also felt that there are international organizations like UNHCR and the LWF or AACC that take care of the needs of these people.[55]

The National Christian Council of Kenya (NCCK)

The Refugee Service Unit (RSU) of the National Christian Council of Kenya (NCCK) was established in January 1983 as a result of the recommendations made by a consultative meeting held at Karen in September 1982. The partners were the Kenyan Government, UNHCR, World Council of Churches (WCC), All Africa Conference of Churches, Kenya Catholic Secretariat, and National Christian Council of Kenya (NCCK). RSU became one of the five departments of the NCCK General Secretariat.

NCCK/RSU is funded mainly by international donations through the office of UNHCR and All Africa Conference of Churches (AACC). RSU does assessment of needs and administration of assistance to the refugees. Three programs that they focused on were the following:

- **Counseling:** They recognized that refugees having suffered much loss would be in need of counseling services in order to cope with

---

54. When I interviewed the pastor in charge of the Anglican cathedral in Eldoret, he was proud to tell me that they had done a good job in assisting these people who had been deprived of their homes as a result of the ethnic clashes. But he also admitted they had not done as much in assisting the external refugees. They had provided them with a place for worship, but they had not done much in terms of providing them with the basic necessities. He was also aware of their acute housing needs because he had paid pastoral visits to them. He told me that more than ten people occupied a one-bedroom house. He was also of the opinion that the external refugee population had UNHCR as a body to help them, and the refugee camps had sufficient facilities like schools for the refugee population. These were resources that he felt the internally displaced population did not have.

55. When I asked a pastor of one of the largest churches in Nairobi what his church does about the refugee problem, he told me that they try to keep away from that because it is something that involves the government and the large international bodies like UNHCR. His reasoning was that ordinary Kenyans found it difficult to tell the difference between genuine refugees and those who were impostors. This was especially so in the urban areas.

the situation in the country of asylum. This service was offered to the refugees in all the stages of their stay.

- Temporary Relief and Assistance Policy: Considering the difficult situation in which refugees find themselves when they have newly arrived in the country, they need financial assistance until they can be self-reliant. They were provided with a monthly allowance for a period of six months. Those who were over fifty-five years of age and unaccompanied minors until the age of eighteen, the sick, mentally and physically handicapped were entitled to monthly allowances until well beyond the six months. They were also entitled to medical assistance through the Free National Health Service. Accommodation was also provided for those with special needs while a long-term solution was being sought.

- The Local Assistance/Development Assistance: This was mainly to assist the refugees to identify means of self -reliance and local integration. In order to do this, they were offered small business loans to help them start a business. They were also supported with training and guided in project formulation, and with extension services. They were also bound by legal contract for the loans granted. The job placement officer familiarized them with the job market while taking record of their skills and educational background. Those who had been granted refugee status were granted work permit class M, which is the official recognition of refugee status in Kenya's Immigration Act, chapter 172.[56] Meanwhile, those with rural or semi-rural backgrounds were assisted to find places in the rural areas, where Kenyan families and other charitable organizations hosted them, as they looked for their livelihood in these rural areas. The social group worker coordinated various social groups initiated by the refugees. The aim of some of these groups was to meet national, ethnic, political or cultural interests of the refugees while others were to be task oriented.

All these services were offered to refugees in Kenya before 1992, when their numbers were small. The number of people that could be assisted in the city increased so the government decided to settle all the refugees in the rural settlements in the camps. This meant that they could not get individualized services.

---

56. Republic of Kenya, *The Laws of Kenya*, 20.

All Africa Conference of Churches (AACC)

All Africa Conference of Churches (AACC) is an ecumenical organization that has been assisting refugees in Africa since the 1960s. Its headquarters is in Nairobi. It has done exemplary work in aiding churches and national associations to help the refugees become self-reliant. They have not done the groundwork itself but have helped individual churches to do the work. Ankrah[57] has written two articles assessing the work done by the AACC for the refugees through the decades of the sixties and nineties. In his first article he applauds the work which in his opinion covered significant ground. But in his second article, Ankrah is more critical because he is aware that though the assistance has continued, the problem of refugees has steadily worsened since the 1970s. The fact that the problem of refugees had become more acute than it was in the1970s and that it had steadily increased showed that there is a flaw in the approach. His analysis regarding the cause of this failure is that Africa has been influenced by the Western theological model, which leads them to respond with charity, instead of looking for the root causes of the problem. He says, "Western theological positions were based on the theory that human suffering must be relieved regardless of the root causes resulting in that suffering, and that the political views of the causes are irrelevant to their present predicament as refugees, the best one can do is simply to concern oneself to alleviating that immediate suffering."[58] He also argues, "The old theology which encouraged the churches in Africa to disregard the causes of refugees initially, and therefore, prevent them from confronting African governments with their actions and consequences of their policies, made it possible for the governments to behave with a lack of justice."[59] There is a growing recognition by many like Okullu and Ankrah, that the church in Africa should not just be the one that runs ambulance service, caring and faring for the refugee casualties without asking for the cause of the casualty.[60] Another critique is that "the contemporary Good Samaritan is one who does not simply provide the first aid to modern-day travelers on the Jericho-Jerusalem road, but who also tackles the underlying problem of robbers preying on the innocent, the high cost of health care, prejudice against the minority."[61]

---

57. Ankrah, "The Stranger Within the Gates," 107–32. His second article is "A Theological Reflection on the Ministry of Churches to Refugees in Africa," 122–34.

58. Ankrah, "A Theological Reflection," 127.

59. Ibid., 128.

60. Okullu, *Church and State*, 140.

61. Ankrah, "A Theological Reflection," 129, quoting Minear, "Terms of Engagement in Human Need," 6.

All these reflections show that churches need to do more about the causes of the refugee problem in Africa since the problem continues to worsen. It causes us to think seriously of what it will take to make the churches become communities that will promote peace and reconciliation. What will it take to be the church of the stranger? In 1997, the World Council of Churches declared that year as the year of solidarity with the uprooted people. One of their key suggestions is that the church all over the world should commit themselves to be the church of the stranger. But to be a church that cares for strangers will take diligent work. What will be those chief components that will keep us in constant check to be the kind of a people who will not only respond to the emergency but will also do something about those situations? How will we prevent and put an end to vicious cycles of violence, famines, wars and continuous displacement of people from their homes? One way to do this will be to develop an ethic for refugees that will guide the church in becoming the church of the stranger.

An Ethic for Refugees: The Church of the Stranger

In developing an ethic for the care of strangers, I will use the four-dimensional method that Glen Stassen and David Gushee have provided as enriched by the pilgrim motif in Hebrews. The four dimensions are: the way of seeing, the way of reasoning, passions and loyalties and basic convictions I suggest that doing character ethics while paying attention to the perspective of the stranger, the process will be transformed. The results of such ethical reflection will be transformational not only for the strangers but also for the hosts.

The Way of Seeing Dimension

First, a character ethic that will not only be focused on individuals but communities that take their pilgrim identity seriously will critically analyze the social, economic and political context. Therefore, we will not just ask the question, who are the powers and authorities in the refugee problem? But we will also find out how these powers impinge on the refugee situation. We will also attempt to see the problem from the perspective of the victims. Such a perspective will cause not just theoretical reflection but a genuine, truthful and honest search for lasting solutions to the problem. We will not stop at the window dressing stage. Yoder tells us that seeing the problem and solution from the perspective of the minority will cause us to look more truthfully. He notes:

> . . . the minority community provides a training ground for cultivating the concrete expectation that things will usually be seen inadequately by those who read events from a posture of control or of seeking to control. Thus we educate ourselves in the reasonable expectation that when we see things differently from others, we will often be seeing them more truly.[62]

The refugee situation in Kenya and in Africa as a whole, seen from the perspective of the refugees, presents us with a hierarchy of powers and authorities that the individual refugee and the churches have to contend with. First are the powers that the refugees run away from in their countries. Various wars and conflicts cause most refugee situations in Africa. The causes of the conflict may be multifaceted but the immediate cause is usually one group denying power to another or one group feeling that they are being oppressed unjustly, so they demand to have a say in running the government. In the case of Sudan, war has continued for over 40 years, due to the stubbornness of the Islamic government in their refusal to share power with the inhabitants of Southern Sudan. In Rwanda, the situation has been ethnic and clan conflicts between the Hutu and Tutsi. The differences between these two ethnic groups existed even before the colonial period, but the gap was enlarged when the colonial masters endorsed the superiority of one group over the other. The letter of Hebrews calls for the practice of hospitality and love for aliens and strangers by a people who know themselves to be pilgrims, who know what it means to be strangers.

The truth of the matter regarding these conflicts and wars is that they would cease if they did not have support and encouragement from external forces and powers that are benefiting from the confusion and chaos of the situation. In chapter 2, we saw that the wars in the Horn of Africa in the sixties and the eighties were mainly undertaken with the funding of the superpowers, who were at that time the USSR and the US. These two powers exchanged loyalties back and forth between the newly independent nations of Sudan, Ethiopia and Somalia. The main purpose was to safeguard their interests in the Gulf area. None of these superpowers were interested in stopping the war, especially if their interests were being threatened. They benefited by selling weapons to these countries that continued to fight. Now that that the Cold War has stopped, these countries that were once used as pawns to protect the superpowers have been forgotten, only to continue to languish in war and confusion.

War causes famine, general economic deterioration, loss of morale, and the spread of diseases like AIDS, cholera, malnutrition, etc. These

---

62. Yoder, *The Priestly Kingdom*, 95.

situations cause refugees to flee their homeland. Thus, it is not only political reasons that cause refugee problems in Africa. Refugees run away because they do not have the social and economic climate to make a living in their countries. This is the reason many critics have argued that the UN definition of a refugee is very limited because it does not take into account the serious economic situations that threaten the lives of people in Africa. According to Okure, you do not have to go to a refugee camp to be confronted with the situation of acute deprivation because the whole continent is like a refugee camp. She says, "Africa as a continent itself is a big refugee camp. One can identify within it the conditions similar to those which obtain in isolated refugee camps."[63] These conditions are a result of the impoverishment of the continent by external organizations such as the World Bank and the IMF. Some of the countries that have been at war for a long time cannot receive any economic help because they have become poor debtors, thus worsening the situation.

The refugees not only have to contend with the difficult conditions that they are escaping from, but they are also confronted with the same conditions or even worse, in the countries that they run to. Because they are strangers, they also have the powers and authorities within the countries of asylum to deal with. Most of the countries of asylum are themselves experiencing social and economic hardships so they do not want to share these few resources with an influx of populations that is coming into the country. To make matters even more complicated, most countries that generate refugees also receive refugees so it becomes like a game of musical chairs.[64] This is the situation that faced Kenya in 1992. The country was facing the ethnic clashes that came as a result of the clamor for a multiparty government. The refugees were not received well because they brought more strain on the meager economic and social resources. Thankfully, even in the midst of these difficulties, these refugees were not forcefully returned to their countries.

African countries as a whole have been commended for their hospitality in hosting large numbers of refugees despite the harsh economic and political problems. However, the situation is changing and the nationals are becoming increasingly hostile to incoming strangers who are most of the time used as scapegoats for the country's problems. In the Kenyan context, the refugees in the urban area face much hostility and harassment from security personnel and even from ordinary citizens. They are arrested and jailed, and the police extort bribes from them because they know that they

63. Okure, "Africa: A Refugee Camp Experience," 12–21.
64. Ibid., 14.

are vulnerable. The government has threatened many times to close the borders to these people because they are accused of bringing arms into the country, thus causing much insecurity.

Apart from governmental powers of asylum-countries, the refugees and the churches also have to contend with the powers of the aid agencies that respond to the problem. The chief respondent to these situations is of course, the UNHCR. But there are other umbrella organizations that work in conjunction with it. UNHCR has been the only organization that has been entrusted with the sole mandate of providing 'durable solutions' to the refugee problem. But one wonders whether UNHCR is really serious in working toward 'durable solutions,' if 'durable solutions' are only limited to voluntary repatriation to the country of origin, local integration in the country of asylum or resettlement in a third country. It is interesting to note that, after fifty years of trying to work for 'durable solutions,' UNHCR has finally realized that it is not enough to respond to refugee situations from a humanitarian angle; they must address the root causes of these problems. Sadako Ogata, writing the foreword to the book celebrating fifty years of UNHCR, had this to say:

> Humanitarian action is of limited value if it does not form part of a wider strategic and political framework aimed at addressing the root causes of conflict. Experience has shown time and time again that humanitarian action alone cannot solve problems which are fundamentally political in nature.[65]

This confession comes in the face of long-term and protracted refugee situations all over the continent. The war situation in Sudan has gone on for about forty years. Refugee camps in Uganda and Tanzania have been there for over thirty years. Though the refugee camps in Kenya are just over ten years old and relatively recent in comparison, the call to work extensively toward durable solutions is more urgent than ever. There really should be a serious search for other avenues to help communities to come together and solve this problem.

Furthermore, the prolonged stay of refugees in camps causes debilitating psychological and emotional effects. Ankrah has observed that:

> It is not the lack of funds which constitutes a threat to the continued dependence of these individuals as such, but it is what such continued dependence will ultimately do to the dignity and the personality of the individual. When a person who is strong and willing to earn his own living is compelled by circumstances to

---

65. Cutts, *The State of the World's Refugees*, x.

be a "pauper" for, say, four years, his self-respect begins to dwindle and his ability and desire to get off the "dole" diminish.[66]

It also a fact of life that if people are left helpless for a long time, the feeling of estrangement, alienation, and rejection continues, and people develop negative feelings like trying to seek vengeance in either misusing or abusing the system. In Kakuma camp, it was observed that the refugees began to develop negative habits such as "recycling." This term is used to explain a situation in which those who come from Sudan cross the border over and over again in order to receive extra ration cards so that they can get extra food. This generates a feeling of lack of trust and suspicion on both sides, between the refugees and the aid workers. In such a situation it is very hard to know what to do. During my visit to Kakuma, we went to the receiving center in Lokichoggio, where the new arrivals are received. There is much screening and some are subjected to staying there for several weeks because they are suspected to be recyclers. UNHCR staff as well as humanitarian workers do not always make morally sound decisions and they have been known to give preferential treatment to some refugees. Some UNHCR have even been known to receive bribes in order to arrange for some refugees to get resettlement. One cannot rule out the fact that when people have been in a situation of extreme need for a long time, the helpers have to learn to detach themselves from the situation, otherwise they cannot deal with it with integrity, or they may experience stress.

These are the examples of the powers and authorities that refugees contend with on a daily basis. The mission of the church that is conscious of her pilgrim identity is to engage these powers[67] in order to see that the situation that causes extreme suffering for a group of humanity is eliminated. We have to be honest that the church universal and especially those in the Western countries have not been active enough to speak against the policies of their governments that impoverish and cause suffering in other nations of the world. They have also not spoken against the sale of armaments that continue to fuel these wars. They have only responded in charitable ways by giving band-aid solutions, like medicine, food, clothes, and rescue workers.

---

66. Ankrah, "The Stranger Within the Gates," 127.

67. I have borrowed the use of these words, "engaging the powers" from Wink who argues that, "The Powers are good. The Powers are fallen. The Powers must be redeemed." It is for this reason that the Powers are not just to be combated or destroyed because they are not simply evil. "Thus the title, *Engaging the Powers*. It is precisely because the Powers have been created in, through, and for the humanizing purposes of God in Christ that they must be honored, criticized, resisted, and redeemed. Let us engage these Powers, not just to understand them, but to see them changed." (Wink, *Engaging the Powers*, 10)

This is long after the effects of war have already taken place. The refugees at Kakuma camp asked me the following question:

> Do we have brothers and sisters in the West who care for us? We thought we all belonged to the universal body of Christ? Why did they preach the gospel to us and now leave us to die with the weapons that they sell to our countries? Surely they are not serious enough otherwise they would stop the wars that are causing all these problems to us? It seems that we are fighting this on our own.[68]

If the church takes her pilgrim identity seriously, they will know that they have to be in solidarity with their brothers and sisters in Kakuma camp. I am not just putting the blame on the Western church; the church in Africa and specifically in Kenya has its share of the blame as well. She has cooperated with the authorities and powers and neglected to speak for "the least of these." We know the church in Kenya for a long time surrendered to the status quo and did not speak against the injustices within their country, let alone those that affect the refugees. The reason is because they have been divided along tribal lines. The only group that spoke against the tribal oaths that were administered during the time of Kenyatta was the East Africa Revival Brethren. This is a group that is informed about their pilgrim identity. They unite with their brothers across East Africa. But even then, they only spoke because some of their members were being affected and not because they had a well-articulated theology of social justice. The only other time that the church spoke with a strong voice was during the time of the tribal clashes, thanks to those leaders who were able to transcend tribal lines in order to speak God's word to those who were victimized.

The church in Kenya has not even spoken about the refugee problem. One can give the excuse that they have been busy with the political issues such as working on the constitution, but it appears that they have not even thought that good relations with needy neighbors should be a central part of that constitution. They have also said that this is a matter that should be left to UNHCR and the Kenyan government. In my opinion, they have neglected an important part of life, where they can make a difference. The church should guide the government to formulate rules and policies for the immigration policy as well as provide direction regarding the response to strangers who are in our land. The Kenyan government has done much in arranging for peace talks between the warring people in Sudan and Somalia, but the average Christian does not know how to deal with strangers. If their pastors do not even preach sermons that speak about the strangers, then

---

68. Refugee Christians from Congo, interview.

it is not a wonder if people remain ignorant and even hostile to strangers. I am aware that we have many problems of our own, especially in trying to make ends meet in difficult economic times, but this should not shut us from those who are needy around us. My next question is, how can we rouse ourselves from this apathetic stance in order to be passionate enough to respond to the refugee problems?

Passion/Loyalties Dimension

In order to develop an ethic for the refugees or churches that care for strangers we should ask ourselves how we can become passionate about this, because passion fuels action. First, I think the Kenyan Christians have not been passionate about the refugee problem because they have lacked the leaders and models that would demonstrate to them that this is where our interest should be. When we had great social injustice in the country outspoken leaders like Bishop Okullu, Bishop Muge, Archbishop Gitari, and Rev. Timothy Njoya were admired and followed because they spoke out against the status quo in Kenya. Their sermons were always featured in the daily newspapers because they spoke what everyone wanted to speak but were afraid to because they would be arrested. They did not fear to challenge the powers that be because they knew that they had protection from above and if need be they were ready to die because they viewed their lives from a pilgrim's perspective.[69] They had the courage that comes from faith. In the same way, we need the leaders to remind people from the pulpit that they have a responsibility to care for our brothers and sisters who are in need. In my interviews with pastors none of them said they had preached a message about refugees in recent times.

Second, we lack the passion that would fuel us to action because we are far removed from the situation. We lack the experience and closeness to those who are suffering. Yoder tells us, that the experience of isolation, oppression, suffering, powerlessness causes us to learn "empathy for others who are the victims; one learns the power game from below and to see how different it looks from there."[70] I have shown that refugee camps have been located in the remotest parts of the country. I think the idea is that when we have them out of sight we will also have them out of mind.[71] In my

---

69. Bishop Muge, of the Diocese of Eldoret, died in a mysterious road accident on August 22, 1990. The church believes he paid with his life for his outspoken criticisms against the government.

70. Yoder, *The Priestly Kingdom*, 94.

71. Jim Wallis recommends that in order to care about the needy we have to go beyond the comfortable confines that keep us away from such people. See Wallis, *Faith*

interviews with the local people, the closer they were to the refugee camps the more passionate and caring they were about the situation. The churches in Kakuma were more aware and more involved in the lives of the refugees than were the churches further away. The churches far away from the camp in Nairobi who had refugee congregations within their services were more aware than the churches that did not have any interactions with the refugees. Such was the case with the members of St. Francis, Karen and St. Luke's, Kenyatta, who had limited interaction with the refugees. In St. Luke's Church, Kenyatta, the members of the youth service were more aware of the refugee problem than members of the older congregation because the young refugees interacted with the youth rather than with the older people. The older generation of refugees had their own service in their language in the afternoon, while the Kenyan congregation met in the morning. The two groups did not meet. I asked the pastors if they had encouraged some of the members to visit the afternoon congregation or if they had visited it themselves, and they had not. The amazing thing is that even while hosting the refugees under their roof they had not preached a single sermon in their congregation about caring for refugees. I encouraged them to do so, especially on June 20th in order to celebrate Africa Refugee Day.

The third reason the Kenyan church has not been passionate about the refugee problem is that they have felt that the problem is too big, and they cannot do anything about it. The decade of the nineties, with the devaluation of the shilling, has been especially traumatic for most Kenyans trying to make ends meet. The economic situation worsened because since Kenya did not have a good record of human rights the world lending institutions decided to cut off economic aid until they could rectify this situation. This resulted in the use of structural adjustment programs in order to try to get the economy on its feet, and this meant that the government had to apply what is called cost-sharing even as they cut down the essential services in the country. It has also meant that the unemployment rates have risen and young professionals have had to take early retirement. This has been the decade that has seen many people leave the country for greener pastures elsewhere. Kenyans used to be very patriotic and many of them did not like to settle in other countries, but now Kenyans have been scattered all over the world.

In 2001, I met a group of Kenyans in the middle of Cape Town, South Africa, selling curios and handcrafts. Without my asking why they had come they told me that they described themselves as "economic" refugees. Thus, with the enormity of the problems facing them back in Kenya, it has

---

Works, 23.

been more than they could handle to see one more needy group added to the number. It was evident that when they realized that they could do something even small to alleviate the situation they were more than willing to do so. After my visit to the refugee camp, I went to my local church. They gave me time to share about the refugee situation and I asked them questions to find out how much they knew about the problem. I was really surprised about how well-informed they were from the media and from scriptures. What they did not know is that they could do something about this situation. They were ready to give whatever they had in the form of clothes and food and they even offered to visit the camp. Two members of a US church that supports me financially visited the camp with me. They brought several boxes of medicine, which greatly helped the clinic. Their lives were changed forever because they were able to interact with the refugee Christians and be encouraged by their faith. Such examples show that if people are given the opportunity to make a difference, they will do something, and even if it is small, their efforts combined will make a big difference.

Another example of passionate people who are eager to give their talents and service to the refugees is the cooperative effort of both the refugees and the Kenyan Christians at the camp. Kakuma Interdenominational School of Mission (KISOM) was started under the leadership of Pastor Tito Mayaribu, who is himself a refugee from Burundi. He got the vision that Kakuma, which has people from eight African nations, is a perfect place to train missionaries for the church of God so that when they return to their countries, they can make a difference. He started with the help of a few people who wholeheartedly bought into the idea. However, he soon experienced heavy opposition from other pastors in the camp who thought he really wanted to make a name for himself. When I visited in the camp in 2001, he was having problems in convincing the members of other denominations within the camp to join in this venture. One of my meetings at the camp that year was with pastors from eight countries representing various denominations. I encouraged them to be united in their efforts to share the gospel because they had a readymade audience in the camp. I also sold them on Pastor Tito's idea of the training school. I did not think much of my talk, but in early 2003 the school was up and running. In fact, they were preparing to graduate their second class of students who had been prepared in various skills such as Bible reading, evangelism, pastoral counseling, and medicine in mission.

This is a concrete example of what it means to engage with the church of the stranger. The refugees are not only trained and equipped but the Kenyans are enriched Christians as they discover their talents and resources in their giving. The beautiful thing about it is that those who teach and prepare these leaders are mainly drawn from the Kenyan Christians who work for the NGOs at the camp. These are ordinary lay people who are imparting to these refugees some of what they have learned from the Word of God. They have not had any formal training at all. The members of the school board are now in the process of affiliating themselves with a recognized Bible school so that they could be sure that they were doing something that was validated elsewhere. It seemed that their efforts to connect with Nairobi Evangelical Graduate School of Theology (NEGST) are bearing fruit.

Yet another reason the Kenyans have not responded to the refugee problem is that their loyalties are ultimately tied to their tribal affiliation rather than to the community of faith. It seems that the churches in Kenya have preached the gospel and it has been a mile wide and an inch deep, so to speak. They have been no more than "preaching stations" as Stassen[72] has said. They have not formed communities aware of their pilgrim identity in order to transcend tribal and ethnic loyalties. They need to know in reality how such loyalties lead to tribal clashes and displacement across the national and ethnic boundaries. They can only learn this practically from suffering the consequences and that is "church of the stranger" in Kakuma.

I met a Christian from one of the areas where the clashes had taken place in Kenya. I asked him why his people killed their neighbors. I was trying to find out why the Christian faith had not made a difference in these areas. His reply was that they were not neighbors; they only lived in close proximity but they were worlds apart. I asked him further, "Did you not go to church together or did you not eat together?" He agreed that they did attend church together but they did not have anything uniting them beyond that. He further expressed the fact that the two groups ate and fellowshipped in their separate worlds. The only ray of hope was the recent formation of what is called Small Christian Communities, which is a kind of cell group in the Catholic Church. This organization has been encouraging Christians to meet in homes to study the Bible together and also to share meals. He said that this was making a difference in that area and if it had been started earlier, it would have prevented some of the conflicts and violence. This hopeful story proves that small groups that break bread together as part of the component of Yoder's church's body politics, can make a difference in how people live on an ongoing basis with each other. As we saw in our study of Hebrews, there is no private Christianity; Christian faith is about incorporation into the fellowship of the people of God, and the journey is made through sharing in suffering together. The staying power is appropriated through faith, and it takes much patience. We serve one another and help

---

72. Stassen and Gushee, *Kingdom Ethics*, 61.

one another to keep the faith. Christ is the example who has gone before, and it is dramatically clear that Christ's ministry entailed the incorporation of outcasts—lepers, prostitutes, tax collectors, women, children, zealots—into one community together. Christ is the high priest who brings healing, and in Kenya and Africa that certainly must include healing of divisions between the tribes and ethnic groups.

Another positive story that proves the same point took place decades ago, involving the East Africa Revival Movement. The group stood against tribal oaths, citing the Bible as grounds for their contention. In 1969, during the Kenyatta era, the government which was under the Kikuyu tried to consolidate the tribal loyalties of the Kikuyu, in an effort to exclude other communities from participation in the government. They tried to get individuals to bind themselves to the tribe through sacrificial offering that involved drinking the blood of a goat. However, this group of Christians said that they would not mix the blood of Christ with that of goats. They made it clear like the book of Hebrews (9:12–14) that the blood of Christ is totally sufficient. This group of Christians alerted the whole church to take a stand against this practice, and some people even died for their faith. The whole church was able to send a message to the president that they would not tolerate such division in the body of Christ and that they would stand together. This only happened because there was a small group of believers who were ready to stand for their faith regardless of tribal loyalties.

The chief characteristic of this group even until this present time is that they meet together in small groups comprised of various tribes and denominations that all feel united by the blood of Christ. They care for one another in tangible and practical ways. Those who come from Uganda are hosted in the homes of the brothers and sisters in Kenya. They address one another as brothers and sisters: *ndugu na dada*.[73] They really take seriously this brotherhood and sisterhood. Whenever a brother or sister is in trouble, they rally together and meet the need. They even arrange for marriage partnerships across tribal boundaries so that no one is left without a spouse. In other words, it is a very close-knit fellowship. One of the important features of their meeting is the sharing of testimonies in which they confess sins from which the Lord has set them free.[74] This group is serious about following Jesus as the pioneer of faith as Hebrews 12:1 urges. They do not just want

---

73. The Kiswahili word for brother and sister.

74. The only negative thing about the group is some of their legalistic tendencies and the fact that they make one feel they do not deserve salvation if they do not have big sins to confess. I remember when I was young, attending one of the meetings and thinking that because I had not committed such sins as adultery or stealing, I did not need to repent.

to read the Bible; they desire to live it in their lives, even sometimes to the danger of legalism. But they have shown that taking Jesus seriously means to recognize that tribal boundaries are null and void in light of our relationship in Christ our pilgrim *par excellence.*

The church in Kenya and the whole of Africa needs to hear this message over and over again. The clashes in Rwanda that caused the 1994 genocide can be attributed to tribal and ethnic loyalties. The same can be said of the Kosovo crisis. The fight toward multipartyism in Kenya was delayed because certain churches were loyal to the President mainly because of his tribe and did not support the rest of the coalition that was working toward greater freedoms for the Kenyan people. We need to reexamine whether Christ is really divided as Paul asked the Corinthians. How committed are we to be brothers and sisters across tribal and racial lines? It was the Dutch Reformed Church that supported the apartheid system in South Africa. We need to repent and ask God to forgive this great sin of division that continues to wreck the body of Christ.

The Way of Reasoning

In developing an ethic that cares for the stranger and the refugee we have to focus also on the dimension of moral reasoning. Stassen and Gushee[75] have shown that there are four levels of moral norms in Christian ethics and we will see how on each level we can receive guidance to respond to strangers in our land. These four levels are: the immediate or particular judgment level, the rules, principles and basic conviction.[76] A way of reasoning that is informed by the perspective of the pilgrim or the stranger will talk not only of norms or rules but the kind of rules and norms that are sensitive to the outsider. It will also focus on virtues and practices that will form people who are conscious of a pilgrim identity. Virtues are those character traits that will form and manifest in a person that will be caring for strangers. Practices are those public and communal activities that will reinforce and consolidate those virtues and values that we hope to see manifested in the community that will be caring for the stranger.

When faced with particular situations and judgments we expect that people will be guided by a well-formed character and the power of intuition, or the constant practice of doing the kind deed to the stranger or outsider. We hope that on this level a person will not use a particular bad deed that happened to them to make a principle or rule for all future acts.

75. Stassen and Gushee, *Kingdom Ethics*, 100–124.
76. Ibid, 100.

For example, if one is treated badly by a certain stranger in a particular place and time one will not use such a situation to say all refugees are bad, or they are dishonest and cheat. This is a level we have to be constantly aware of because many times the way we treat people is based on a preconceived stereotype. Because of one negative interaction, we make judgments that will encompass all situations despite the change of circumstances. Sometimes we also completely write off people because of a single act in which they did not measure up, and we do not give them a chance to improve or show that they are capable of a better deed. We have several relevant examples in the Bible that can give us moral guidance as to what we can do in our own particular situation.

Thankfully, in an ethic of the stranger, we will not just act on the level of particular situations. We are sinners prone to make biased judgments, so we need some rules to guide us. Rules will apply not only to immediate situations, but also to all similar cases. A rule will also tell us what to do or not to do. In the moral code of Israel there are several rules that tell us how to treat strangers. Here are a few of them (NRSV):[77]

> **Exodus 22:21** You shall not wrong or oppress a resident alien, for you were aliens in the land of Egypt.
>
> **Exodus 23:9** You shall not oppress a resident alien; you know the heart of an alien, for you were aliens in the land of Egypt.
>
> **Leviticus 19:33** When an alien resides with you in your land, you shall not oppress the alien.
>
> **Leviticus 19:34** The alien who resides with you shall be to you as the citizen among you; you shall love the alien as yourself, for you were aliens in the land of Egypt: I am the LORD your God.
>
> **Deuteronomy 10:19** You shall also love the stranger, for you were strangers in the land of Egypt.

There are other rules that direct the Israelites on the rights and privileges of the Strangers—that they were to be included in various feasts as well as be provided for by the tithe. One of the rules that is prevalent in the New Testament is the one that instructs the people of God to practice hospitality. One of the most important characteristics of the church leaders was hospitality.

Because modern refugees have to deal with governments it is important not only to operate within the biblical rules that we have, but to know

---

77. Tzoref, "Knowing the Heart of the Stranger," 119–131; see also Jipp, *Divine Visitations and Hospitality to Strangers*.

the rules and legislations of the various governments in the countries of asylum. In Kenya, the Refugee Bill that has been proposed since 1990 did not pass until 2019. The government has been evasive and has delayed in making specific legislation because they then can easily operate in the area of general principles and guidelines that are given by the United Nations and the Organization of African Unity (OAU). There has been nothing to pin them down when a specific violation has been done against the refugees, even when it has clearly been observed that the principles have been violated. Our work therefore as Christians in Kenya is to see that we hold our government accountable in making sure that all refugees are recognized and protected under the law. Furthermore, we must help to ensure that it works according to the established principles, not only of the UN, but also of the Word of God on how strangers are supposed to be treated.

This leads us now to discuss moral norms on the principles level. Principles usually support rules or criticize rules. They are more general than rules and do not tell us what to do directly or concretely. Principles that would help us in responding to strangers include the command that we are to love our neighbors as we love ourselves. We are to love our enemies. (It might be the case that our neighbors are those who have treated us badly.) We are also told to do to others what we would like to be done to us. We have observed that these principles are too general, but the level of rules or a specific act will tell us how to put into practice concretely what it means to love our neighbor or our enemy. The story of the Good Samaritan is such a story that embodies what the love of neighbor means by spelling out the specific acts of compassion that were done. The specific rules in Romans 12:9ff spell out what love for neighbor means, which includes contributing to the needs of the saints, extending hospitality to strangers, blessing those who persecute you, not repaying evil for evil, and feeding your enemy if they are hungry.

It seems that these rules and principles are what guided those who drafted the articles for the OAU, because they included the key principle that "granting asylum should be considered a humanitarian act, not an act of aggression." This has been very important in helping African nations who have granted asylum to those who have fled from war in their own countries, so that they would not be construed as enemies except where it has been established that they were being charged for crimes committed in their home countries. They have also followed the principle that those who have been granted asylum should be settled far from the border so that they would not become a target of attack from the home country. Or that those who are in the neighboring country should not launch an attack on their country.

However, laws can be criticized or changed when human lives are in danger. The principle that a ruler who has been granted asylum should not use the neighboring country to launch an attack was demonstrated by the relations between Uganda and Tanzania in the 1970s and 1980s. Idi Amin had overthrown the elected President Obote who had also overthrown the monarch, the Kabaka. Obote was granted asylum by Nyerere in Tanzania and it was obvious that they had to prepare for war so that Obote would be returned to power. One can say that it was legitimate in this case to overthrow Idi Amin because he had committed several atrocities against the Ugandan people and others within East Africa. But this proves that a higher principle is sometimes considered more important so that specific rules can be broken.

The weakness of not putting forth specific legislation but operating on the level of principles has also undermined the whole principle of asylum in Africa, especially when it takes several years, and when people in the country are treated badly. This explains the situation of the Rwandan refugees in Uganda. They had been kept in camps for long and were not really treated well, and felt that they needed to go back to their country. After several years they violated the principle that the country of asylum should not be used for launching an attack. They did this in 1993, resulting in the atrocities of the genocide in 1994. It was a battle between those who feared being ousted from power back in Rwanda and the refugees from Uganda, but it wreaked havoc on the innocent civilian population.

It is important to ground the rules and principles on specific practices that demonstrate in real life the kind of people who will care for the refugee. One such key practice is the love of strangers (*philoxenia*) or hospitality.

Hospitality is an important practice that is not only rooted in the Christian faith but also within the African community. The hosting of many refugees in Africa has been attributed to the African spirit of hospitality. Hospitality was very foundational to the life of the early church. It was not really an option that they could choose to do or neglect. In her book, *Making Room for God: Recovering Hospitality as a Christian Tradition*,[78] Christine Pohl shows that this was central to the spread of the gospel in the early church. It is a rich tradition that is seen throughout the history of the lives of the people of God right from the Old Testament. Several narratives in the Old Testament are given to show the centrality of this practice among the people of God. Abraham, who is known as the father of the Jews, is given as a supreme practitioner of hospitality. The writer of Hebrews reminds his readers to emulate Abraham and Sarah, who in their practice of hospitality welcomed angels (Heb 13:2). That this continued to be an important

---

78. Pohl, *Making Room*. See also Pohl and Donley, *Responding to Refugees*. This is a valuable small booklet that gives practical suggestions on how to respond to refugees and is directed mainly to Christians in the West.

practice for the early Christians is shown by the teachings in the *Didache* guiding the believers on how they were to put this to work.

The explanation for the importance of this practice in the early church is that the public accommodations like hotels and inns were often not in good condition, so the Christians offered one another accommodation in their homes. Riddle shows that in the early church Christianity was spread in the homes because of the hospitality that the believers practiced. He says, "It is of primary importance that in the beginning, it was people not documents who spread the news about Jesus. It was the spoken word—the human voice—which carried the message."[79] He also reports that Papias, Bishop of Heirapolis, preferred to learn more about the teaching of Christ by word of mouth than through the books.[80] This was possible because hospitality was a common practice in the Christian households. Pohl argues that once hospitality was severed from the household/church setting a new set of dynamics entered. She says that the church/household setting for the practice of hospitality is "the most significant institutional base for transcending social difference and creating community."[81] She shows that activities that were once located in the household—work, religious observance, care for the sick and welcome of strangers—are now located in their own spheres. This hinders us from practicing hospitality because it has become specialized and impersonal. She also observes that in a setting where the practice has been taken over by professionals, though the physical needs are met, "needs for a social identity and connection are not only overlooked but sometimes intensified."[82] Now it has become almost difficult for Christians to practice hospitality, especially in very institutionalized settings. Pohl shows that institutionalized help was set up because of the unpredictability of voluntary service, but now it has become a hindrance because it lacks that personal and human element.[83] She says:

> Our sense of personal capacity to respond to the needs of strangers is undermined by the authority of large institutions designed to meet their needs. However, given our uncertain sense of personal responsibility, any total rejection of institutional measures would be both naïve and risky. The task is to find practices that join personal relations with predictable care . . . Returning the care of the strangers to the vicissitudes of individual kindness

79. Riddle, "Early Christian Hospitality," 145.
80. Ibid., 149.
81. Pohl, *Making Room*, 164.
82. Ibid.
83. Ibid.

is not an option; but without personal involvement, strangers become detached and vulnerable.[84]

No doubt, it has been difficult for Christians in Kenya to know how to meet the needs of strangers because of all the large bodies like UNHCR and World Food Program (WFP) already involved in this service. These Christians consider their personal efforts more of a hindrance than a help in the refugee situation, because they feel unable to match the political and financial power of these agencies. Nonetheless, they need to be encouraged by the fact that the personal human touch cannot be replaced, even by humanitarian organizations. Christians must find a way to minister to the needs of these strangers in their midst, even if it is to inform these larger organizations that they need to exercise that human touch as they serve these vulnerable human beings. Christians can also practice hospitality in their churches and homes whenever individual strangers visit their congregations. This practice in the church can be strengthened by the sharing of meals, the understanding that they are all united in the body through baptism and the fact that they affirm the value of every individual.

Within the African social system hospitality has also been a key practice. One can learn of this importance by the use of the proverbs that testify to the fact that guests are important. Two sayings in my language are, *ibu toek ropta* "Visitors bring blessing, or rain." Another one is, *toot kebou*, "Visitors are really at the mercy of their hosts." These sayings reveal that the stranger is viewed as one who is able to bring blessing, yet he or she is a vulnerable person. This is why many African societies value visitors, and do not generally look at strangers with fear or suspicion.

On the other hand, Gaim Kibreab also has warned that hospitality is on the decline in Africa because of the prevalence of poverty. He says we cannot depend on the continuance of this practice, especially if this is viewed as a vehicle to respond to the economic needs of the people. I assert that this is where the solidarity of the body of Christ should begin to emerge. Rich Christians in the West should demonstrate their love for God and the strangers in these African countries by extending their assistance in tangible ways. Maybe by meeting the needs of congregations in Africa they will empower African Christians to respond to the specific needs of the refugees and offer care for the strangers in their midst. This all follows the wisdom of the African proverb: *Mgeni siku ya kwanza, siku ya pili mpe jembe* ("One is a guest for two days; on the third day you should give a hoe"). This means that in the protracted situations in which the refugees are left idle for a long time in a country of asylum, Christians both in

---

84. Ibid.

Kenya and those abroad, should find creative ways to give the refugees a "hoe." This will ensure that they can have a sustainable livelihood rather than depending on handouts. Certainly, the practice of hospitality is one that can ensure that this will happen.

Apart from the practice of hospitality, there are virtues that need to be embodied in those who are to be caring to strangers. These virtues that are key elements in the pilgrim motif in the book of Hebrew are compassion, caring, kindness, courage, partnership and teamwork. Most African peoples also practiced a rite of passage in which they hoped to inculcate these virtues into the lives of the young members of the society. The Nandi, for example, practiced circumcision for both male and female. The most important thing was not just the physical operation but the informal education and training that followed. The young people were taught to know that vulnerability and pain were part and parcel of living. They learned to endure deprivation and hardship as a way of life. Usually they lived out in the bush, being exposed to the harsh elements for several months before they could rejoin the community. They also learned the value of cooperation, teamwork and partnership because those who were initiated lived together for a period of time, sharing meals together and anything else that they had. This is a practice we have almost lost and the virtues, too, are no longer being taught in the school system. Recently Christians in my community have decided to incorporate this into the church as a form of discipleship. They circumcise the boys only, not the girls because they have come to the judgement that the practice of clitoridectomy is oppressive. During the seclusion period instead of teaching the values of tribal lifestyle they teach them the Word of God. They also take time to teach them about their sexuality and their personal responsibility within the society. In my community this ceremonial rite of passage was the time when the boys were prepared to be leaders, mainly warriors and defenders of the community. I think this can be a valuable institution to incorporate into the Christian faith. A relevant equivalent teaching can be given for the girls so that they feel they have been prepared for the virtues of motherhood and other responsibilities that the society is calling them into. I remember when I was in high school, the school arranged that our class would spend a weekend outside of school when we would be taught the foundations of living and maturing into adulthood. We learned about boy/girl relationships, the health of our bodies, our sexuality and the value of staying sexually pure, the importance of careers, the importance of marriage and how to choose a life partner when that time came. Of course, we were also taught the importance of our devotion to God and service to the community. It was basically a well-rounded time of retreat. That was a formative time in my life because I remember making a commitment to live a

God-honoring life. That is an equivalent of what I could call a rite of passage ceremony, but done within the Christian community.

Basic Convictions Dimensions

Stassen and Gushee show the importance of grounding our Christian ethics in theological convictions rather than in enlightenment universal principles that do not really have any intrinsic connection to our life. They say that our ethics have to be related to the "larger drama of the reign of God, which is characterized by salvation, justice, peace, joy and God's presence."[85] The variables in this dimension include: God and human nature, forgiveness and discipleship, Christlikeness and justice, and the mission of the church. We will look at how each of these variables will be worked out in an ethic of refugees for a community that cares for strangers.

An ethic for the care of strangers will be grounded in the character of God, who has demonstrated concern about strangers and those who are vulnerable and marginalized in the society, from the book of Genesis onward, and including the book of Hebrews. God's concern for the stranger is demonstrated by the fact that the people whom he chose as his light to the nations were constantly reminded that they had been strangers/aliens in Egypt, so they would know how to treat strangers. God further showed his care through the severe consequences that would befall them if they did not care for the stranger. One author says that the important festivals that we celebrate in the Christian calendar reveal a God who comes to us as a stranger. At Christmas we celebrate the coming of a child for whom there was found no room in the inn. He came to his own and they did not receive him. At Easter, we celebrate the One who walked with the disciples on the road to Emmaus as a "stranger" and they could not recognize him until the breaking of bread. On Pentecost we celebrate the One who comes and surprises his followers with strange tongues. When his people did not get the point that they were not to oppress the widows, the orphans and the strangers, he took them into exile in Babylon so that they would learn what it meant to be strangers. Even in exile, he tells them to be a blessing in their situation and to pray for the welfare of this city that was not their own. So, we have a God who is a caring stranger, who knows what it means to be a stranger because he was incarnate on this earth. This is why he calls his people, the church, to also live as aliens and exiles. Elliott has put it this way:

---

85. Stassen and Gushee, *Kingdom Ethics*, 60.

> The Bible in an important sense is a book written by refugees for refugees. It was written about a man called Abraham who along with his family was called to leave his land and become a sojourner, a resident alien, in a foreign land. Abraham is recognized as a father of a pilgrim people. The Jewish people are the people of *Gola*, the people of dispersion, "strangers in a strange land," ever seeking a permanent home.[86]

Not only will we pay attention to the character of God, it is also important to have a realistic view of human nature. Stassen and Gushee argue that the way we understand human nature will influence our ethics. They note, "Jesus was realistic about human nature, diagnosing the vicious cycles that we get stuck in."[87] The fact that one has become a refugee does not exempt him or her from the emotions of human life. In fact, we have to pay attention to these more than ever before. Refugees experience extreme deprivation, hunger, disease, poor sanitary conditions, alienation, loss of identity, rejection by host country, ignorance of language of host country, and confinement in camps. They know the insecurity that we saw the letter to the Hebrews speaking to. Children are separated from their parents and husbands from wives. Women are exploited and sexually violated, often by people who are expected to be their saviors. These kinds of conditions produce a hostile and volatile people.[88] This usually rubs off on those who respond to their needs, so we need to be aware as Christians that if we are serving in situations where we are exposed to extreme deprivation we need a strong sense of grace and strength from God to continue to minister. Most of the Christian refugee workers whom I interviewed said that their faith in God really helped them to be wholeheartedly there for the people. They knew that they did not have strength on their own. Their faith also helped them to treat the people with dignity and value them as people who are highly esteemed by God. Thus, a realistic view of human nature will help to give us a realistic view of those whom we deal with—as sinners and yet as those who are valuable to God. As a result, we will communicate this sense of value to them so that they can be on the road to recovery.

This dimension also offers the variables of forgiveness and discipleship. These are very crucial in an ethic for refugees. The importance of forgiveness is one aspect that we cannot underestimate. If anything is clear in

---

86. Elliott, "The Bible from the Perspective of the Refugee," 50.
87. Stassen and Gushee, *Kingdom Ethics*, 61.
88. The security staff at the UNHCR camp are aware that refugees are people who are volatile because of the conditions of life to which they have been exposed. We were warned by them not to stay in the camp beyond 6:00 p.m. in the evening.

the letter to the Hebrews, it is Christ as the High Priest who brings the gift of forgiveness, reconciliation, and who heals us from our alienation. Most refugees flee their countries because of conflicts and difficult conditions. Some have been the cause of strife and some have been the victims. Both parties need forgiveness and reconciliation. Many refugees carry memories of traumatic situations that caused them to leave their homeland and most of them say that it is their faith in God that has helped them to forgive their tormentors, even as they have received forgiveness for their own wrongdoing. But it should not end there; they need to grow in their Christlikeness and discipleship, so that they not only receive forgiveness but they in turn become agents of reconciliation in their communities.

This brings us to the level of Christlikeness and justice. An ethic of refugees will include this component because those who have experienced injustice need to be redeemed to the point that they themselves become the agents of peace and reconciliation. A refugee who is Christian will know that his or her Christianity will not just be confined to the inward life because they will see how it affects them in their walk. Most of the refugees I interviewed could see how God had intervened in remarkable ways in their lives and they also wanted to see this change come into their communities. The graduates of Kakuma Interdenominational School of Mission (KISOM) know that the gospel of peace is not just for peace between humans and God but between human beings who are in real-life situations of conflict. They have witnessed the cruel effects of human conflicts, and have taught us Kenyans not to take the peace that we have in our country for granted. One lady whom I talked with from Burundi told me sincerely, "When I was at home, the church was not serious to teach us that not loving our neighbors will cause such havoc in our lives. Now I know the importance of loving my neighbor. If we Christians had loved our neighbors, we would not be refugees in a foreign land."

This leads us to the last variable of this dimension, which I consider the most crucial of all, that is, the mission of the church in the world. We started this chapter by attempting to understand what Yoder and Okullu say the mission of the church is. I believe that an ethic that does not include this variable will be skewed. It is one thing to form individuals who are motivated to work for the kingdom, but the church gathered together is the greatest force of social change. No government or society can beat this voluntary, international, interdenominational multiracial group of people who are united together by the blood of Christ. Jesus said, "I will establish my church and the gates of hell will not prevail against it." The church has not fully realized its power for change in the world and that is why its effect in the world has not been felt. It is now being given recognition in the US as a faith-based organization, and as such, a force to be reckoned with and to pay attention to. For the most part, we have not known what our true identity is and how powerful the force of the church is for transforming our world.

When I sat down with pastors representing the eight nations out of which the refugees in the Kakuma camp are drawn, for the first time, I witnessed the power of God to change the world through the church. After I had shared the importance of unity in the body of Christ for the purpose of reaching the communities in the camp and later in their own countries, we joined hands and sang:

> If you believe and I believe and we together pray,
>
> The Holy Spirit will come down and Africa will be changed/saved/healed
>
> And Africa will be changed
>
> And Africa will be changed
>
> The Holy Spirit will come down and Africa will be changed!

The church in Kenya can learn from these refugees, coming from eight different nations, singing together of the Holy Spirit bringing change to Africa, how the church itself can be changed and healed across our ethnic divisions.

I believe that in order to make a difference in our communities, the church needs to recover that identity of being "pilgrims and exiles." We are those called to be a pilgrim people of God *in* the world but not *of* the world. I like the way Stassen and Gushee have described the mission and identity of the church as "a Christ-following countercultural community that obeys God by publicly engaging in working for justice and refusing to trust in the world's powers and authorities."[89] I think we have trusted too much in the powers and authorities of the UN, UNHCR, the government of Kenya, or the governments of the refugee-generating countries to help us obtain durable solutions for the refugee problem. But what we have seen is that instead of the problem getting better it is getting worse. Kakuma camp, that was meant to be a temporary settlement, is now into its tenth year and refugees keep streaming in. This is in no way trying to diminish the work that these bodies have done, but the church to whom God has entrusted the care of the world has not done its part. We are being called upon to rise to the occasion.

What is the church to do then in this context? Stassen and Gushee describe the church's mission in three ways corresponding to Jesus' teaching on the Sermon on the Mount of being salt, light and showing good deeds. They further explain this threefold mission of the church: "as a pioneering

---

89. Stassen and Gushee, *Kingdom Ethics*, 467.

model for human community, a caring community for the human family and a disciple-making community obeying Christ's commands."[90]

First, we have to repent that we have trusted in other lords and authorities and not really strived to seek first the Kingdom of God and his righteousness. As I showed earlier, many times the church in Kenya has sought the blessing of the state and forgot her role to be with those who are suffering. Part of the pioneering mission of the church—following Jesus Christ, the Pioneer of our faith—means joining God where he is, and that is, ahead of the society: "To respond to God is always to pioneer because God's will is always ahead of where society is. God's rule cannot be reduced to the way things are; it includes judgment and change."[91] I think the worst sin that has divided the church worldwide has been the sin of ethnocentrism. We have been loyal to our cultural groupings rather than to the lordship of Jesus Christ. We have also been loyal to our nationalities rather to the body of Christ that transcends national boundaries. The fact that all these nations have come together in Kenya should wake us up to the fact that evil knows no national and human boundaries. At the same time, we are assured that the grace of God demonstrated through our acts of kindness can go even further, reaching beyond any boundary, to bring transformation to our brothers and sisters who have been ravaged by war and economic deprivation. Like the prophets of old we should not just be confined to our national concerns. If evil is happening in Uganda then we should denounce it, and by partnerships with the churches there, seek to support our brothers and sisters so that we can help to build a society. Okullu, a true pilgrim, spoke against the atrocities during the time of Idi Amin and called upon the world not to stand silent while such evil was being committed. He also hosted families in his home who fled from the persecutions of Idi Amin.

Second, we will work for peace in the neighboring countries. Fortunately, the government of Kenya has been working for peace in these neighboring countries by coordinating peace talks. Christians should not just be satisfied to be innocent and inactive bystanders, or to compliment the good that the government is doing. But they can become involved in the efforts of gathering Christian leaders from these countries in order to work for reconciliation. Thankfully such efforts are being seen in the pioneering work of FECCLAHA (Fellowship of Christian Councils and Churches in the Great Lakes Areas and the Horn of Africa) and also other Christian bodies like ALARM (African Leadership and Reconciliation Ministries).[92]

---

90. Ibid., 473–83.
91. Ibid., 474.
92. I will give more information about these two bodies in chapter 7.

These efforts should be lauded, but there should be more Christian participation in them as well. Other efforts should be promoted and supported on the grassroots level, at the camp or within the Kenya community that seeks to understand the cause of the conflicts and attempts to work together.

Christians should also be creative in working toward new ways of helping the refugees not to live an idle existence while in the camp. The efforts of KISOM in preparing church leaders to return to their countries are examples of such creative ways. There is need to give these people other socio-economic skills so that they can earn their livelihood when they return home; this is part of the principle of giving the people a "hoe." There are also other humanitarian efforts that should be done within the countries where the conflicts originated so that when refugees return home, they can find an economically and socially stable place to resettle in.

All these can happen if the church worldwide and more particularly in Kenya discover their pilgrim identity. This will sharpen their focus and fuel commitment to work for peace and durable solutions in the neighboring countries. When this happens, we will witness to one of the greatest global transformations in the twenty-first century.

Conclusion

We started by asking ourselves what is the mission of a church that is conscious of her pilgrim identity in Kenya. We were guided in this discussion by the pilgrim motif in Hebrews as well as the reflections of Okullu, an Anglican churchman, and Yoder, a theological ethicist. We identified four key points regarding the mission of the church that is aware of her pilgrim status in the world. They are as follows: to announce the lordship of Christ to powers and authorities, to be an agent of social change, to be a paradigm of what society should be, and to serve the society through its manifold ministries. Then we looked at how the Kenyan church has fulfilled that function, noting both the strengths and weaknesses. We noted that the major weakness that has prevented the church in Kenya from being a church of the stranger and fulfilling its mission in Kenya has been tribal loyalty rather than loyalty to the lordship of Christ.

With this in mind, we asked ourselves how we the church in Kenya become that community that transcends ethnic barriers and welcomes the stranger. How can we be the church of the stranger instead of being that which looks like us? I used Stassen's and Gushee's four-dimensional Method of Concreteness in Christian ethics as informed by the pilgrim motif in order to develop an ethic for the stranger. We have seen that this method helps us to examine our biases and loyalties in all areas. In the perception dimension, we will pay attention to the stranger in order to curb the tendency to side with the powers and authorities. In the loyalties dimension, we will critique loyalties directed to the ethnic or tribal group rather than to the body of Christ. Furthermore, we will pay attention to the rules and guidelines that talk about the treatment of the stranger in the Old Testament, in the life of Jesus and in the early church, and also those from the international organizations such as the UNHCR. In order to ground these rules in the concrete life of the church, through the recovery of the practice of hospitality as a central characteristic of the pilgrim people of God. In the basic convictions dimension, we will emphasize discipleship grounded in the virtues of courage, caring and concern for the other. We will borrow from the African institution of the rites of passage that was used to form the leaders for the African community. We will use their key principles in order to develop Christian communities that are conscious of their role in the world. We will do this training in discipleship, paying close attention to the mission of the church in the world. In this way we hope we will have developed an ethic that will be caring to the refugee and form a church community that is conscious of its pilgrim existence in the world.

7

Recommendations and Conclusion

> The tragedy of refugees and displaced persons is so immense and so complicated that it needs all of us for its solution.
>
> —Jesuit Refugee Service, *Displaced in Africa*

Introduction

THE REFUGEE PROBLEM IN Africa is enormous, and it continues to grow every day with no signs of decreasing. Millions of lives have been lost through the wars and unrest in the various parts of Africa. Thousands are displaced, and countless others have spent their lives in hopeless situations in refugee camps across Africa with no hope of returning to their homelands in the near future. The world community, especially the church, cannot afford to remain silent or complacent about this. The need to work for durable solutions is more urgent than ever before.

I have sought to provide a Christian response to the refugee problem in Kenya. My attempt was to fill the gap in the literature by presenting a biblical-theological response.[1] I hope these findings will be applicable to situations elsewhere in Africa and the rest of the world. Here is a summary of the study:

Chapter 1 lays out the general scope of the problem, discussing the rationale for a Christian theological response to the refugee problem. Kenya prides itself in being 80 percent Christian, but its response to the refugees has been on the whole negative. My concern is to motivate the church to live up to its true identity of being a pilgrim and an alien, and thereby respond with compassion by being a voice for and to those who are suffering exclusion from

---

1. Veney, "The Politics of Refugee Relief Operations" and Okoro, "Africa's Refugee Problem." They have studied the refugee problem from a political/social perspective but their findings indicate that the response to refugees in Kenya is hostile and sometimes outright cruel. The study by Kibreab, *Reflections on the African Refugee Problem*, has shown that African hospitality is on the decline.

their lands. My hope is that the church will draw its response from the study of the pilgrim motif in Hebrews, leading to the recovery of the practice of hospitality rooted both in the biblical message and in the history of the Christian church, as well the African tradition. Therefore, the aim of this chapter is that the church, acknowledging its pilgrim existence, will make hospitality the principle component of its ethic in caring for the refugees.

In chapter 2, I showed the root cause of the problem of refugees is linked closely with the economic disparity between the northern and southern countries. This gap has been widened by the continuous interference of the northern countries, promoting their own interests in Africa. The intrusion was first felt in the great plunder of African peoples during the era of the slave trade and it continued into the colonial times. Another root cause of the refugee influx directly related to colonialism is the creation of arbitrary boundaries, which has been a source of wars between several countries as they struggle to determine where their borders lie. A good example of this are the Somali people who have been fighting for the establishment of a greater Somalia because they are scattered over four countries, Kenya, Ethiopia, Djibouti and Somalia. The forty-year conflict between Northern and Southern Sudan is rooted in the British colonial policy that failed to prepare the South for independence. The conflicts in Rwanda and Burundi have their source in ethnic and clan conflicts that were present even before outside interference. However, these potential conflicts were aggravated by the Belgian policies of 'divide and rule' and also by the decision to favor one group over the other. The wars in the Horn of Africa after independence were fueled by the Cold War climate between the US and USSR, with these powers supplying weapons to protect their interests in Africa. Poor leadership and violation of human rights in many African countries have aggravated the situation. In fact, all these problems have been worsened by unfavorable environmental conditions in this region. The countries that have suffered from the scourge of war have also gone through severe drought and shortage of rain, resulting in adverse hunger situations.

In chapter 3, I indicated that those who have shouldered the responsibility of the refugee problem have been the host countries, which are in no better shape than the incoming population, thereby putting a strain upon their economies. Though they have done a great job in responding with African hospitality, the situation has worsened by the continuous flow of refugees and the dwindling resources. This has resulted in poor relations between the host community and the refugee population. On the other hand, there are success stories of the cooperative efforts and good working conditions initiated by UNHCR and NGOs, especially church-affiliated ones such as AACC and LWF. What has been found to be the secret of success in these refugee situations is not only the humanitarian aid projects but also those that emphasized zonal development, especially when it includes the host population. Efforts to consolidate this kind of deal were pursued through conferences like ICARA I and II (International Conference on Assistance to Refugees in Africa). Evidence about the follow-up of these programs is not available, so it is difficult to assess their long-term success and effectiveness.

Chapter 4 shows Kenya as a latecomer in hosting a large refugee population. It is only since 1992 that the refugee population increased to over 500,000. These numbers have now reduced due to voluntary repatriation of the Somali. Kenya started with ten camps but now only two remain at Kakuma and Dadaab. The government tried to respond favorably, but with great difficulty, because of the unstable political climate that the country was facing at particular times. UNHCR worked closely with the government in order to try to help the populations in the camps. Other implementing partners of UNHCR include NGOs, especially the Christian ones, such as LWF (Lutheran World Federation), which in collaboration with Jesuit Refugee Services, provides leadership in camp management; NCCK, which supports reproductive health, working under IRC (International Rescue Committee), and World Vision, which is in charge of shelter and the general infrastructure of the camp.

In general, most Kenyan Christians except those who live near and work in the camps, do not have direct exposure to the refugee problem. Though they are sympathetic, they lack first-hand knowledge about the situation. They have read about it in the papers or listened to it on the radio. Some churches in Kenya have hosted refugees in congregations, especially by offering them their premises for school or church service. But even in such cases, there are not many interactions between the host population and the refugees. In general, relations between the host community, the Turkana and the refugees have not been favorable. However, there are noteworthy individual stories of cooperation between the Turkana Christians and the refugees. One such case is the story of Simon Narogoi, a Turkana who pastors a Congolese church in the camp. Pastor Namuya is the pastor of the Full Gospel Church, Kakuma, a church where refugees and the host community worship together. Kakuma Interdenominational School of Mission (KISOM) is another effort of exemplary cooperation between Kenyan Christians and refugees. The aim is to train and equip refugee church leaders so they are prepared to spread the Gospel in their countries when peace returns. Such efforts have encouraged refugees, who give testimony that if it were not for their faith and the encouragement and support of other Christians, the conditions in the camp would be unbearable.

In chapter 5, I demonstrated that the book of Hebrews offers encouragement to Christians who are facing harsh conditions by reminding them that their identity is that of pilgrim or alien. This is an identity that they share with heroes of faith throughout the history of the people of God in ancient Israel, as well as the early church. A study in the book of Hebrews shows that the pilgrim motif presents a paradigm of what the true identity for the Christian entails. It also plays a central role in comforting Christians who are going through hard times and exhorting them to maintain faith, hope, and courage on their pilgrimage to the eternal city.

The pilgrim motif in Hebrews presents a special message for Christians in Africa facing extremely harsh social, economic and political conditions as manifested by the refugee problem. They are reminded to focus on Jesus Christ, who is the author and finisher of their faith. They are encouraged by the reassurance that they have a community of faith that is standing with them, "a cloud of witnesses," cheering them along the way so that they would not give up. They are also urged to maintain courage, perseverance and hope, which are important components of faith in the book of Hebrews, so that when they complete the race they will be welcomed into their eternal home.

In chapter 6, I argued that through the pilgrim motif in Hebrew and works of Bishop Okullu and theological ethicist John Howard Yoder, present what the mission of the church in the world is. We are shown that the church is God's primary instrument in bringing transformation in society. It is called to announce the lordship of Jesus Christ over the powers and authorities, in order to bring change across ethnic and national boundaries, and to serve the community through being and doing God's will and purpose. The church in Kenya has met this criterion to a certain extent by standing against the socio-political powers and helping the nation toward multiparty democracy.[2] However, the church has been plagued by temptations to seek power by aligning with the status quo and tribal-ethnic loyalties, rather than commitment to the lordship of Jesus Christ. They have not responded adequately to the refugee problem, because they have not fully grasped their pilgrim identity so they been preoccupied with national issues, rather than being in solidarity with the strangers within their borders. They have also felt that the problem was too much for them, so they have left it to international bodies like UNHCR. The antidote is for the church in Kenya to be a church of the stranger and this means developing an ethic for refugees using the four-dimensional Method of Concreteness in Christian

---

2. See Githiga, *Church as the Bulwark against Authoritarianism*. He has given a good analysis of the participation of the church in Kenya in social justice issues.

ethics.³ This also means that Christians must pay attention to the social context, their loyalties, the way they reason and their basic convictions from a perspective of the stranger. The result is an ethic that cares for the stranger rooted in the character of God, who has told us to care for the stranger. This will heal the apathy and hostility that have engulfed the church and the nation in the midst of this crisis, and will supply the resources of hospitality and compassion to the needy in Kenya. Indeed, they will learn that with the strangers in the midst they will not only give to them but they will receive what it means to be a pilgrim community.

Recommendations to the Churches in Kenya/Africa

In many African countries the church has unrivaled political power which it can use to good effect to bring about desirable economic, political and social change.⁴ The church is the only institution that reaches where people are. It is the only grassroots institution in rural Africa. Mugambi says:

> In Africa the Church remains the most influential and most sustainable social institution especially in the rural areas. Political parties, trade unions and cooperatives are transient, because the leadership changes from time to time and accountability is difficult to achieve. Owing to this transient nature of such agencies of social mobilization, leaders have tended to use these organizations more for their own interests than for the interests of the members. Churches in contrast have permanence that transcends particular national boundaries and generations of leaders. Deriving their mandate from the Bible, their accountability can be assessed on the basis of Biblical insights.⁵

Due to its strategic position, the church informed by her pilgrim's stance is able to play a key role in responding to the refugee issues in Africa. But it cannot do this if it sits on the sidelines or is not properly informed. One of my findings showed that the pastors and congregations that were far removed from contact with refugees, as well as those who had refugee congregations, did not feel adequate to address these issues. Through conferences that raise awareness to key issues as well as promoting direct contact with refugees, churches will be guided on what it means

---

3. See Stassen and Gushee, *Kingdom Ethics*, 55–124.

4. Kinoti, *Hope for Africa*, 11. See also Okullu, *Quest for Justice*, 126.

5. Mugambi, *From Reconstruction to Liberation*, 225. See also Mugambi, "The Christian Ideal of Peace," 70–96.

to be the church of the stranger. One such conference was organized for church leaders by AACC in 1990.[6] One of the activities of this conference was to arrange for the delegates to visit a refugee camp. This experience was life-changing for most of them, who were confronted for the first time with the enormity of the problem. This conference also understood the response of the church in three categories: addressing root causes, responding to needs, and raising awareness.[7] I will use these three elements in presenting my recommendations to the church.

Addressing Root Causes

The conference noted that it is not enough to assist refugees; churches must work toward removing the root causes of the refugee problem and raising awareness about the refugee situation in Africa.[8] The violation of human rights is one central cause of the refugee problem that churches must address. They need to be courageous to challenge their governments to uphold human rights. Many countries have signed international covenants and are members of the United Nations. The OAU has set up a commission on the African Charter on Human and People's Rights which entered into force in 1986. As many as forty members have signed it. African nations need to be reminded that they have to be responsible for what they have signed. Since the work of advocacy is very sensitive and we know many church leaders have suffered reprisals, such efforts need to be fortified through cooperative efforts with other ecumenical bodies and NGOs. The case of Kenya Christians during the fight for multiparty democracy is a good example. If the Christians had not presented a united front, combined with unfailing support from ecumenical bodies such as NCCK (National Christian Council of Kenya), and AACC, including the moral and financial input from Christians outside Kenya, the cause would have failed. The overthrow of the apartheid system in South Africa is another example. The church was the only voice that could not be silenced, through such outspoken leaders as Bishop Tutu, who did not give up through the hard and silent years. They were eventually rewarded. Christians in Kenya should urge the government to recognize all refugees under the newly-enacted Refugee Bill. They should work in solidarity with other groups like the Refugee Consortium

---

6. Deliberations from that conference are recorded in ACCC, "The Refugee Problem." This conference took place too long ago. We need one now. I am not aware if one has been organized in the recent past.

7. ACCC, "The Refugee Problem," 15–33.

8. Ibid., 5.

of Kenya and the Law Society of Kenya to see that legal aspects of the refugee problem are addressed.

Churches and other religious organizations should work for transformation of society by using the school system to teach about human rights and good values for community living. The school syllabus of Christian Religious Education, Islamic Religious Education, Hindu Religious Education, and Social Ethics is a natural vehicle within the Kenyan educational system. Church members should also be educated in matters concerning refugees. This can be done through cell groups, Bible study sessions, Sunday school, youth rallies, and organized seminars. The Catholic Church is doing a commendable job through the Small Christian Communities. They have produced material to expose Christians to various social and political issues, including the refugee problem.[9] This need not be theoretical because the refugee community is within reach to demonstrate the reality.

The church in Kenya has been plagued by tribal and ethnic conflicts they can learn much from the refugee community on how to transcend these narrow confines in order to work together as a united body of Christ. I showed in my findings how pastors in the refugee community are reaching out across tribal lines and showing that the body is larger than the small ethnic community. Those who are pilgrims band together in order to support one another along the journey. Thus, the literal church of the stranger can teach the rest of the church in Kenya what it means to live true pilgrim existence. This will help to heal all the tribal tension and work to forge unity in the body of Christ that will be a powerful witness to the world.

Churches can seek durable solutions by working toward peace in the countries where the refugees originate. They need to inform their congregations that there are alternative ways of resolving conflict rather than war, and to promote peaceful coexistence between potential enemies. I need to commend the efforts of one Catholic priest who has worked toward peaceful existence in a volatile situation. His name is Father Bernhard Ruhnau, 68, and he has been a Catholic priest for over thirty years in Turkana District.[10] His nickname is *Apa Merireng* (white skin). He has mastered the language of the Turkana, Toposa and Karamojong of Kenya, Uganda and Sudan. He works tirelessly to resolve conflicts among these warring nomadic tribes. He was a refugee in East Germany after the Second World

---

9. The study guide for the refugee problem, *Displaced in Africa*, is produced by the Jesuit Refugee Service. It is arranged in such a way that Christians, at the end of each session, are motivated toward practical action and not just theoretical reflection. JRS, *Displaced in Africa*.

10. His story appeared in the *East African Standard*, December 18, 2002, "Nomadic Priest on a Peace Mission."

War and this has inspired him to appreciate peace and to care for those who are the victims of war. His is a good example of how pilgrim existence informs action. He says, "I visit pastoralists in their *adakar* (Turkana settlements) to preach love and peace between them and their neighbors. The only way to deal with nomads and gain their appreciation is to be with them at the same level."[11] He has helped the settlements to be stocked with cattle so that they do not go raiding. He has motivated the young men to form the Young Herdsmen Association whose aim is to unite pastoralists from Kenya and Uganda so that they can work together for peace. He also combines his efforts with NGOs like World Vision and Oxfam to help in the developmental needs of the community.

Because church leaders in Kenya are usually respected, they can facilitate peace talks with warring parties in protracted war cases, like the one between North and South Sudan. There it might work for church leaders to cooperate with their Muslim counterparts to arrive at a peaceful solution for a war that has lasted over forty years. Church leaders are involved in the recent peace talks convened by the Kenyan government, but it might also help to involve the Muslim religious leaders because one of the tenets of Islam is that it is a religion of peace. Muslim scholars are working with the faculty of Fuller Theological Seminary to develop a Muslim just peacemaking theory, in order to articulate the practical steps of peacemaking that are fitting for Muslims, analogous with *Just Peacemaking: Ten Practices for Abolishing War*.

Responding to Needs

The church informed by the pilgrim motif should not only identify the needs of the refugees both short-term and long-term, they will also look for how the refugee community can be a resource to the rest of society. When this is done, they can isolate those areas where they can make a significant contribution on their own, and those where they can work in cooperation with other bodies. Usually the large organizations like UNHCR and WFP are more structured to meet logistical needs like shelter and initial food ratios, but they are not attuned to personal and social needs, such as the need to make the refugees feel a sense of welcome and receive humane treatment.

Congregations that are close to the refugee camps should be encouraged to participate in welcoming refugees, especially at the reception centers. I visited one of these centers and it was a pitiful sight. Most of the refugees have walked long distances to get there, and they are tired, hungry, and thirsty, but nobody is there to attend to them. Some stay there for

11. Ibid.

several weeks until they are proved to be genuine refugees. When people are at the most vulnerable stage of their lives, they remember every kind or cruel deed done to them. I hope what they do remember will be the good deeds of the Christians. Churches at this point can also provide support services for those who are extremely vulnerable—like children, women, the old, the sick and the disabled.

I am aware that Kenyan Christians might not have the skills, abilities, trained personnel, and material resources to respond adequately to the refugee problem. In the presence of large organizations like UNHCR and the multitude of needs, one can feel powerless and helpless. It is therefore important to teach and train Christians in the face of these new circumstances that hospitality, which is rooted both in our Christian and traditional African societies, is a dynamic tool of social encounter and healing.[12] We should dispel wrong notions that hospitality has to involve the serving of elaborate meals and modern entertainment settings. Or the fact that it is one directional from the stronger to weaker. Hospitality is a reciprocal practice that transforms both the host and the guest, an ethic central to the book of Hebrews, against the Greco-Roman context of benefaction and patronage.[13] Preparing simple meals and inviting people to share them in the home and in church can transform enemies into friends. In my community, sharing a meal always seals social transactions, such as peace agreements and marriage negotiations. Those who have disagreed would show their sign of reconciliation by drinking milk from the same gourd.

The importance of meals in the practice of hospitality is one that should be explored, because it is affirmed and enriched by various traditions. The pilgrim motif in Hebrews is tied closely to the practice of hospitality and care for others in the community. Yoder also emphasized the Lord's table or Eucharist, as a practice that will distinctly show the church as a community that cares for both the physical and spiritual needs of people.[14] Phol also states, "The table is central to the practice of hospitality in the home and in the church—the nourishment we gain there is physical, spiritual and social. Whether we gather around the table of the Lord's Supper or for a church potluck dinner, we are strengthened as a community."[15] We should also learn from the African-American church tradition that has

---

12. I am not aware of books or resources in Africa that provide hands-on guidance on hospitality in recent times. Maybe that is a clarion call for me to write one.

13. Whitlark, *Enabling Fidelity to God*, 1–14. See also his discussion on symmetrical and asymmetrical reciprocity (38–48).

14. Yoder, *Body Politics*, 14–27.

15. Pohl, *Making Room*, 158.

preserved this practice from their African origins. Jualynne Dodson and Cheryl Townsend Gilkes say:

> African American church members in the United States feed one another's bodies as they feed their spirits or, more biblically, one another's "temples of the spirit." In the process an ethic of love and emphasis on hospitality emerge, especially in the sharing of food, which spill over into the large culture.[16]

They further explain: "This love and this hospitality remind the congregation that they are pilgrims and strangers, and that as they feed somebody one day, they may stand in need on (sic) another."[17] Thus, there is the need for the church in Kenya to strengthen the teaching and practice of hospitality.

Churches should also provide pastoral care and counseling. The kind of terror, hardship and trauma the refugees go through makes the need for pastoral attention and caring very crucial and essential. This can be enhanced if pastors facilitate links and contact between refugees and their home churches, so those refugees can feel connected with the people that they left at home. One true observation is that "refugees endure a double exile—exile from their native country and also from their local church and parish."[18] It is also a pity that only during times of exile the church teachings of loving one's neighbor begin to make sense.[19] So it seems the teachings about peace should begin with the church members who have many times allowed tribal loyalties to override their faith in Jesus Christ.

One of the long-term needs for the refugees is education and training, especially peace education. These people who have suffered the trauma of being uprooted from their communities will later be fervent ambassadors of peace and reconciliation in their communities. In this context the cooperative effort of Kakuma Interdenominational School of Mission (KISOM) is a wonderful opportunity to provide refugees with skills and abilities, not only in preaching and sharing the Gospel but also in mediation, conflict transformation and peaceful coexistence. This school was started through the initiative of a refugee, Tito Mayaribu from Burundi, who had the foresight that by bringing eight nations together in one place, God was providing a wonderful opportunity to spread his good news to these nations. Kenyan Christians have joined him to assist in the preparation of God's people for the work of ministry. Above all, this ministry is

---

16. Dodson and Gilkes, "There is Nothing Like Church Food," 520–21.
17. Ibid., 535.
18. Anderson, "Refugees in East Africa in America," 16–21.
19. One lady from Burundi told me that now that she was in a refugee camp, she understood the need to value all people equally.

a beacon of hope for the refugees and proof to Kenyan Christians that God can transform dry (Kakuma is literally a desert) and hopeless circumstances into a place where life-giving water is flowing. A fulfillment of the words of Isaiah the prophet, "I am doing a new thing, now it springs forth, do you not perceive it? I will make a way in the wilderness . . . For I will give water in the wilderness, rivers in the desert, to my chosen people, the people whom I formed for myself" (Isa 43:19).

Raising Awareness

One other important aspect of responding to the refugees is to raise awareness regarding their situation. The spirit of urgency needs to be fostered in Kenya where refugees are tucked away in the remotest part of the country, far removed from public view. During my research, most of the people I talked to had not had any close contact with the refugees. It seemed so remote and such a huge issue that they felt they could not do anything about it. Churches can rectify this through using the annual Refugee Sunday (a Sunday close to June 20th, which is Africa Refugee Day) as a day when special prayers, gifts and messages can be sent to the refugees. They can also use this day to disseminate materials such as videos, photographs and published literature on refugee life. I indicated before that the pastors I interviewed had not preached a sermon on God's concern for the refugees. They should use that Sunday to preach about them or better still to invite some of the refugee pastors and their church members to share their stories with the Kenyan congregations. The Kenyan churches will not remain the same after such an encounter. Large churches such as Nairobi Pentecostal or Nairobi Chapel, which have access to radio and TV broadcasts, can take advantage of such avenues to bring to light those things that affect the wellbeing of the refugee.

Congregations can also arrange time to visit the refugee camps. Such visits can be made through the local administrative officer and the community services coordinator of UNHCR.[20] People need not be bothered about what to carry as gifts to the camp. Many times the refugees are just touched by the concern of people who want to visit, and they usually surprised just by their hospitality.[21] In all our efforts to help refugees we should realize that

20. For visitors from outside, arrangements are made through UNHCR and the Ministry of Home Affairs, Refugee Service Department.

21. During my visit to Kakuma in January 2003, I was impressed by the hospitality of the refugee community. The Burundi community treated me to a Burundi delicacy for my lunch. The Ethiopian community invited me to an Ethiopian coffee-making ceremony to celebrate a newly-wed couple. After enjoying the Congolese music, I shared drinks with them.

they are human beings who need to feel that they are making a contribution to the larger society. We should desist from making them feel like objects of charity, with only needs to be met. Rather, we should treat them as dignified human beings created in the image of God who have valuable talents, skills and experiences to share. Thus, the goal should be to provide them with opportunities to utilize their full potential, even in the restrictive circumstances in which they live. The refugee community has creative skills borne out of adversity. One lady from Burundi told me she had learned to grow vegetables in cans because of the scarcity of water.

Pastors in Kenya have a unique role in helping their congregations realize their calling as the pilgrim people of God, especially with people who are leading that kind of existence right in their midst. They can connect their congregations with the refugee Christians so that they can keep in touch constantly resources of being a pilgrim people. This would give the Kenyans a great opportunity of encouraging the refugees to grow in their walk of following Jesus in the hard road of the refugee camp. The book of Hebrews, which is a letter of encouragement for those going through hard times is also a rich source to draw the themes of hope and endurance in the midst of suffering. Ever since I met the refugee Christians at Kakuma I have kept in touch with them. They have been a channel for great joy and inspiration to me.[22] The refugees have impressed me with the ability to hope even in adverse circumstances.

However, they still do get discouraged when nothing seems to happen to change in their circumstances. They need to hear that other people are caring and praying for them. They desire to know that their sufferings are not in vain even as they are conformed to the image of Christ. But they also need tangible brothers and sisters who can walk this pilgrim way with them. I hope the Kenyan Christians will take this call seriously and walk alongside them because they will understand their calling better if they do so. I suggest that this can be done if Kenyan churches adopt a church in the refugee camp and develop strong ties through mutual visits, sponsoring some pastors for training as well all other forms of social interaction.

To Christian NGOs

Christian NGOs informed by a pilgrim identity should work at building partnerships, and coordinate their activities so that there is no duplication and competition for limited resources. They should also learn to listen to the perspective of those who are below by seeking to empower them in matters

22. See Appendix C for my letter to refugees.

that affect them. In my opinion those NGOs working in Kakuma are already making progress along these lines. They focus on capacity building, providing skills to the refugees as well as operating on their areas of strength; World Vision is focused on infrastructure and shelter, LWF on camp management, JRS on education, Don Bosco on vocational training and NCCK on reproductive health. Their constant complaint is scarcity of resources in the midst of plenty of needs. I was impressed with the dedication and commitment of many of the workers who see their service, not just as a job but as a calling from God.[23] Many of them go beyond their call of duty to minister to the needs of the refugees.

However, I feel they need to expand their capacity by seeking cooperation with the local churches. It seemed to me that most of the individuals as well as the organizations did not have strong links with the local churches and these churches have great potential for being connected to the work directly. The local churches were not informed about what the NGOs were doing and did not report to them. I asked one pastor if they knew what NCCK was doing in the refugee camps and he did not know. The coordinator of the NCCK reproductive program at the refugee camp also admitted that their work in the camps was better known outside Kenya than locally. The reason for this may stem from the fact that most of these organizations are funded from outside. It is not a wonder that many Christians in Kenya are not involved. They may feel that they are bypassed and not given a chance to be part of the solution. Therefore, there is need to encourage grassroots initiatives of church groups and individuals who would offer voluntarily to work among the refugees and to promote peace and reconciliation in the area.

NGOs also need to integrate human rights into their work with governments. This is a risky business. I have known of some NGOs who were expelled from Kenya because of what was termed involvement in politics. However, this can be avoided if NGOs work together as a united front and then speak with one voice about matters that are sensitive. This will protect them against the victimization and isolation of one group by the government. The pilgrim motif demonstrates that in banding together as a community of pilgrims there is strength in unity.

I also would like to present a challenge to organizations that have only focused on the spiritual nurture of people to the neglect of the physical, to be a part of the work among the refugees. It may not mean that they become part of the refugee workers cadre directly, but they could use their voice and

23. In my interviews with many workers, one of my main questions was what motivated them to continue in such a difficult task. Many responded that it was their faith in God and the fact that they are making a difference in the Kingdom of God by helping the refugees.

influence in their constituencies to promote concern for refugees and the need to work for peace. One such organization that has not been involved in the work directly is the Association for Evangelicals of Africa (AEA). It was founded in 1966 to give leadership to the evangelical churches in Africa. Its motto is "To mobilize and empower evangelical churches and mission agencies for the total evangelization and effective transformation of Africa."[24] It has a membership of seventy million evangelicals and forty national fellowships all over the continent.[25] This body can have significant influence to promote peace and reconciliation in Africa through its many projects and commissions. Such projects include two theological institutions in Africa, Nairobi Evangelical Graduate School of Theology (NEGST) and Bangui Evangelical School of Theology (BEST). NEGST is now working in close partnership with KISOM to provide trained personnel for refugee pastors.[26] Through the Christian Learning Material Center (CLMC) and Theological Education by Extension, teaching resources and material can be made available for the transformation of the African continent.

An indirect result of AEA work is the recent formation of ALARM (African Leadership and Reconciliation Ministries). Rev. Celestin Musekura, an ordained Baptist minister who was born and raised in Rwanda, himself a refugee, founded the organization to respond to the ethnic conflicts and genocide that happened in Rwanda in 1994. He graduated from NEGST with an MDiv. Realizing that the church is caught up in this vicious cycle of war, poverty and more violence, this organization is committed to training and equipping church leaders with skills in mediation, conflict resolution, and trauma counseling for reconciliation ministries all over Africa. Its leaders believe strongly that "the future of Africa relies not on economic growth, good politics, or even the respect of human rights or the healing of ethnic hostilities, but on the deepening of the church and her leaders."[27] They provide these skills and tools close to home where pastors can put them to immediate use. ALARM is also committed to empowering pastors' wives and women leaders to play key roles in teaching, discipleship and counseling in their communities. It also produces teaching and preaching outlines on issues such as reconciliation, forgiveness, love and trust. This group is doing tremendous work, especially touching lives in the rural areas

24. Association for Evangelicals in Africa, *AEA: A Symbol of Evangelical Unity in Africa*, 3.

25. Ibid., 1.

26. I hope to teach Christian Ethics at NEGST when I complete my work. It will be a great opportunity to train Christian leaders from all over Africa, who I hope will influence their nations toward peace.

27. African Leadership and Reconciliation Ministries (ALARM), Inc., *Pamphlet*, 1.

where the need is acute. Most of Africa's refugees come from rural settings. In year 2001, ALARM and church partners conducted twenty-seven training conferences in eight central and eastern African countries, educating 3,538 men, women and youth leaders.[28] If one organization can do this in one year, what can happen if more people are involved?

The Kenya Government

The Kenya government has done much to assist the refugees, even in the midst of struggling to meet the concerns of her own people. But there are still many areas where they have been criticized for not doing their part. One aspect is in the area of security and the protection of the lives of the refugees. It is obvious to anybody that the places where the refugees are located are volatile security zones. Because they are close to the borders that are really porous, the government is unable to control the flow of arms into the country. One recent effort to rectify this was the research done on the possession of weapons in the West Pokot, which found out that there are 127,000 unlicensed guns in this region.[29] The response to the offer of amnesty to those who surrendered their guns was good. Seven thousand guns were brought forward and they were destroyed publicly to show the government's commitment to security.[30] The new government has also threatened harsh measures upon members of the police and security personnel who in the past have extorted bribes from refugees.[31] The effort by the government to facilitate peace talks between the warring parties in Somalia and Sudan is also commendable. Though the road is long and hard, some progress is being made.

However, I feel that the government still needs to do more by working closely with UNHCR to provide services to the refugee community. One needed service is to make sure that the refugees can be granted refugee status. The government needs the assurance from the international community that they will not single-handedly shoulder the burden of meeting the needs of refugees when this happens. Kenya government in the spirit of true African hospitality should also look for creative ways to integrate and gainfully engage the refugees who have lived long in the country by providing them with ways and means to earn a living without interfering

28. Christina Spear Richardson, letter to author, October 1, 2002.
29. *Daily Nation*, May 6, 2003.
30. *Daily Nation*, May 20, 2003.
31. A refugee thanked the new government for this change. *Daily Nation* "Letters to the Editor," May 6, 2003.

with touchy issues of land. This can be done in the spirit of the African proverb of "providing a hoe" to a guest who has stayed for more than three days. Some refugees have stayed in the camps for over ten years and they are not gainfully employed. There is need for Kenya to address this seriously, in collaboration with UNHCR and the neighboring countries. Progress in the right direction might be witnessed if Kenya continues to improve on her human rights record, through constant review and the teaching of human rights in our school curricula. Instilling values in our youth should be the focus, such as dialogue and cooperation across racial, ethnic, religious, and ideological boundaries.

To UNHCR

It is important for the UNHCR, not only to respond to situations when the damage has been done, but also to work at preventive measures by dealing with the root causes. This will mean working closely with other international development agencies to alleviate poverty conditions that cause wars in many African countries. They should learn now that it is over fifty years since it was established durable solutions should go beyond what they offer. In the spirit of African hospitality of providing "a hoe" they should promote means for sustainable livelihoods for the refugees.

In his speech at this year's Africa Refugee Day, the High Commissioner stressed the need to keep the refugee problem in Africa on the world map.[32] After the end of the Cold War, Africa's needs have lost strategic priority, because attention has been turned elsewhere. Lubbers called for commitment to 4Rs, namely: Repatriation, Reintegration, Rehabilitation, and Reconstruction.[33] He also urged multilateral partnerships to integrate relief and development. He stressed the need for burden sharing to alleviate the strain on the host governments and called for New Partnerships for Africa's Development (NEPAD) to help utilize the productive capacity of the refugees so that they can be self-reliant and help to develop their host communities as well.[34]

Sadako Ogata, a former UNHCR high commissioner, said in the same vein, "If human security is our goal, then we must analyze refugee questions in a broader context—by linking the humanitarian dimension of forced human displacement with development, security, human rights and

---

32. UNHCR, "Lubbers, Ogata call for a new approach to the refugee situation in Africa."

33. Ibid.

34. Ibid.

governance-related issues."³⁵ She also emphasized that strategies for refugees must be multidimensional and integrated, involving protection during armed conflict and empowerment through education (especially for girls), skills, training and community development. She noted that if peace returned to the country of origin, attention should be given on how displaced people can participate in rebuilding their country.

When wars have occurred, UNHCR should promote and use multinational forces to keep peace in the areas that are volatile. They should also focus on peacekeeping regional efforts by cooperating with organizations such as the African Union (formerly OAU).

Christians Worldwide

The church as the worldwide body of Christ is the strongest force for social change, if we can only discover her identity as the pilgrim people of God. Christians in the West in true solidarity with their fellow pilgrims in the rest of the world have a great responsibility to educate their constituencies on the refugee problems of the world and to suggest ways and means for responding as churches and governments.³⁶ One important area where they can make a difference is to influence their governments to formulate policies that are favorable both to refugees and immigrants in their country, as well as to keep Africa as a key foreign policy issue. They should tell their governments to stop supporting the groups that cause terrorism and help those that promote human rights and multiparty democracy. They should work for peace by promoting the principles of just peacemaking theory.³⁷ This is a valuable asset that should help the US and other governments to use peaceful means rather than war or the supply of firearms, in order to promote world peace. There is also need for repentance and humility on the part of Western Christians whose governments have been the cause of war and instability in most countries. I believe the vibrancy of the Christian faith all over the world will be maintained if congregations and individuals will connect with and support refugees and immigrants in a tangible way.

---

35. Ibid.

36. See Pohl and Donley, *Responding to Refugees*, 23–62.

37. Many scholars who wanted to give an alternative to the just-war theory have developed just-peacemaking theory. The ten practices of preventing war are discussed in detail in Stassen, *Just Peacemaking: Ten Practices for Abolishing War*. See also just-peacemaking theory based on the teachings of Jesus in the Sermon on the Mount, *Just Peacemaking: Transforming Initiatives for Justice and Peace*.

They are the ones who can teach us what it means to walk the pilgrim path, showing that we need each other in the journey.

Conclusion

This study has been an attempt to show that Christians in Kenya, and all over the world, can learn much about what it means to live as a pilgrim and alien through the lives of the refugees and the internally displaced peoples in our world. It does not mean we glorify the conditions under which the refugees live; on the contrary it calls us to work for durable solutions, especially peace in our world, so that no one has to live under that threat of loss of life, family and homeland. Though we are realistic about the world we live in, where we are continually confronted with hatred, conflict and evil, but we are reminded by the life of the refugees that we are not to be overcome by evil but to overcome evil with good. This will result in an ethic of compassion, caring and hospitality. When we are tempted to give up because the task is too great, we are reminded that we serve a great God and nothing is too hard for God. We also know that when we do seemingly small, insignificant deeds by serving "the least of these," it matters in the eternal scheme of things, when He will say, "Well done, good and faithful servant." This story from *The Secret Place: Devotions for Daily Worship*, is a fitting encouragement to continue in the good work.

> An illustration I've heard tells of a man walking along a beach where thousands of starfish had washed up on the shore. One by one, the man picks up the starfish and tosses them into the life-giving water. A passerby watches for a moment and asks, "Why are you doing that? What does it matter? You'll never be able to help them all!" Without pausing, the man picks up another starfish and replies, "It matters to this one."
>
> As I become aware of all the needy people that surround me, I am tempted to be discouraged by the relatively few people I'm able to help in my small counseling ministry. But when Satan whispers, "What does it matter? You'll never be able to help them all," Jesus comes and helps me focus on the individuals with whom I'm involved at that time. Lovingly he speaks the words that give me the incentive I need to press on: "It matters to this one."[38]

---

38. Hayes, *The Secret Place*, 58.

Appendix A
Definition of Key Terms

Refugees: The definition of this term has been the subject of much discussion. One begins with the 1951 U.N. Convention Relating to the Status of Refugees and its 1967 Protocol, which extended the Convention's provisions to current refugees. This definition was designed to meet the needs of individuals fleeing persecution in the post-war era. The Convention defines the refugee as follows:

> Any person who, owing to a well-founded fear of being persecuted for reasons of race, religion, nationality, membership of a particular social group or political opinion, is outside the country of his nationality and is unable or, owing to such fear, unwilling to avail himself of the protection of that country, or who, not having a nationality is outside the country of his former habitual residence, is unable or, owing to such fear, is unwilling to return to it.[1]

Elizabeth Ferris notes three important exclusions[2] in this definition. First, it excludes those individuals who have been displaced by violence or warfare and who have not been singled out for individual persecution. It also excludes those whose have been displaced because of violence and have not left the country of origin. Third, it excludes those whose livelihoods are threatened by economic conditions in their countries, forcing them to search for a better existence. It also leaves out those for whom environmental situations have caused them to move to other places. For those in third-world countries, political, economic and environmental conditions intertwine, causing refugee flows both within and outside the country. And there is internal displacement for those who do not cross international borders.[3]

Recognizing the limitation of this definition, in 1969 the Organization of African Unity (O.A.U.) developed the Convention Governing the

---

1. UNHCR, *Convention and Protocol Relating to the Status of Refugees*, 14.
2. Ferris, *Beyond Borders*, 12. These would still fall under the category of refugees.
3. Though I recognize those internally displaced as refugees, my focus in on refugees from outside.

Specific Aspects of Refugee Problems in Africa. The O.A.U. definition therefore includes:

> Every person who, owing to external aggression, occupation, foreign domination, or events seriously disturbing public order in either part or the whole of his country of his nationality, is compelled to leave his place or habitual residence in order to seek refuge in another place outside his country of origin or nationality.[4]

This convention reflects the reality of the African situation but it still excludes internally displaced people or those who are uprooted by economic disasters. To find a definition that will include everyone is difficult, and of course, there is a danger that if the definition is too broad it will not serve the neediest people. According to Elizabeth Ferris, Christian organizations such as World Council of Churches (W.C.C.) and other NGOs have always had the liberty to extend the definition, and, as she says, they have "shown greater flexibility in working with uprooted people, including internally displaced people, than either governments or intergovernmental organizations."[5]

I use both the U.N. and O.A.U. definitions because refugees are a clearly defined group within our borders. From the situations in African countries, it is obvious that Africans have suffered all sorts of deprivations arising from diverse situations—political, environmental, and economic. However, because tribal affiliations in Africa have been used to separate people, whether they belong to the same nation or not, we need to use the word "refugee" also to refer to those who suffer internal displacement. This includes those who suffered as a result of tribal clashes in 1992 as well as in 2007/2008 in Kenya.[6] It should be noted that when we focus on the needs of refugees, it does not mean we do not have our own needy people to attend to. I know Kenyans struggle with the issue of how we can respond to refugees, some of whom appear well-to-do, when we have our own pressing needs. But the presence of refugees in our country is a unique opportunity that should sensitize us to their unique dilemma and should also make us concerned about those who are needy among our own people.

Pilgrim: In its most classic and generic usage, the word "pilgrim" has a twofold dimension. It means one who makes a journey to a sacred place. But it

---

4. *OAU Convention Governing the Specific Aspects of Refugee Problems in Africa.*
5. Ferris, *Beyond Borders*, 20.
6. I have not given a detailed analysis of the ethnic clashes in Kenya except insofar as they affected the response to the refugees who came from outside Kenya. However, I believe the guidelines for a Christian response to strangers, whether internal or external, remains the same.

also gives the sense that all of life is a pilgrimage. More specifically, the word "pilgrim" is rooted in a very rich religious tradition. Upon hearing the word, one immediately gets the visual image of a band of people on a journey, with their hearts set on a goal or destination, which is usually an earthly sacred place. Such a journey is purposeful because it is usually planned and deliberately arranged for, and in most cases, it is undertaken along with a group of people who share the same purpose.

The concept of Christian pilgrimage has biblical roots in both the Old and New Testaments. Thus, I use this word in two ways: first, to refer to the Christian life as a whole. The physical journey of the Israelites from Egypt to the Promised Land is equated to the Christian walk of faith from the kingdom of darkness to the kingdom of light, or the journey from earth to our heavenly destination.

Second, more particularly, I use the word "pilgrim" to refer to the refugees as those who have set their hearts on a pilgrimage. If they have espoused the Christian life, then they are not just refugees living a haphazard existence, but they are pilgrims journeying towards a specific destination. Most of them did not deliberately set out on the physical journey, but if they view their existence in this manner—not just as helpless victims who were pushed out of their land, but as purposeful pilgrims on a journey of faith, both literally and figuratively— then this brings an added dimension of purpose and meaning to their existence. It can transform the hopeless, dreary existence at the refugee camp to a life of hopeful expectation—not just for the durable solutions of the UNHCR, but for the ultimate manifestation of the kingdom of God. Thus, the word "pilgrim" denotes more than the physical experience of merely existing in a foreign land; it includes a sense of purpose and psycho-spiritual awareness that radically alters the quality of that existence. This understanding, therefore, is that although life on earth is temporary and fleeting, it also has a dimension of purpose that should inform everything the pilgrims do.

That said, I hope this Christian goal is not seen just as a pie-in-the-sky idea. It is a life of determination and expectation that, by clinging to faith, refuses to give in to the despair of what is around it. This is a life caught in the reality of experiencing the worst thing that could happen to anyone, and the hopeful expectation that there is a better world awaiting them that they can call home. They know they have lost what they call home here on earth, temporarily or permanently, and yet they anticipate a place they will call home, both physically and spiritually. And because they are caught in that ongoing tension of the "now and the not yet," they are the ones who can best exemplify to Christians everywhere the essence and meaning of eschatological expectation. That is why I hope the Christians in Kenya can learn from the refugees what it means to live as aliens, exiles, and pilgrims who are looking for a city whose architect and founder is God. The refugees are a part of the "cloud of witnesses" that the epistle to the Hebrews talks about, who urge the rest of the world to run the race with perseverance.

Hospitality: Hospitality in both the biblical and the African tradition is not just about entertaining family and friends; it reaches to the arena of one who is the "other," the stranger, the outsider, the foreigner. In most African languages, the same word is used for both stranger and guest. To show how hospitality was built into the structure of life of the Kipsigis people, Chepkwony tells us that whenever a meal was prepared, it was normal to leave one portion, known as "*kimyet ab lakwa*," set aside, so that if a stranger would show up after an evening meal there would be something to offer. It is also a normal practice in most African homes to prepare more food than for those who regularly eat because there is the expectation that a stranger will arrive.

Christians have a rich biblical heritage of hospitality. For ancient Israel, it was one of the central pillars of their identity as the people of God. Abraham, who is considered the father of the nation and of the faithful, is lifted up as the prime practitioner of hospitality. In the book of Hebrews, Christians are urged to emulate not only Abraham's example of faith (Heb. 11:11–17) but also his practice of hospitality (Heb 13:2).

Therefore, as Pohl shows us, although throughout the history of the church the practice has lost this radical meaning of reaching out to those on the margins of society, we can still recover the essence of this virtue to be practiced within the Christian church. I contend that those who need this hospitality the most are "those who are disconnected from basic relationships that give a secure place in the world."[7] I agree with Pohl that "this condition is most clearly seen in the state of the homeless people and the refugees."[8] Thus, this work focuses on how we can be hospitable to one specific category of people, the refugees.

Hospitality as a practice is potentially subversive, upsetting the status quo, and it is full of risks. It is about giving those who have been displaced a legitimate place to belong and to be. It is not about making a people constantly dependent on handouts, as some have done, thus making people more vulnerable than when they started. Rightfully applied, this practice can be a tool for empowerment, restoration, and transformation for those who have been excluded. In recovering this concept, especially in the public arena of the nation and the church, we also are recovering our rich biblical heritage

---

7. Pohl, *Making Room*, 13.
8. Ibid.

and church history and a traditional African practice. One Kiswahili proverb addresses the protracted refugee situations that seem to be prevalent all over Africa by saying, *Mgeni siku ya kwanza, siku ya pili mpatie jembe.* It literally means "one is a guest only for two days; on the third day give him/her a hoe to dig." Such is the wisdom that we need in our complex world, where insecurities thrive and people are not sure who is a genuine stranger.

Appendix B

Interview Questions

Questions for Kenyan Christians

1. Name
2. Age
3. Place of origin
4. Denominational background
5. What do you know about the refugee problem?
6. What is your source of knowledge: a) radio; b) television; c) personal contact; d) friends; e) newspapers; f) sermons?
7. What biblical knowledge do you have about refugees?
8. Do you see any benefits in having refugees in our country?
9. Do you see any negative effects?
10. What do you think the government should do about these people?
11. What do you think the church should do?

Questions for refugees

1. Name
2. Country of origin
3. Denominational background
4. Marital status
5. How many children (if married)?
6. Previous profession
7. Academic qualifications
8. When did you come to the present camp?
9. How did you become a refugee? Did war start in your village? Did you leave before it started or did you leave after it had started?

10. Describe your journey
11. Discuss your present circumstances in the camp (e.g., What do you do? How do you spend the day or are you employed or taking some training?)
12. If you had the opportunity to talk to leaders of your country, what would you tell them?
13. Are you a Christian/baptized?
14. Has your faith in God helped you as a refugee?
15. Are there times when you wonder about God's goodness?
16. If you had the opportunity to talk to Christians who are not from your country, what would you tell them?

Questions for leaders of Christian organizations who have participated in refugee work

1. Name
2. Male/Female
3. Position in the organization
4. When did you start involvement in the refugee work?
5. Are those services direct or indirect?
6. Do you see any progress in your work? Are there any permanent solutions in sight?
7. Have you changed your strategies since you got involved in the work?
8. What do you think is the solution in the future and how are you going to attain it?

Appendix C

Letter to the Refugees

December 10, 2003

Dear Brothers and Sisters in Kakuma Refugee Camp:

It is with great joy and pleasure that I write this letter to you at the completion of my work. This has been a long, hard road of three years, but when I think of how long you have been in the refugee camp, this is nothing compared to that.

First, I want to thank you for the support and encouragement that you have been to me. When I came to Kakuma the first time in August 2001, I did not know how you would receive me. But you welcomed my friends and me into your fellowship with open arms. This visit was memorable to us, and we have the pictures as a reminder of the wonderful time we spent together. My most memorable time was when we had a meeting with the pastors in Kakuma who were from eight different nations. After sharing a message on the unity of the body of Christ and illustrating it with my prosthetic leg (which shocked many of you because you did not know I had an artificial leg), we all sang together the song I taught you: "If you believe and I believe and we together pray, the Holy Spirit will come down and Africa will be saved." That was a powerful moment, and I believe God will answer our prayers one day and we will see you all back in your countries, or wherever the Lord will lead you to continue doing his work.

When I came back in January 2003, I had mixed feelings. I hoped I would see some of you again, and yet I also hoped that some of you would have left to go home or elsewhere. But to my surprise, many of you were still there! I met Pastor Tito on the first day, and I was happy that his family had joined him in the camp. It was great to reunite with all those friends I had met the last time, now even more zealous in their faith in God. Pastor Gatera was looking more mature, especially having been entrusted with the responsibility of leading the refugee pastors. My visit to the Congolese Fellowship gave me such great joy. I still listen to the songs we sang together, with evangelist Malula leading us and beating the drums. I just felt so loved and accepted being with you. You comforted my heart at a time when I was grieving the loss of my mother. I was happy to meet with the ladies, though I regret that I did not have much time with them. It also gave me such joy that KISOM is now up and running and that there is a full-fledged board made up of Kenyan Christians who are willing to offer their services so that you can be mutually enriched. I am sure the third graduation event of KISOM in mid-February was a great time of celebration. I am sorry to have missed that one. However, I am just happy for the way the Lord is putting things together, bringing teachers and people who care to continue to encourage you.

Now, let me share in brief what I have been reading and writing. As I told you, I am writing on how we as Christians can recover our identity as pilgrims, aliens, and exiles. I have focused my study on the book of Hebrews, which is really a letter of encouragement written to believers who are facing hard times. They were facing trials because they were believers in Jesus Christ. I have learned a lot from it and also practically from you about what it means to live as a people in exile from your home countries. You know better than many what that means, so you are our teachers. You have taught me a lot about the pilgrim faith so that this work is not merely theoretical. I know you live this kind of life, and I am encouraged.

Let me summarize some key things that I have learned from reading the word of God and from seeing your lives and walk of faith. I have learned that people who have a pilgrim faith are people who know their God. I believe that because you are in a strange land, you have learned that God is the mighty, all-present God, and nothing is too hard for him. He is God for you in Kenya as he was in Rwanda, Burundi, or Sudan. This means you can call upon him at any time and everywhere, and he will respond. You can come boldly to his throne of grace and obtain mercy and grace in your time of need. I know how tough it is sometimes to get the officials at UNHCR to listen to you. You get to the gate and you are screened thoroughly before you can go anywhere, so you feel that your life is restricted. But our God is the king of the universe, and you can approach him and tell him all your needs straight away, and he will answer. He says in Jeremiah to "call unto me and I will answer you and tell you great and hidden things you have not known."

You have also learned seriously that your name is "Refugee." You are not the first ones to own that name. Our biblical examples of faith, in fact, confessed this without being ashamed of their identity. My sister Florence wrote me a letter the other day, and she unashamedly indicated on the envelope that she is a refugee in Kakuma. Sister Florence's honesty encouraged my friend who saw the verse in Hebrews in a new light. The good thing is that when we own our identity, claiming that we do not belong to our present world, literally in your case, or living in that understanding that this world is not our home, then God is not ashamed to be called our

God. He will show up in our situation of need. God's heart is especially inclined to those who are needy, and he cares especially for the stranger who can easily be taken advantage of.

Based on what you have shared, the other thing your situation has taught you is that God has given you companions to be with you along this pilgrimage of life. He has put you into a family of people who love him and who will also care for you. These people may not be your blood relatives, or people from your country, but God has truly given you brothers and sisters from all over the world. When the writer of Hebrews was encouraging his fellow believers, who were going through a lot of trials, he told them that they have this great cloud of people—all these saints from the Old Testament who are encouraging them to run the race with perseverance and not to lose heart. He told them finally that they have the ultimate example of who is Jesus, and he has finished the race. So, my dear brothers and sisters, even though you are going through hard times in the camp, the Lord knows you individually, and also as a group. I think of Brother Gatera's testimony of how he got married in the refugee camp; God provided him with a wife and a family to celebrate with him. Yes, God is a God who surprises us in circumstances that we think we are not able to go through.

So, this is a letter of encouragement from me to you. I know the days are long and difficult in dry Kakuma, but all I can tell you is that God is with you there. He will not leave you nor forsake you. He has an answer for you. He will provide for you. Be diligent to do these things: Never neglect to meet with your brothers and sisters for fellowship. The evil one wants to isolate you by separating you from others. He tells you that no one cares about you but then he will kill you when you are alone. So, meet with your brothers and sisters, even if sometimes you disagree with them. Just meet with them because they will support you in your walk. Support one another, especially in these hard times.

Another instruction that God wants for all of us as aliens and exiles is to take on a new sense of urgency when we live in such situations. Read the book of Hebrews, especially chapters 11, 12 and 13. Also, read what the prophet Jeremiah wrote to the people of God in exile. Read his letter in Jeremiah 29:4–14. He says in summary, marry, build houses, plant gardens (this may not be possible at Kakuma but I know my sisters from Burundi were planting a few things in pots), pray for the city or land that you are in. I am convinced it is because of your prayers that we went through last year's elections in Kenya quite peacefully. Pray for the Turkana, and the neighboring people, and work with them. Thank Pastor Simon, a Turkana who is a pastor among the Congolese. Meet and get to know people who are from another part of the world, and fellowship with Christians from another church. Have meetings together jointly with Christians from other parts of Africa, even if you do not understand their language. Above all, continue to care and support one another, not neglecting to show hospitality to the strangers—those who come to you—because you know what it means to be a stranger. Take advantage of the opportunities that LWF and UNHCR give you to learn. Attend KISOM classes; they are not just for a few people but for you all to grow in the word of God.

My brothers and sisters, be encouraged in the Lord. It is difficult to stop writing but I need to do so. When I finally complete my work and I return to Kenya, I will come to visit you as soon as I am able. I long to see you all. My love to all the pastors in the United Refugee Churches, the students and teachers at KISOM, the Women's Fellowship. I hear brother Malula has gone to Australia. The LORD be praised. I will end my letter with the prayer that Hebrews ends with: "Now may the God of peace, who brought back from the dead our Lord Jesus, the great shepherd of the sheep, by the blood of the eternal covenant, make you complete in everything good so that you may do his will, working among us that which is pleasing in his sight, through Jesus Christ, to whom be glory forever and ever. Amen."

Your sister in the Lord,
Emily J. Choge

Bibliography

Primary Sources

Interviews

Ajuoga, Nick, Vicar, St. Luke's Parish, Kenyatta. Interview by author. Tape recording. Nairobi, February 7, 2003.
Bwayo, David Wangaya, Pastor, Kakuma Christian Church. Interview by author. Tape recording. Kakuma, January 21, 2003.
Congolese Community Church, Kakuma Refugee Camp. Interview by author. Tape recording. Kakuma, January 17, 2003.
Ekai, Abong, Akolong and Natapar of World Vision. Interview by author. Tape recording. Kakuma, January 21, 2003.
Gatera, Jean Pierre, Pastor, Somali Fellowship. Interview by author. Tape recording. Kakuma, August 2001.
Gatera, Jean Pierre, Pastor and Chairman, United Refugee Churches. Interview by author. Tape recording. Kakuma, January 20, 2003.
Gur, Peter Yuol, Pastor Episcopal Church of Sudan. Interview by author. Tape recording. Kakuma, January 20, 2003.
Kamau, Evangeline, LWF, Community Services Coordinator. Interview by author. Tape recording. Kakuma, January 23, 2003.
Kankuri, Hannele, LWF, Director. Interview by author. Tape recording. Kakuma, January 23, 2003.
Kogo, Thomas, Anglican Bishop, Diocese of Eldoret. Interview by author. Tape recording. Eldoret, January 28, 2003.
Lodio, Jacob, Pastor AIC Sudan, Kenya. Interview by author. Tape recording. Kakuma, January 20, 2003.
Mengistu, Admasu, Pastor, Ethiopian Evangelical Church. Interview by author. Tape recording. Kakuma, January 20, 2003.
Mutoka, Benjamin Tanguli, Pastor Kitale Deliverance Church. Interview by author. Tape recording. Kakuma, January 18, 2003.
Namuya, Francis Erupe, Pastor, Kakuma Full Gospel Church. Interview by author. Tape recording. Kakuma, January 18, 2003, Kakuma.
Narogoi, Simon, Pastor Congolese Community. Interview by author. Tape recording. Kakuma, January 17, 2003.
Nyamai, Director, World Vision, Kakuma. Interview by author. Tape recording. Kakuma, January 20, 2003.
Ochilo, Polycarp, Director, Refugee Department, AACC. Interview by author. Tape recording. Nairobi, January 21, 2003.

Omusundi, Archdeacon, St. Matthews, Eldoret. Interview by author. Tape recording. Kakuma, January 16, 2003.
Onyango, Morris, Director, Peace building Programme, Kakuma. Interview by author. Tape recording. Kakuma, January 23, 2003.
Refugee Christians from Congo. Interview by author. Tape recording. Kakuma, January 16, 2003.
Riungu, Joyce, Director Reproductive Health, NCCK, Kakuma. Interview by author. Tape recording. Nairobi, February 13, 2003.
St. John's Parish, Cheptingting. Interview by author. Tape recording. Cheptingting, January 26, 2003.
Tuong, John Mayul, Pastor Evangelical Lutheran Church of Sudan. Interview by author. Tape recording. Kakuma, January 21, 2003.
Turkana Ladies, World Vision, Kakuma. Interview by author. Tape recording. Nairobi, February 4, 2003.
Wuor, James Ruot, Pastor Baptist Church of Sudan, Kakuma. Interview by author. Tape recording. Kakuma, January 21, 2003.

Unpublished Material

African Leadership and Reconciliation Ministries (ALARM), Inc. *Pamphlet*. Dallas: ALARM.
Association for Evangelicals in Africa (AEA). *AEA: A Symbol of Evangelical Unity in Africa*. Pamphlet. Nairobi: AEA.
Chungi, Jane. Letter to the author. May 2001.
Jesuit Refugee Service. *Displaced in Africa (Bible-study Guide)*. Rome: Jesuit Refugee Service, International Office.
———. *Scholarship Programme Brochure*. Rome: Jesuit Refugee Service, International Office, 2003.
Kakuma Interdenominational School of Mission (KISOM). *Mission Statement*. Kakuma, 2001.
Kakuma Interdenominational School of Mission (KISOM). *Sample Diploma*. Kakuma.
The Lutheran World Federation, Department of World Service. *Overview of Kakuma Refugee Camp*. Geneva.
The Lutheran World Federation. *Community Service Handout*. Geneva, January 2003.
Ministry of Health, UNICEF. Kenya Red Cross Society. *A Manual for Health Workers Nairobi*. Nairobi.
National Christian Council of Kenya and Joyce Ruingu. *Reproductive Health Training Manual*. Nairobi.
Refugee Insights. Quarterly Newsletter of the Refugee Consortium of Kenya 1 (April 2001) 7.
Richardson, Christina Spear. Letter to the author. October 1, 2002.

UNHCR Publications

United Nations High Commissioner for Refugees (UNHCR). *Community Services Brochure*. Kakuma Sub-Office, January 2003.

———. Convention and Protocol Relating to the Status of Refugees, Text of the 1951 Convention Relating to the Status of Refugees Text of the 1967 Protocol Relating to the Status of Refugees Resolution 2198 (XXI) adopted by the United Nations General Assembly with an Introductory Note by the Office of the United Nations High Commissioner for Refugees. https://cms.emergency.unhcr.org/documents/11982/55726/Convention+relating+to+the+Status+of+Refugees+%28signed+28+July+1951%2C+entered+into+force+22+April+1954%29+189+UNTS+150+and+Protocol+relating+to+the+Status+of+Refugees+%28signed+31+January+1967%2C+entered+into+force+4+October+167%29+606+UNTS+267/0bf3248a-cfa8-4a60-864d-65cdfece1d47.

———. *Dadaab Refugee Camps*. Profile. Nairobi: Public Information Section, 2001.

———. *Information Bulletin*. UNHCR. November 1996.

———. *Kenya and Somali Cross-border Operation: Finding Solutions*. Information Bulletin Nairobi: Public Information Section, 1996.

———. *Kenya/Somali Programme*. Information Bulletin. Nairobi: Public Information Section, 1998.

———. *Poetry Book*. Peace Education Programme. UNHCR Regional Service Center.

———. *State of the World's Refugees 2016: A World in Turmoil*. Oxford: Oxford University Press, 2016.

———. *Teachers Resource Notes: Peace Education Programme*. Nairobi: UNHCR Regional Centre, 2001.

Publications by Refugees

Tasew, Yilma Tafere, *Agonizing Wound*. Wellington, New Zealand: Refugee and Migrant Service, 2001.

Secondary Sources

ACCC. "The Refugee Problem: A Time Bomb in Africa." A Report on the Seminar on Awareness Building for Church Leaders held from 12th–16th November 1990. Blantyre, Malawi.

Achiron, Marilyn. "A Timeless Treaty Under Attack." *Refugees* 2, no. 123 (2001) 6–29.

Achtemeier, Paul J., Joel B. Green and Marianne Meye Thompson. *Introducing the New Testament: Its Literature and Theology*. Grand Rapids: Eerdmans, 2001.

Acquah, Benjamin K. "The African Economic Crisis: A Review of the Present State of the African Economy." In *Vision for a Bright Africa: Facing the Challenges of Development*, edited by G. Kinoti and Peter Kimuyu, 42–61. Nairobi: African Institute for Scientific Research and Development, 1997.

Adelman, Howard, and John Sorenson eds., *African Refugees: Development Aid and Repatriation*. Boulder, CO: Westview, 1994.

Adepoju Aderanti, "The Dimension of the Refugee Problem in Africa," *African Affairs* 81, no. 322 (January 1982) 24–25.

Aguilar, Mario I. *The Rwanda Genocide: And the Call to Deepen Christianity in Africa*. AMECEA Gaba Publications Spearhead Nos. 148-150. Eldoret, Kenya: AMECEA Gaba, 1998.

Aitken, Ellen Bradshaw. "The Body of Jesus Outside the Eternal City: Mapping Ritual Space in the Epistle to the Hebrews." In *Hebrews in Contexts*, edited by Gabriella Gelardini and Harold W. Attridge, 194–209. Ancient Judaism and Early Christianity 91. Leiden: Brill, 2016.

All Africa Conference of Churches. "Too Many Refugees. News: All Africa Conference of Churches, Nairobi." *One World* 115 (May 1986) 19.

Allison, Dale C., Jr. *The End of the Times Has Come: An Interpretation of the Passion and Resurrection of Jesus.* Philadelphia: Fortress, 1985.

Anderson, George M. "Refugees in East Africa: An Interview with John Guiney." *America* 183, no. 12 (October 21, 2000) 16–21. https://www.americamagazine.org/issue/385/article/refugees-east-africa.

Ankrah, Kodwo E. "The Stranger within the Gates: The Care of Refugees in Africa." In *Windows on Africa: A Symposium*, edited by Robert T. Parsons, 107–32. Leiden: Brill, 1971.

———. "A Theological Reflection on the Ministry of Churches to the Refugees in Africa." In *The Church and the Future of Africa*, edited by J. N. K. Mugambi, 122–34. Nairobi: All Africa Conference of Churches, 1997.

Arnold, Serge. "Les 'Enfants Meres' de la Tragedie: Tanzania and Zaire." *SEDOS Bulletin* 28 (November 1996) 311.

Arowele, P. J. "The Pilgrim People of God (An African's Reflection on the Motif of Sojourn in the Epistle to the Hebrews)." *Asia Journal of Theology* 4 (1990) 438–55.

Attridge, Harold W. *The Epistle to the Hebrews: A Commentary on the Epistle to the Hebrews.* Hermenia. Philadelphia: Fortress, 1989.

———. "Paraenesis in the Homily (*Logos Paraclesis*). The Possible Location of, and Socialization in, the 'Epistle to the Hebrews.'" *Semeia* 50 (1990) 211–26.

Aukot, Ekuru. "'It is Better to Be a Refugee Than a Turkana in Kakuma': Revisiting the Relationship between Hosts and Refugees in Kenya." *Refuge* 21, no. 3 (2003) 73–83.

Awad, Abdallah Suliman el. "Human Resources Under Threat: The Case of Muslim Refugees." In *Islam in Africa: Proceedings of the Islam in Africa Conference*, edited by Nura(sic) Alkali, Adamu, Anwal Yadudu, Rashid Molem and Haruna Sahihi: 364–72. Ibadan, Nigeria: Spectrum, 1993.

Backhaus, Knut. "How to Entertain Angels: Ethics in the Epistle to the Hebrews." In *Hebrews: Contemporary Methods—New Insights*, edited by Gabriella Gelardini, 149–75. Biblical Interpretation Series 75. Leiden: Brill, 2005.

Balz, Horst. "Early Christian Faith as 'Hope Against Hope.'" In *Eschatology in the Bible and in Jewish and Christian Tradition*, edited by Henning Graf Reventlow, 31–48. JSOT Supplement Series 243. Sheffield: Sheffield Academic, 1997.

Barrett, C. K. "The Eschatology of the Epistle of Hebrews." In *The Background of the New Testament and Its Eschatology: Studies in Honour of C. H. Dodd*, edited by W. D. Davies and David Daube, 363–93. Cambridge: Cambridge University Press, 1964.

Barrett, David. "AD 2000: 350 million Christians in Africa." *International Review of Mission* 59, no. 233 (January 1970) 39–54.

———, ed. *Kenya Churches Handbook: The Development of Kenyan Christianity 1498–1973.* Kisumu: Evangelical Publishing House, 1973.

Barriagaber, Assefaw. "Political Violence, Refugee Situations, and the Internalization of Regional Conflicts: A Six Nation Analysis (Chad, Djibouti, Ethiopia, Kenya, Somalia, Sudan)." PhD diss., Carbondale, IL: Southern Illinois University, 1990.

Bauer, Walter, Fredrick W. Danker, William F. Arndt and F. W. Gingrich. *Greek-English Lexicon of the New Testament and Other Early Christian Literature*. 3rd ed. Chicago: University of Chicago Press, 2000.

Bayart, Jean-Francois. *The State in Africa: The Politics of the Belly*. London: Longman, 1993.

Bedell, Kenneth. "Refugee Aid for Soweto Students." *Christian Century* 95 (10 May 1978) 506–8.

Bediako, Kwame. "Africa in the New World Christian Order." Presented for the Payton Lectures at Fuller Theological Seminary, Pasadena, California, October 12, 2000.

———. *Christianity in Africa: The Renewal of Non-Western Religion*. Edinburgh: Edinburgh University Press, 1995.

———. "Unmasking the Powers: Christianity, Authority, and Desacralization in Modern African Politics." In *Christianity and Democracy in Global Context*, edited by John Witte, 207–19. Boulder, CO: Westview, 1993.

Belcher, Wendy L. "The Africans." *Sojourners* 20 (October 1991) 40–41.

Bellino, Michelle J. "Youth Aspirations in Kakuma Refugee Camp: Education as a Means for Social, Spatial, and Economic (Im)mobility." *Globalisation, Societies & Education* 16, no. 4 (August 2018) 541–56.

Berkhof, Hendrikus. *Christ and the Powers*. Scottdale, PA: Herald, 1962.

Berquist, Jon L. "Critical Spatiality and the Book of Hebrews." In *Hebrews in Contexts*, edited by Gabriella Gelardini and Harold W. Attridge, 181–93. Ancient Judaism and Early Christianity 91. Leiden: Brill, 2016.

Betz, Otto. "Firmness in Faith: Hebrews 11:1 and Isaiah 28:16." In *Scripture: Meaning and Method: Essays Printed to Anthony Tyrrell Hanson*, edited by Barry P. Thompson, 92–113. Hull, UK: Hull University Press, 1987.

Biber, Freni. "Politischen Nomaden." *Zeitschrift für Mission* 13/3 (1987) 147–53.

Bonhoeffer, Dietrich. *The Cost of Discipleship*. 1959. Reprint, New York: Touchstone, 1995.

———. *Ethics*. 1955. Reprint New York: Simon & Schuster, 1995.

Bovon, Francois. *The New Testament Traditions and Apocryphal Narratives*. Translated by J. Haappiseva-Hunter. Allison Park, PA: Pickwick Publications, 1995.

Brawley, Robert L. "Discursive Structure and the Unseen in Hebrews 2:8 and 11:1: A Neglected Aspect of the Context." *Catholic Biblical Quarterly* 55 (1993) 83–89.

Brooks, Hugh C., and Yassin El-Ayouty eds. *Refugees South of the Sahara: An African Dilemma*. Westport, CT: Negro Universities Press, 1970.

Brown, R. "Pilgrimage in Faith: The Christian Life in Hebrews." *Southwestern Theological Journal* 28 (1985) 28–35.

Buchanan, George Wesley. *To the Hebrews: Translation, Comment and Conclusions*. Anchor Bible 36. Garden City, NY: Doubleday, 1972.

Bulley, A. D. "Heb.11: Death and Rhetoric in the Hebrew, 'Hymn to Faith.'" *Studies in Religion* 25 (1996) 409–23.

Burnet, Régis, Didier Luciani, Geert Van Oyen, eds. *The Epistle to the Hebrews: Writing at the Borders*. Leuven: Peeters, 2016.

Cannon, Katie G. *Black Womanist Ethics*. Atlanta: Scholars, 1988.

Carlston, C. E. "Commentaries on Hebrews: A Review Article." *Andover Newton Review* 1/2 (1990) 27–45.

———. "Eschatology and Repentance in the Epistle to the Hebrews." *Journal of Biblical Literature* 78 (1959) 296–302.

Catholic Church. "Africa: The Pastoral Care of Refugees Conference Report." *SEDOS Bulletin* 25 (15 February 1993) 46–50.

———. "1998 Maputo Consultation for a More Co-ordinated Pastoral Response to the Refugee Crisis in Africa: Final Statement-29 January 1998." *SEDOS Bulletin* 30 (April 1998) 126–28.

Chepkwony, Adam. "African Religion in the Study of Comparative Religion: A Case Study of Kipsigis Religious Practices" PhD diss., Moi University, Eldoret, Kenya, 1997.

Christian Century. "Multinational Force Headed for Zaire." *Christian Century* 113 (November 20–27, 1996) 1140–41.

———. "Refugees Crowd the Congo." *Christian Century* 78 (September 6, 1961) 1043.

———. "War Flares in Central Africa." *Christian Century* 111 (13 November 1996) 1103–4.

Christianity Today. "'Perhaps the World's Worst Refugee Problem.'" *Christianity Today* 4 (6 June 1980) 53.

Clay, Jason, and Bonnie Holcomb. *Politics and the Ethiopian Famine, 1984–1985*. Cambridge, MA: Cultural Survival, 1986.

Cockerill, Gareth Lee. *The Epistle to the Hebrews*. Grand Rapids: Eerdmans, 2012.

Colijn, Brenda B. "'Let Us Approach': Soteriology in the Epistle to the Hebrews." *Journal of the Evangelical Theological Society* 39 (1996) 571–86.

Compton, Ruth. "Out of Sight, Out of Mind: African Refugees Are Forgotten in the Wake of the Kosovo Crisis." *Christian Social Action* 12 (July/August 1999) 25–27.

Cone, James H. *A Black Theology of Liberation*: Twentieth Anniversary Edition. Maryknoll, NY: Orbis, 1990, 2001.

Copeland, Warren R. *And the Poor Get Welfare: The Ethics of Poverty in the United States*. Nashville: Abingdon, 1994.

Cosby, Michael R. *The Rhetorical Composition and Function of Hebrews 11 in the Light of Example Lists in Antiquity*. Macon, GA: Mercer University Press, 1988.

Crisp, Jeff. "Africa's Refugees: Patterns, Problems and Policy Challenges." In *New Issues in Refugee Research*, Working Paper no. 28. Geneva: UNHCR, 2000.

Croy, N. C. "A Note on Hebrew 12:2." *Journal of Biblical Literature* 114 (1995) 117–19.

Cutts, Mark, ed. *The State of the World's Refugees: Fifty Years of Humanitarian Action*. New York: Oxford University Press, 2001.

Davidson, Basil. *Africa in History: Themes and Outlines*. Rev. ed. New York: Simon & Schuster, 1991.

De Montclos, Marc-Antoine Perouse and Peter M. Kagwanja, "Refugee Camps or Cities? The Socio-economic Dynamics of the Dadaab and Kakuma Camps in Northern Kenya." *Journal of Refugee Studies* 13 (2000) 205–22.

deSilva, David A. *Despising Shame: Honor Discourse and Community Maintenance in the Epistle to the Hebrews*. Atlanta: Scholars, 1995.

———. "Entering God's Rest: Eschatology and the Socio-Rhetorical Study of Hebrews." *Trinity Journal* 21 (2000) 25–43.

———. "The Epistle to the Hebrew in Social-Scientific Perspective." *Restoration Quarterly* 36 (1994) 1–21.

———. "Exchanging Favor and Wrath: Apostasy in Hebrews and Patron-Client Relationships." *Journal of Biblical Literature* 115 (1996) 91–116.

———. *Perseverance in Gratitude: A Socio-Rhetorical Commentary on the Epistle to the Hebrews.* Grand Rapids: Eerdmans, 2000.

Dodson, Jualynne, and Cheryl Townsend Gilkes. "There is Nothing Like Church Food": Food and the US Afro-American Tradition: Re-membering Community and Feeding Embodied S/spirit(s)." *Journal of the American Academy of Religion* 63 (1995) 520–21.

Doornobs, Martin. "Church and State in East Africa: Some Unresolved Questions." In *Religion and Politics in East Africa: The Period Since Independence*, edited by H. B. Hansen, 260–70. London: Currey, 1995.

Dougherty, James E. *Horn of Africa.* Cambridge, MA: Institute of Foreign Policy Analysis, 1982.

———. *A Map of Political Strategic Conflict.* Cambridge, MA: Institute for Foreign Policy Analysis, 1982.

Easter, Matthew C. *Faith and the Faithfulness of Jesus in Hebrews.* Society for New Testament Studies Monograph Series 160. Cambridge: Cambridge University Press, 2014.

Eaton, Heather. "Rwanda: Survival of the Dominant." *Theology and Public Policy* 8 (1996) 80–94.

Ellingworth, Paul. "Jesus and Universe in Hebrews." *The Evangelical Quarterly* 58 (1986) 337–50.

———. *The Epistle to the Hebrews: A Commentary on the Greek Text.* Grand Rapids: Eerdmans, 1993.

Elliott, John H. "The Bible from the Perspective of the Refugee." In *Sanctuary: A Resource Guide for Understanding and Participating in the Central American Refugee Struggle*, edited by Gary MacEòin, 49–54. San Francisco: Harper & Row, 1985.

Eriksson, L.-G., Göran Melander, and Peter Nobel. *An Analysing Account of the Conference on the African Refugee Problem, Arusha, May 1979.* Uppsala: Scandinavian Institute of African Studies, 1981.

Evans, Michael Anthony "An Analysis of U.N. Refugee Policy in the Light of Roman Catholic Social Teaching and the Phenomena Creating Refugees." Ph.D. diss., Graduate Theological Union, Berkeley, 1991.

Ferris, Elizabeth G. *Beyond Borders: Refugees, Migrants and Human Rights in the Post-Cold War Era.* Geneva: WCC Publications, 1993.

Fitzpatrick, Brenda. "Speaking for Themselves: WCC and Christian Communicators in Africa, Lesotho, 1991." *One World* 168 (August–September 1991) 6–7.

Ford, Margaret. *Janani: The Making of a Martyr.* London: Marshall, Morgan & Scott, 1978.

Frame, Randall L. "A Familiar Tragedy: Mozambique Civil War Escalates; Photo." *Christianity Today* 32 (7 October 1988) 28–29.

France, R. T. "The Writer of Hebrews as a Biblical Expositor." *Tyndale Bulletin* 47 (1996) 245–76.

Fretheim, Terence E. *The Suffering of God: An Old Testament Perspective.* Overtures to Biblical Theology. Philadelphia: Fortress, 1984.

Fukui, Katsuyoshi, and John Markakis. *Ethnicity and Conflict in the Horn of Africa.* London: Currey, 1994.

Gatwa, Tharcisse, "Mission and Belgian Colonial Anthropology in Rwanda. Why the Churches Stood Accused in the 1994 Tragedy? What Next? *Studies in World Christianity* 6 (2000) 1–20.

Getui, Mary N., and Peter Kayandogo, eds. *From Violence to Peace: A Challenge for African Christianity*. Nairobi: Acton, 1999.

Gielty, Ellen. "The Church and the Refugee Crisis in Africa." *SEDOS Bulletin* 26 (1915, 15–April March 1994).

Gifford, Paul. *African Christianity: Its Public Role*. Bloomington: Indiana University Press, 1998.

Githiga Gideon. *The Church as the Bulwark Against Authoritarianism: Development of Church-State Relations in Kenya, with Particular Reference to the Years after Political Independence 1963–1992*. Oxford: Regnum, 2001.

Gorman, Robert F. *Coping with Africa's Refugee Burden: A Time for Solutions*. Dordrecht: Nijhoff, 1987.

Gray, Patrick. *Godly Fear: The Epistle to Hebrews and Greco-Roman Critiques of Superstition*. Academia Biblica 16. Leiden: Brill, 2004.

Greene, Stephen G. "The Horror and Hope of Rwanda: Some Charities Believe Crisis May Focus Attention on Africa's Long-Term Needs," *Chronicle of Philanthropy* 6/1 (1994) 12–16.

Greenlee, J. H. "Hebrews 11:11: Sarah's Faith or Abraham's?" *Notes on Translation* 4/1 (1990) 37–42.

Grogan, G. W. "The Concept of Solidarity in Hebrews." *Tyndale Bulletin* 49 (1998) 159–73.

Gushee, David P. "Remembering Rwanda: Church Failure." *Christian Century* 121/8 (April 20, 2004) 28–31.

Guthrie, Donald. *Hebrews*. Tyndale New Testament Commentaries. Downers Grove, IL: InterVarsity, 2015.

Guthrie, George H. *The Structure of Hebrews: A Text-Linguistic Analysis*. Novum Testamentum Supplement 73. Leiden: Brill, 1994.

Gutierrez, Gustavo. *A Theology of Liberation: History, Politics and Salvation*. Translated by Sister Caridad Inda and John Eagleson. 1973. Reprint, Maryknoll, NY: Orbis, 2001.

Hamm, Dennis. "Faith in the Epistle to the Hebrews: The Jesus Factor." *Catholic Biblical Quarterly* 52 (1990) 270–91.

Hammond, Laura. Review of *Losing Place: Refugee Populations and Rural Transformations in East Africa* by Johnathan Bascom. *Journal of Refugee Studies* 13 (2000) 203–5.

Hamrell, Sven, ed. *Refugee Problems in Africa*. Uppsala: Nordiska Afrikainstitutet, 1967.

Hansen, Bernt Holger, and Michael Twaddle, eds. *Religion and Politics in East Africa*. London: Currey, 1995.

Harrell-Bond, Barbara E. "What Are Camps Good for? The Plight of Refugees in Sub-Saharan Africa." *Insights Development Research* 44 (December 2002).

Hatch, John. "Historical Background of the African Refugee Problem." In *Refugees South of the Sahara: An African Dilemma*, edited by Hugh C. Brooks and Yassin El-Ayouty, 1–16. Westport, CT: Negro Universities Press, 1970.

Hauerwas, Stanley. *A Community of Character: Toward a Constructive Christian Social Ethic*. Notre Dame, IN: University of Notre Dame Press, 1981.

———. *Dispatches from the Front: Theological Engagements with the Secular*. Durham: Duke University Press, 1994.

———. The *Suffering Presence: The Theological Reflections on Medicine, the Mentally Handicapped, and the Church*. Notre Dame: University of Notre Dame Press, 1986.

Hauerwas, Stanley, and William H. Willimon. *Resident Aliens: Life in the Christian Colony*. Nashville: Abingdon, 1989.

Hayes, Kathleen, ed. *The Secret Place: Devotions for Daily Worship* 66, no. 3 (November 20, 2003). Valley Forge, PA: American Baptist Churches.

Hays, Richard B. *The Moral Vision of the New Testament: A Contemporary Introduction to New Testament Ethics*. San Francisco: HarperCollins, 1996.

———. "'Here We Have No Lasting City: New Covenantalism in Hebrews.'" In *The Epistle to the Hebrews and Christian Theology*, edited by Richard Bauckham et al., 151–73. Grand Rapids: Eerdmans, 2009.

Healey, Joseph, and Donald Sybertz, eds. *Towards an African Narrative Theology*. Maryknoll, NY: Orbis, 1999.

Healy, Mary. *Hebrews*. Grand Rapids: Baker Academic, 2016.

Heil, John Paul. *Hebrews: Chiastic Structures and Audience Response*. CBQ Monograph Series 46. Washington, DC: Catholic Biblical Association of America, 2010.

Hoerber, R. G. "On the Translation of Hebrews 11:1." *Concordia Journal* 21 (1995) 77–79.

Holborn, Louise W. *Refugees: A Problem of Our Time: The Work of the United Nations High Commissioner for Refugees, 1951–1972*. Vol. 1. Metuchen, NJ: The Scarecrow Press, 1975.

Holzer, Elizabeth. *The Concerned Women of Buduburam: Refugee Activists and Humanitarian Dilemmas*. Ithaca, NY: Cornell University Press, 2015.

Houten, Christiana van. *The Alien in Israelite Law*. JSOTSup 107. Sheffield: JSOT Press, 1991.

"How Somali Refugees are Ruining the Environment." *Daily Nation*, September 16, 1992.

Howell, Leon. "Justice and Service." *One World* 102 (January–February 1985) 24–37.

Hughes, Philip E. "Christology of Hebrews." *Southwestern Journal of Theology* 28 (1985) 19–27.

Hurst L. D. *The Epistle to the Hebrew: Its Background of Thought*. Society for New Testament Studies Monograph Series 65. Cambridge: Cambridge University Press, 1990.

Hydman, M. Jennifer. "Geographies of Displacement: Gender, Culture and Power in UHNCR Refugee Camps, Kenya (United Nations High Commissioner for Refugees, Persecution, Violence)." Ph.D. diss., University of British Columbia, Canada, 1996.

Hyndman, M. Jennifer, and Bo Victor Nylund. "UNHCR and the Status of Prima Facie Refugees in Kenya." *International Journal of Refugee Law* 10 (1998) 21–48.

"Illegal Arms Pose Threat to Everyone." *Daily Nation*. February 15, 2001.

Jacob, Sol. "Southern Africa Today -Refugees and Exiles: A Challenge to the Churches." *Journal of Theology for Southern Africa* 61 (1987) 1959–72.

Jacobsen, Karen. "Livelihoods in Conflict: The Pursuit of Livelihoods by Refugees and the Impact on the Human Security of Host Communities." *International Migration Review* 40, no. (2002) 94–117.

Jacques, Andre. "The Stranger within Your Gates: Uprooted People in the World." *Risk* 29, no. 1–87 (1986) vii–viii.

Jamieson, R. B. *Jesus' Death and Heavenly Offering in Hebrews*. Society for New Testament Studies Monograph Series 172. Cambridge: Cambridge University Press, 2019.

Jewett, Robert. *Letter to the Pilgrims: A Commentary on the Epistle to the Hebrews*. New York: Pilgrim, 1981.

Jipp, J. W. *Divine Visitations and Hospitality to Strangers in Luke-Acts. An Interpretation of the Malta Episode in Acts 28:1–10*. Novum Testamentum Supplements 153. Leiden: Brill, 2013.

Johnsson, W. G. "The Cultus of Hebrews in Twentieth-Century Scholarship." *Expository Times* 89 (October–September 1977/1978) 104–8.

———. "Issues in the Interpretation of Hebrews." *Andrews University Seminary Studies* 15 (1997) 169–87.

———. "The Pilgrim Motif in the Book of Hebrews." *Journal of Biblical Literature* 97 (1978) 239–51.

Jones, Camilla, Trish Hiddleston, and Christine Mccormick. "Lessons from Introducing a Livelihood Project for Unaccompanied Children into an Existing Child Protection Programme in the Dadaab Refugee Camps in Kenya." *Children and Youth Services Review* 47 (December 2014) 239–45.

Kaiser, Walter. "The Old Promise and the New Covenant." *Journal of the Evangelical Theological Society* 15 (1972) 16–17.

Kalisha, Wills. "Writing the In-between Spaces: Discovering Hermeneutic-Phenomenological Seeing in Dadaabi Refugee Camp, Kenya." *Phenomenology & Practice* 9/1 (2015) 55–69.

Käsemann, Ernst. *The Wandering People of God*. Translated by Roy A. Harrisville and Irving L. Sandberg. Minneapolis: Augsburg, 1984.

Katola, Michael. "The Refugees and the Displaced in Africa: A Challenge to Christians." *Africa Journal of Theology* 17 (1998) 141–51.

Kayandogo, Peter. "Who is My Neighbour? A Christian Response to the Refugees and the Displaced in Africa." In *Moral and Ethical Issues of African Christianity: Exploratory Essays in Moral Theology*, edited by J. N. K. Mugambi and A. Nasimiyu Wasike, 171–84 Nairobi: Initiatives, 1992.

Keller, Katie. "Drought in Africa Is More Than a Lack of Rainfall." *One World* 99 (October 1984) 12–14.

Kerkhofs, Jan, ed. "Living in the Shadow of Death: The Plight of African Refugees." *Pro Mundi Vita Dossiers: Africa Dossiers* 16 (January 1981) 1–27.

Kibreab, Gaim. *Reflections on the African Refugee Problem*. Trenton, NJ: Africa World, 1985.

———. *Refugees and Development in Africa: The Case of Eritrea*. Trenton, NJ: Red Sea, 1986.

Kifle, Melaku. "Intra-Continental Migration Patterns, Problems and Opportunities." *Reformed World* 41/7–8 (1991) 260–65.

Kim, D. "Heb 10:32–13:1: Perseverance in Hebrews." *Skryfkerk* 18 (1997) 280–90.

Kimuyu, Peter K. "A Christian Response to the Economic Crisis in Africa," In *IFES Anglophone Africa Vision for a Bright Africa*, 104–25. Kampala, Uganda: IFES Anglophone Africa, 1997.

King, Martin Luther, Jr. *Strength to Love*. Philadelphia: Fortress, 1963.

Kinoti, George. *Hope for Africa: And What the Christians Can Do.* Nairobi: African Institute for Scientific Research and Development, 1994.

Kinoti, G. and Peter Kimuyu. *Vision for a Bright Africa: Facing the Challenges of Development.* Christian Perspectives. Nairobi: International Fellowship of Evangelical Students/The African Institute of Scientific Research and Development, 1997.

Kironde, Apollo. "African Evaluation of the Problem." In *Refugees South of the Sahara: An African Dilemma,* edited by Hugh C. Brooks and Yassin El-Ayouty, 104–14. Westport, CT: Negro Universities Press, 1970.

Koenig, John. *New Testament Hospitality: Partnership with Strangers as Promise and Mission.* Overtures to Biblical Theology. Philadelphia, Fortress, 1985.

Koester, Craig R. "The Epistle to the Hebrews in Recent Research." *Currents in Research: Biblical Studies* 2 (1994) 123–45.

———. *Hebrews.* Anchor Bible 36. New York: Doubleday, 2001.

———. "'In Many and Various Ways': Theological Interpretation of Hebrews in the Modern Period." In *Hebrews in Contexts,* edited by Gabriella Gelardini and Harold W. Attridge, 299–315. Ancient Judaism and Early Christianity 91. Leiden: Brill, 2016.

Korten, David C. *When Corporations Rule the World.* San Francisco: Berrett-Koehler, 1995.

Kwayera, Juma. "US to Resettle Thousands of Somalis." *East African Standard.* January 21, 2002.

Laansma, Jon C. *The Letter to the Hebrews. A Commentary for Preaching, Teaching, and Bible Study.* Eugene, OR: Cascade Books, 2017.

———. "Hebrews: Yesterday, Today, and Future: An Illustrative Survey, Diagnosis, Prescription." In *Christology, Hermeneutics, and Hebrews: Profiles from the History of Interpretation,* edited by Jon C. Laansma and Daniel J. Treier, 1–32. London: T. & T. Clark, 2012.

Lane, William L. "Standing Before the Moral Claim of God: Discipleship in Hebrews." In *Patterns of Discipleship in the New Testament,* edited by R. N. Longenecker, 203–24. Grand Rapids: Eerdmans, 1996.

———. *Hebrews 1–8, Hebrews 9–13.* Word Biblical Commentary 47A & B. Dallas: Word, 1991.

Larbi, Emmanuel Kingsley. *God and the Poor.* Accra, Ghana: Centre for Pentecostal and Charismatic Studies, 2001.

Lee, Becky R. "Your Kingdom Come: Reflections Upon the Tanzanian Sojourn of the Rwanda Hutu." *Grail* 13 (June 1997) 75–81.

Lee, Gregory W. *Today When You Hear His Voice. Scripture, the Covenants, and the People of God.* Grand Rapids: Eerdmans, 2016.

Lindars, Barnabas. "The Rhetorical Structure of Hebrews." *New Testament Studies* 35 (1989) 382–406.

———. *The Theology of the Letter to the Hebrews.* New Testament Theology. Cambridge: Cambridge University Press, 1991.

Long, T. G. "Bold in the Presence of God." *Interpretation* 52 (1998) 53–69.

Longenecker, Richard N. "The Obedience of Christ in the Theology of the Early Church." In *Reconciliation and Hope: New Testament Essays on Atonement and Eschatology Presented to L. L. Morris on His 60th Birthday,* edited by Robert Banks, 142–52. Grand Rapids: Eerdmans, 1974.

Lowe, Kathy. "Scathing Self Criticism for African Church Aid." *One World* 53 (January–February 1980) 10–11.

"Lubbers, Ogata Call for a New Approach to the Refugee Situation in Africa." *UNHCR New Stories*, June 19, 2003.

Mackie, Scott. "Entrance and Draw-near Terminology (*proserchōmetha* and *eiseleusesthai*) in the Context of the Warnings to Not 'Drift Away'—The Pilgrimage of Faith." Unpublished paper.

MacRae, George W. "The Heavenly Temple and Eschatology in the Letter to the Hebrews." *Semeia* 12 (1978) 179–99.

———. "A Kingdom That Cannot Be Shaken: The Heavenly Jerusalem in the Letter to the Hebrews." In *Studies in the New Testament and Gnosticism*, edited by Daniel J. Harrington and Stanley B. Marrow, 98–112. Good News Studies 26. Wilmington, DE: Glazier, 1987.

Malina, Bruce J. *The New Testament World: Insights from Cultural Anthropology*. 3rd ed. Louisville: Westminster John Knox, 2001.

Markakis, John. *Resource Conflict in the Horn of Africa*. London: Sage, 1998.

Marshall, Bruce D. "Christ and the Culture: The Jewish People and Christian Theology." In *The Cambridge Companion to Christian Doctrine*, edited by Colin E. Gunton, 81–100. Cambridge Companions to Religion. Cambridge: Cambridge University Press, 1997.

Martin, Michael Wade, and Jason A. Whitlark. *Inventing Hebrews: Design and Purpose in Ancient Rhetoric*. SNTSMS 171. Cambridge: Cambridge University Press, 2018.

Matera, F. J. "Moral Exhortation: The Relation between Moral Exhortation and Doctrinal Exposition in the Letter to the Hebrews." *Toronto Journal of Theology* 10 (1994) 169–82.

Matthews, Z. K. "The Ecumenical Programme for Emergency in Africa." *Ecumenical Review* 19 (1976) 173–75.

Mayotte, Judy A. *Disposable People: The Plight of Refugees*. Maryknoll, NY: Orbis, 1992.

Mazrui, Ali A. *The African Condition: A Political Diagnosis*. Cambridge: Cambridge University Press, 1980.

———. *The Africans: A Triple Heritage*. Boston: Little, Brown, 1986.

———. *Africa Since 1935. UNESCO General History of Africa*. Paris/Berkeley: UNESCO/University of California Press, 1993.

———. "Human Rights Between Rwanda and Reparations: Global Power and the Racial Experience." *Encounters* 2, no. 1 (1996) 3–22.

———. "Religion and Political Culture." *Journal of the American Academy of Religion* 53 (1985) 817–39.

McClellan, Joel. "Geneva: ICARA II Conference Links Refugee Care to Development Aid." *One World* 99 (October 1984) 4–5.

McClendon, James William. Jr. *Biography as Theology: How Life Stories Can Remake Today's Theology*. New ed. Philadelphia: Trinity, 1990.

McCleod, D. J. "The Doctrinal Center of the Book of Hebrews." *Bibliotheca Sacra* 146 (1989) 291–300.

McConnel, Michael. "Swiss Sanctuary: Chocolate, Clockwork." *Christianity and Crisis* 46/11 (1986) 269–70.

McCullough, J. C. "Hebrews in Recent Scholarship." *Irish Biblical Studies* 16/2 (1994) 66–86.

McKelvey, R. J. *Pioneer and Priest: Jesus Christ in the Epistle to the Hebrews.* Eugene, OR: Pickwick Publications, 2013.

Meier, John P. *The Mission of Christ and His Church: Studies in Christology and Ecclesiology. Good News Studies.* Wilmington, DE: Glazier, 1990.

Mengelle, E. "La Estructura de Hebreos 11,1." *Biblica* 78 (1997) 534–42.

Michaels, J. Ramsey. *Hebrews.* [Linda Belleville on *1 Timothy*, and Jon Laansma on *2 Timothy, Titus*]. Cornerstone Bible Commentary. Carol Stream, IL: Tyndale House, 2018.

Minear, Larry. "Terms of Engagement in Human Need." *The Ecumenical Review* 42 (1990).

Mitchell, Alan C. *Hebrews.* Sacra Pagina. Collegeville, MN: Liturgical, 2007.

Moffatt, James. *Hebrews.* International Critical Commentary. Edinburgh: T. & T. Clark, 1924.

Monaghan, Christine, and Elisabeth King. "How Theories of Change Can Improve Education Programming and Evaluation in Conflict-Affected Contexts." *Comparative Education Review* 62 (2018) 365–84.

Mongi, Albert, Sam Obol and Luminita Oancea. "Refugee Participation in Camp-Management." *Transformation* 12 (June 1995) 23–27.

Montefiore, Hugh. *Hebrews.* Harper's New Testament Commentaries. London: A. & C. Black, 1964.

Mugambi, J. N. K. "The Christian Ideal of Peace and Political Reality in Africa." In *From Violence to Peace: A Challenge to African Christianity*, edited by M. N. Getui and P. Kanyandogo, African Christianity Series, 70–96. Nairobi: Acton, 1999.

———. *From Liberation to Reconstruction: African Christian Theology after the Cold War.* Nairobi: East African Educational, 1995.

Muggah, Robert, ed. *No Refuge: The Crisis of Refugee Militarization in Africa.* London: Zed, 2006.

Mulloor, A. "The Pioneer of Salvation and the Merciful High Priest." *Jeevadhara* 27 (1997) 123–32.

Musa-Habtu, Azieb. "Refugee Women Suffer: Africans' Vulnerability to Sexual Assault." *One World* 192 (January–February 1994) 15–16.

Muzorewa, Gwiyai H. *The Origins and Development of African Theology.* Maryknoll, NY: Orbis, 1985.

Mwangi, Oscar Gakuo. "Securitisation, Non-refoulement and the Rule of Law in Kenya: The Case of Somali Refugees." *International Journal of Human Rights* 22 (Dec 2018) 1318–34.

Mwereke, Thadei. "Problem of Refugees in Africa South of the Sahara: The Legacy of Foreign Intervention." Licentiate in Sacred Theology, Berkeley, California 1994.

Myths and Truths: The Facts about Refugee Self-Sufficiency and Economic Contribution in Nairobi. Kenya: Refugee Consortium of Kenya, 2015.

Nash, Scott. *The Church as Pilgrim People: Hebrews–Revelation.* Macon, GA: Smyth & Helwys, 2019.

Nelson, Richard D. *Raising Up a Faithful Priest: Community and Priesthood in Biblical Theology.* Louisville: Westminster John Knox, 1993.

Ngewa, Samuel, Mark Shaw and Tite Tienou. *Issues in African Christian Theology.* Nairobi: East African, 1998.

Ngugi, Kamou, ed. *Baseline Report.* London: Article 19 Eastern Africa, 2011.

Niebuhr, H. Richard. *Christ and Culture.* New York: Harper & Row, 1951.

Nielsen, Carl F. "Looking for Peace: Burundians Want to Go Home." *One World* 195 (May 1994) 5–6.

———. "Somalia/Djibouti: The Landscape Tells the Story of an Everyday Crisis." *One World* 64 (March 1981) 3–4.

Nindi, B. C. "The Problem of Refugees in Africa: A Case Study." *Institute of Muslim Affairs Journal* 8 (July 1987) 387–96.

Nyberg, Richard. "Churches Grapple for Unity Amid Great Lakes Crisis: Zaire, Rwanda, Burundi." *Christianity Today* 41 (3 February 1997) 82.

Nzau, Mumo. *Transitional Justice and After: Kenya's Experience with IDP Resettlement and Peacebuilding since the 2007/2008 Post-election Violence*. Nairobi: Catholic University of East Africa Press, 2016.

O.A.U. Convention Governing the Specific Aspects of Refugee Problems in Africa. Adopted by the Assembly of Heads of State and Government at Its Sixth Ordinary Session, Addis-Ababa, 10 September 1969. Geneva: UNHCR, 1974.

Obeng, Emmanuel A. "Religious Dimensions of Refugee Suffering," In *From Violence to Peace: A Challenge to African Christianity*, edited by M. N. Getui and P. Kanyandogo, 121–33. Nairobi: Acton, 1999.

O'Brien, Peter T. *The Letter to the Hebrews*. Pillar New Testament Commentary. Grand Rapids: Eerdmans, 2010.

———. *God Has Spoken in His Son. A Biblical Theology of Hebrews*. Downers Grove, IL: InterVarsity, 2016.

Oden, Amy G., ed., *And You Welcomed Me: A Sourcebook on Hospitality in Early Christianity*. Nashville: Abingdon, 2001.

O'Fahey, R. S. "The Past in the Present?" In *Religion and Politics in East Africa: The Period Since Independence*, edited by Holger B. Hansen, 32–44. London: Currey, 1995.

Ogletree, Thomas, W. *Hospitality to the Stranger: Dimensions of Moral Understanding*. Philadelphia: Fortress, 1985.

Olofin, Sam. "The African Economic Crisis, the Debt Burden and Macroeconomic and Mismanagement by Internal and External Managers." In *Vision for A Bright Africa: Facing the Challenges of Development*, edited by G. Kinoti and P. Kimuyu, 63-103. Nairobi: IFES Anglophone Africa/AISRED, 1997.

Oka, Rahul Chandrashekhar. "Coping with the Refugee Wait: The Role of Consumption, Normalcy, and Dignity in Refugee Lives at Kakuma Refugee Camp, Kenya." *American Anthropologist* 116 (March 2014) 23–37.

Okoro, Ethelbert Ihuarulam. "Africa's Refugee Problem: Politics and Somali Refugees in Kenya." PhD diss., Howard University, 1995.

Okullu, Henry. *Church and Politics in East Africa*. Nairobi: Uzima, 1974.

———. *Church and State in Nation Building and Human Development*. Nairobi: Uzima, 1984.

———. *A Quest for Justice: An Autobiography of Bishop John Henry Okullu*. Kisumu: Shalom, 1997.

Okure, Teresa. "Africa: A Refugee Camp Experience: Concept of Africa as Refugee Camp." In *Migrants and Refugees, Concilium* 4, edited by Lisa Sowle Cahill and Dietmar Mieth, 12–21. London: SCM, 1993.

Opala, Ken. "US Keeps Eye on Moi Exit." *Daily Nation*, April 13, 2001.

Otunga, Maurice Michael and Joseph Abangite Gasi. "Pastoral Care of Nomads, Refugees & the Displaced." *AFER* 36 (1994) 249–52.

Parrat, John. *Reinventing Christianity: African Theology Today*. Grand Rapids: Eerdmans, 1995.
Parsons, Mikael C. "Son and High Priest: A Study in the Christology of Hebrews." *Evangelical Quarterly* 60 (1988) 195–216.
Pirouet, M. Louise. "The Churches and Human Rights in Kenya & Uganda since Independence." In *Religion and Politics in East Africa*, edited by Holger B. Hansen, 247–59. London: Currey, 1995.
———. "The Churches and Refugees in Africa." In *Christianity in Africa in the 1990s*, edited by Christopher Fyfe and Andrew F. Walls, 82–91. Edinburgh: Centre of African Studies, University of Edinburgh, 1996.
Pobee, John. "An African Christian in Search of Democracy." In *Christianity and Democracy in a Global Context*, edited by John Witte, 267–85. Boulder, CO: Westview, 1993.
Pohl, Christine D. "Biblical Issues in Mission and Migration." *Missiology* 31/1 (2003) 4–15.
———. *Making Room: Recovering Hospitality as a Christian Tradition*. Grand Rapids: Eerdmans, 1999.
Pohl, Christine D., and Ben Donley. "Responding to Refugees: Christian Reflections on a Global Crisis." *Crossroads Monograph Series on Faith and Public Policy* 28. Wynnewood, PA: Evangelicals for Social Action, 2000.
Preston, Paul. *Evangelicals and Politics in Asia, Africa and Latin America*. Cambridge: Cambridge University Press, 2001.
Prunier, Gérard. *The History of a Genocide: 1959–1994*. London: Hurst, 1995.
———. *The Rwanda Crisis: History of a Genocide*. New York: Columbia University Press, 1997.
Pursilus, Darrel J. *The Cultic Motif in the Spirituality of the Book of Hebrews*. Lewiston, NY: Mellen Biblical, 1993.
Rad, Gerhard von. *The Problem of the Hexateuch and Other Essays*. Translated by E. W. T. Dicken. New York: McGraw-Hill, 1966.
Rassmussen, Larry L. *Earth Community and Earth Ethics*. Maryknoll, NY: Orbis, 1996.
Rawlence, Ben. *City of Thorns: Nine Lives in the World's Largest Refugee Camp*. New York: Picador, 2016.
Regional Surveys of the World: Africa South of the Sahara. 33rd ed. New York: Europa, 2004.
Reidy, William. "Southern Africa's Refugees." *One World* 120 (November 1986) 7–8.
———. "WCC Sahel Programme." *One World* 119 (October 1986) 16–17.
Republic of Kenya. *Laws of Kenya: The Immigration Act Chapter 172*. Rev. ed. Nairobi: Government Printer, 1984.
Rhee, Victor (Sung Yul). *Faith in Hebrews: Analysis within the Context of Christology, Eschatology and Ethics*. Studies in Biblical Literature 19. New York: Lang, 2001.
Riddle, D. W. "Early Christian Hospitality: A Factor in Gospel Transmission." *Journal of Biblical Literature* 57 (1938) 145.
Rodney, Walter. *How Europe Underdeveloped Africa*. Washington, DC: Howard University Press, 1974.
Rogge, J. R. "Africans' Displaced Population: Dependency or Self-Sufficiency?" In *Population and Development Projects in Africa*, edited by J. I. Clarke et al., 68–83. Cambridge: Cambridge University Press, 1985.
Ross, M. W. *Kenya from Within: A Short Political History*. London: Routledge, 1968.

Salih, Mohammed and John Markakis. *Ethnicity and State in Eastern Africa.* Uppsala: Nordiska Afrikainstitutet, 1998.
Schrage, Wolfgang. *The Ethics of the New Testament.* Translated by David E. Green. Philadelphia: Fortress, 1988.
Schreiner, Thomas R. *Commentary on Hebrews.* Nashville: Holman, 2015.
Schreiter, Robert J. *Faces of Jesus in Africa.* Faith and Culture Series. Maryknoll, NY: Orbis, 1991.
Scott, E. F. *The Epistle to the Hebrews: Its Doctrine and Significance.* Edinburgh: T. & T. Clark, 1922.
———. *Rethinking Realized Eschatology.* Macon, GA: Mercer University Press, 1988.
Shacknove, Andrew E. "Who is a Refugee." *Ethics* 95 No 2 (January 1985) 274–84.
Shiffman, Lawrence H. *The Eschatological Community of the Dead Sea Scrolls: A Study of the Rule of the Congregation.* SBL Monograph Series 38. Atlanta: Scholars, 1989.
Shriver, Donald W. *An Ethic for Enemies: Forgiveness in Politics.* New York: Oxford University Press, 1995.
Sider, Ronald J. *One-Sided Christianity? Uniting the Church to Heal a Lost and Broken World.* Grand Rapids: Zondervan, 1993.
———. *Rich Christians in an Age of Hunger: Moving from Affluence to Generosity.* New ed. Dallas: Word, 1997.
Small, Brian C. *The Characterization of Jesus in the Book of Hebrews.* Biblical Interpretation Series 128. Leiden: Brill, 2014.
Smith, R. Drew. "Acts of Mercy: Spirit of Community in Africa." *Christian Century* 111 (June 1–2 1994) 556–58.
Soding, T. "Zuversicht ünd Geduld Im Schauen auf Jesus. Zum Glaubensbegriff des Hebraerbriefes." *Zeitschrift für die neutestamentliche Wissenschraft* 82 (1991) 214–41.
———. "Gemeinde auf dem Weg: Christsein Nach dem Hebraerbrief." *Bibel und Kirche* 48/4 (1993) 180–87.
Spicq, Ceslas. *L'Epitre aux Hebreux.* 2 vols. Etudes Biblique. Paris: Gabalda, 1952–53.
———. *Theological Lexicon of New Testament.* Edited and translated by James D. Ernest. Vol. 2. Peabody, MA: Hendickson, 1994.
Stanley, S. "The Structure of Hebrews from Three Perspectives." *Tyndale Bulletin* 45 (1994) 245–71.
Stassen, Glen. "Critical Variables in Christian Social Ethics." In *Issues in Christian Ethics, A Festschrift Honoring Dr. Henlee Barnette*, edited by Paul D. Simons, 57–76. Nashville: Broadman, 1982.
———, ed. *Just Peacemaking: Ten Practices for Abolishing War.* Cleveland: Pilgrim, 1998.
———. *Just Peacemaking: Transforming Initiatives for Justice and Peace.* Louisville: Westminster John Knox, 1992.
Stassen, Glen H. and David P. Gushee. *Kingdom Ethics: Following Jesus in Contemporary Context.* Downers Grove, IL: InterVarsity, 2003.
Stassen, Glen H., John Howard Yoder, and D. M. Yeager. *Authentic Transformation: A New Vision of Christ and Culture.* Nashville: Abingdon, 1996.
Stott, John. *Issues Facing Christians Today.* New ed. London: HarperCollins, 1999.
Sugirtharajah, R. S. *The Bible and the Third World: Precolonial, Colonial and Postcolonial Encounters.* Cambridge: Cambridge University Press, 2001.

Suleiman, Naid Mohammed Ahmad. "A Historical Basis of Sudanese Refugee Problems: 1900 to the Present: A Critical Reading into the Power, Structure, State and Society in Sudan." PhD diss., Temple University, 1994.

Sullivan, Clayton. *Rethinking Realized Eschatology*. Macon, GA: Mercer University Press, 1988.

Swanson, James A., John R. Kohlenberger III, and Edward W. Goodrick, *The Exhaustive Concordance of the Greek New Testament*. Grand Rapids: Zondervan, 1995.

Swetnam, J. "Hebrews 11– An Interpretation." *Melita Theologica* 42, no. 2 (1990) 97–114.

Tanenbaum, Marc H. "Moral Considerations: The Value of Human Life." In *American Refugee Policy*, 107–13. Minneapolis: Winston, 1984.

Tedla, Stephanos. "The Refugee Problem in Africa Address; 7th SECAM Assembly; Zaire." *AFER* 27 (April 1984) 115–19.

Thompson, James W. *The Beginnings of Christian Philosophy: The Epistle to the Hebrews*. Catholic Biblical Quarterly Monograph Series 13. Washington, DC: Catholic Biblical Association of America, 1982.

———. "The Appropriate, the Necessary, and the Impossible: Faith and Reason in Hebrews." In *The Early Church in Its Context: Essays in Honor of Everett Ferguson*, edited by Abraham J. Malherbe et al., 302–17. Novum Testamentum Supplement 90. Leiden: Brill, 1998.

———. "The Hermeneutics of the Epistle to the Hebrews." *Restoration Quarterly* 38 (1996) 229–37.

Throup, David. "Render to Caesar the Things That Are Caesar's: The Politics of Church State Conflict in Kenya 1978–1990." In *Religion and Politics in East Africa*, edited by Holger Bernt Hansen and Michael Twaddle, 143–76. London: Currey, 1995.

Thurman, Howard. *Jesus and the Disinherited*. Boston: Beacon, 1976.

Toussaint, Stanley D. "The Eschatology of the Warning Passages in the Book of Hebrews." *Grace Theological Journal* 3 (Spring 1982) 67–80.

Townsend, Jim. *Hebrews: Pilgrim's Progress or Regress*. Colorado Springs: David C. Cook, 1987.

Trevisanut, Seline. "International Law and Practice: The Principle of Non-Refoulement And the De-Territorialization of Border Control at Sea." *Leiden Journal of International Law* 27 (2014) 661–75.

Trexler, Edgar R. "Serving All Those in Need." *Lutheran World* 24 (1977) 435–37.

Tutu, Desmond M. *Crying in the Wilderness: The Struggle for Justice in South Africa*. Grand Rapids: Eerdmans, 1982.

———. *No Future without Forgiveness*. New York: Doubleday, 1999.

———. "Postscript: To Be Human Is to Be Free." In *Christianity and Democracy in Global Context*, edited by John Witte, 311–20. Boulder, CO: Westview, 1993.

Tzoref, Shani. "Knowing the Heart of the Stranger: Empathy, Remembrance, and Narrative in Jewish Reception of Exodus 22:21, Deuteronomy 10:19, and Parallels." *Interpretation* 72 (2018) 119–31.

VanElderen, Marlin. "Ecumenism Made Disunity a Puzzle: Ministry with Refugees in Botswana." *One World* 82 (December 1982) 18–19.

Vanhoye, Albert. "La Teleiosis Du Christ: Pont Capital de Christologie Sacerdotale d'Hebreux." *New Testament Studies* 42 (1996) 321–38.

———. *Structure and Message of the Epistle to the Hebrews*. Subsidia Biblica 12. Rome: Pontifical Biblical Institute Press, 1996.

Veney, Cassandra Rachel. "The Politics of Refugee Relief Operations in Kenya." PhD diss., University of Missouri, Columbia, 1995.

Vennaelghem, Marc. "Mozambican: To Gazankulu, S. Africa." *One World* 115 (May 1986) 4–6.

Verdirame, Guglielmo. "Human Rights and Refugees." *Journal of Refugee Studies* 12 (1999) 57–77.

Volf, Miroslav. *Exclusion and Embrace: A Theological Exploration of Identity, Otherness and Reconciliation*. Nashville: Abingdon, 1996.

Waliggo, John M. "African Christology in a Situation of Suffering." In *Faces of Jesus in Africa*, edited by Robert J. Schreiter, 164–80. Maryknoll: Orbis, 1991.

Walker, Peter W. L. *Jesus and the Holy City: New Testament Perspectives on Jerusalem*. Grand Rapids: Eerdmans, 1996.

Wallis, Jim. *Faith Works: Lessons from the Life of an Activist Preacher*. New York: Random House, 2000.

———. *The Soul of Politics*. San Diego: Harcourt Brace, 1995.

Walls, A. F. "Africa and Christian Identity." *Mission Focus* 4, no. 7 (1978) 11–13.

———. "Towards an Understanding of Africa's Place in Christian History." In *Religion in a Pluralistic Society*, edited by J. S. Pobee, 180–89. Studies on Religion in Africa 2. Leiden: Brill, 1976.

Walzer, Michael. *Spheres of Justice: A Defense of Pluralism and Equality*. New York: Basic, 1983.

Ward, Kevin. "Ugandan Christian Communities in Britain." *International Review of Mission* 89, no. 354 (July 2000) 320–28.

West, Gerald. O., and Musa W. Dube, eds. *The Bible in Africa: Transactions, Trajectories and Trends*. Leiden: Brill, 2000.

Westcott, B. F. *The Epistle to the Hebrews*. London: Macmillan, 1892.

Whitlark, Jason A. *Enabling Fidelity to God. Perseverance in Hebrews in Light of the Reciprocity Systems of the Ancient Mediterranean World*. Colorado Springs: Paternoster, 2008.

Wilkinson, Ray. "'Life is a Classroom, A Street Without Guns and Field Without Mines': Millions of Children Have Been Helped in the Last Decade but the Plight of Many Others Remains Desperate." *Refugees* 1, no. 122 (2001) 6–21.

———, ed. "Quote Unquote." *Refugees* 3, no. 120 (2001) 24.

———. "The Refugee Convention at 50." *Refugees* 2, no. 122 (2001) 2.

Wink, Walter. *Engaging the Powers: Discernment and Resistance in a World of Domination*. Minneapolis: Fortress, 1992.

———. *Naming the Powers: The Language of Power in the New Testament*. Philadelphia, Fortress, 1984.

———. *Unmasking the Powers: The Invisible Forces that Determine Human Existence*. Philadelphia: Fortress, 1986.

Witte, John, ed. *Christianity and Democracy in a Global Context. Collection of Essays*. Boulder, CO: Westview, 1993.

World Council of Churches (WCC). "Hunger in Africa." *One World* 112 (January–February 1986) 22–23.

———. "Sudan: Mobilizing Energies and Pooling Resources Sudan Council of Churches WCC." *One World* 112 (January–February 1986) 18–19.

———. "The Way to Freedom: Ecumenical Movement and the Role of Namibian Churches in Building a New World." *One World* 148 (August–September 1989) 4–6.

———. "Troubled South Africa; [Refugees; News; Photos]." *One World* 110 (November 1985) 18–19.

Wright, C. J. H. "A Christian Approach to Old Testament Prophecy." In *Jerusalem Past and Present in the Purposes of God*, edited by P. W. L. Walker, 1–20. Grand Rapids: Baker, 1994.

———. *An Eye for an Eye: The Place of Old Testament Ethics Today*. Downers Grove, IL: InterVarsity, 1983.

———. *God's People in God's Land: Family, Land, and Property in the Old Testament*. Grand Rapids: Eerdmans, 1990.

Yancey, Philip. "The Other Side of Thanksgiving: Overseas Assistance Is Torn between Relief and Development." *Christianity Today* 26 (26 November 1982) 22–29.

Yeo, K. K. *What Has Jerusalem to Do with Beijing? Biblical Interpretation from a Chinese Perspective*. 2nd ed. Eugene, OR: Pickwick Publications, 2018.

Yoder, John Howard. *Body Politics: Five Practices of the Christian Community before the Watching World*. Scottdale, PA: Herald, 1992.

———. *The Christian Witness to the State*. Scottdale, PA: Herald, 2002.

———. *For the Nations: Essays Evangelical and Public*. Grand Rapids: Eerdmans, 1997.

——— *The Politics of Jesus: Vicit Agnus Noster*. 2nd ed. Grand Rapids: Eerdmans, 1994.

———. *The Priestly Kingdom: Social Ethics as Gospel*. Notre Dame: University of Notre Dame Press, 1984.

———. *The Royal Priesthood: Essays Ecclesiological and Ecumenical*. Grand Rapids: Eerdmans, 1994.

Index of Authors

Adelman, Howard, 17
Allison, Dale C. Jr., 100n18
Ankrah, Kodwo E., 159, 163
Arowele, P. J., 9, 109–12, 131, 135
Attridge, Harold W., 95n7, 101, 113, 117–18, 121–22, 125, 128
Aukot, Ekuru, 49n39, 82n75, 84n83

Barrett, C. K., 108
Barrett, David, 131
Bayart, Jean-Francois, 36n80
Bediako, Kwame, 132n165
Berkhof, Hendrikus, 140
Brooks, Hugh C., 17
Brown, R., 132
Buchanan, George Wesley, 107
Burnet, Régis, 144

Chepkwony, Adam, xviii, 11, 206
Clay, Jason, 26n49
Cosby, Michael R., 121
Cutts, Mark, 17

Davidson, Basil, 19
deSilva, David A., 9, 95n7, 114–15, 114n109, 115n112, 115n113, 122, 122n130, 127–29, 129n150, 134n169, 135n174
Dodson, Jualynne, 194
Donley, Ben, 174n78
Dyrness, William, xi

El-Ayouty, Yassin, 17
Ellingworth, Paul, 102n24, 123n131, 125
Elliott, John H., 178
Evans, Michael Anthony, 4, 17, 22n39, 28, 43

Ferris, Elizabeth G., xvi, 11, 16n5, 203, 204
Fukui, Katsuyoshi, 16

Gatwa, Tharcisse, 32n73
Gilkes, Cheryl Townsend, 194
Githiga Gideon, 151–53, 154n48, 155–56, 188n2
Gorman, Robert F., 17
Gushee, David P., 140, 140n5, 160, 171, 178–79, 181, 183
Guthrie, Donald, 100n15

Hamm, Dennis, 117
Hamrell, Sven, 17
Hatch, John, 18–19
Hays, Richard B., 100n15
Holborn, Louise W., 17
Holcomb, Bonnie, 26n49
Hyndman, M. Jennifer, 43n15

Jewett, Robert, 9, 103–4, 104n43, 105, 108n65
Johnsson, W. G., 9, 107–8, 108n65, 108n69, 109

Kagwanja, Peter M., 83
Käsemann, Ernst, 9, 101, 101n24, 102–3, 103n34, 104, 106–9, 109n79, 113n99, 117, 132
Kibreab, Gaim, 2n4, 10, 17, 20, 27n55, 40, 48n33, 49n40, 53, 176, 185
Kifle, Melaku, 15
Kimuyu, Peter K., 36n80
Kinoti, George, 35
Koester, Craig R., 115, 134

Lane, William L., 9, 95n7, 105 – 06, 123n133, 124, 124n135, 127, 127n148
Lindars, Barnabas, 117
Longenecker, Richard N., 117
Luciani, Didier, 144

Mackie, Scott, 113n99
Markakis, John, 16, 21–22, 24
Martin, Michael Wade, 105n50
Mazrui, Ali A., 18n22, 40, 130
Mugambi, J. N. K., 189
Mwereke, Thadei, 6, 17, 34

Nash, Scott, 9
Ngugi, Kamou, 12n39

Obeng, Emmanuel A., 45n20
Oden, Amy G., 12n38
Okoro, Ethelbert Ihuarulam, 60n2, 65n14, 67, 74, 75, 76, 87, 185n1
Okullu, Henry, xix, 7, 8, 139, 139n3, 139n4, 140-46, 149-51, 153, 159, 166, 180, 182-83, 188
Okure, Teresa, 162

Pirouet, M. Louise, 46n25
Pohl, Christine D., xix, 9, 10, 12, 95n6, 174-75, 174n78, 206
Prunier, Gérard, 31n66

Rad, Gerhard von, 98n10

Rhee, Victor (Sung Yul), 117–18, 117n118, 118n121, 118n122, 122n131, 123n134, 124n135
Riddle, D. W., 175
Rogge, J. R., 47

Salih, Mohammed, 16
Sorenson, John, 17
Spicq, Ceslas, 108
Stassen, Glen H., ix, xiii, 13, 13n40, 140, 140n5, 160, 169, 171, 178-79, 181, 183, 201n37
Suleiman, Naid Mohammed Ahmad, 23

Thompson, James W., 101n24, 114–15n109, 117–18, 118n119
Townsend, Jim, 9
Tutu, Desmond M., 190

van Oyen, Geert, 144
Veney, Cassandra Rachel, 2, 49, 60, 69, 71, 72, 185n1

Wallis, Jim, 166n71
Westcott, B. F., 124
Whitlark, Jason A., 105n50, 193n13
Wink, Walter, 140n6, 164n67

Yeo, K. K., 107
Yoder, John Howard, xix, xixn11, 6-7, 98, 98n12, 138-39, 139n2, 139n4, 140-48, 148n31, 149-50, 160, 166, 169, 180, 183, 188, 193

Index of Subjects

Addis Ababa Agreement (1972), 23, 51, 53
African Charter on Human and People's Rights, 190
African Evangelistic Enterprise (AEE), 46n25
African Leadership and Reconciliation Ministries (ALARM), 182, 198
African theology, 111–12
Africa Refugee Day, 167, 195, 200
Algerian War of Independence, 20, 42
aliens, x, xviii, 9, 50, 70, 90, 93, 94n1, 95–99, 95n6, 96, 97n9, 98n11, 111, 123, 124–25, 124n35, 127–29, 128n151, 132, 137, 139, 161, 172, 178–80, 185, 188, 202, 206, 211, 212
All Africa Conference of Churches (AACC), 46, 156, 157, 159–60
Amin, Idi, 29, 66, 134, 154, 174, 182
Anglican Church Diocese of Eldoret and Nairobi, 85
Angola, 21

Baptism, 7, 147, 176
Biafran war, 21
binding and loosing, 148
breaking of bread, 7, 147, 178
British colonial policy, 186
Burundi, 15n4, 16, 22, 31, 32–35, 66, 85, 87n88, 88, 91, 131, 168, 180, 186, 194, 194n19, 195n21, 196, 211, 212

Catholic Relief Services (CRS), 45–46
Church World Service, 46

colonialism/colonization, ix, xv, 6, 18, 20, 35–36, 40, 61, 130, 152–53, 152n42, 186
Congo, 19, 21, 22, 23, 32n70, 33, 34, 37, 39, 41, 42, 48, 51, 66, 84–85, 87n88, 88, 90n95, 91, 131, 187, 195n21, 210, 212
Convention Governing the Specific Aspects of the Refugee Problems in Africa, xvi, 21, 69, 70

displacement, ix, xvi–xvii, 1, 3, 15, 18, 27, 28, 30, 31, 32, 34, 37, 38, 61, 96, 160, 169, 200, 203, 204
Djibouti, 15n4, 19, 25, 34, 186
drought, 16, 22n39, 24, 28, 29, 37, 37n82, 39, 56, 59, 64, 186

East African Cooperation, 30
East Africa Revival Movement (EARM), 155, 170
economics
 economic assistance, 26, 167
 economic challenges/hardship, xv, xvi, 2, 3, 6, 10, 29, 41, 43, 59, 60n2, 69, 131, 134, 161, 162, 204
 economic conditions, xvi, 4, 12, 31, 34, 48, 49, 50n45, 60, 62, 130, 131–32, 160, 162, 167, 188, 203
 economic growth/development, 18, 18n22, 40, 43, 52, 146, 198
 economic disparity, 16, 20, 57, 147, 176, 182, 186
 economic factors, 23, 24, 25, 64
 economic justice/injustice, 7, 36
 "economic" refugees, 167
 economic systems, 19, 37, 55, 140, 141

237

Eldoret, 29, 85–86, 134, 157, 166n69
Emergency Action in Africa (EPEAA), 46
environment
    environmental conditions, xvi, 80, 186, 203, 204
    environmental degradation, 47–48, 83
    environmental disasters, 15, 21, 26, 37
    environmental protection, 75
Eritrea, 15n4, 23, 25, 26, 27, 27n55, 51, 52, 53, 88
Eritrean Liberation Front (ELF), 27
Ethiopia, ix, 2, 3, 3n7, 5, 8, 15n4, 16, 19, 22, 22n39, 23, 24, 25, 26, 26n49, 27–29, 27n55, 34, 35, 39, 51, 53, 61, 62, 66, 77, 88, 90n94, 92n96, 131, 156, 161, 186, 195n21
eschatology, 109, 111
ethnic clashes, xviin6, 3, 59, 64, 157n54, 162, 204n6
exile, xviii, 4, 7, 9, 11, 20, 29, 30, 31, 49n40, 94, 95, 98–99, 110–11, 122–23, 123n134, 128, 130, 132, 135, 178, 181, 194, 206, 211–12
exodus, 11, 107–8

Fellowship of Christian Councils and Churches in the Great Lakes Areas and the Horn of Africa (FECCLAHA), 182

Gnostic-Redeemer Myth, 101, 104, 107
Green Revolution, 28
Guinea-Bissau, 21, 53

Habyarimana, Juvenal, 31
hospitality
    African hospitality, ix, xviii, 2, 2n4, 39, 40, 185n1, 186, 199, 200
    definition of hospitality, xviii–xix, 206–7
humanitarian aid, 16, 29, 32, 38, 49n39, 54, 57, 58, 187
human rights violations, 25, 36
Hutu, 30–33, 31n66, 48, 92, 161

International Conference on Assistance for Refugees in Africa (ICARA I), 49, 54–55, 56, 187
International Conference on Assistance for Refugees in Africa (ICARA II), 54–56
International Rescue Committee (IRC), 45, 79, 187
Inter-Governmental Authority on Drought and Development (IGADD), 25

Jesuit Refugee Service (JRS), 77, 78–79, 156, 185, 187, 191n9

Kagnew Station, 26
Kakuma Refugee Camp, xiii, 25, 56, 72, 82, 89, 210
Kasha, 24
Katanga region, 20–21
katapausis (rest), 107
Khartoum government, 23–25
Kipsigis, xviii, 11–12, 206

Lakwena, Alice, 30
land
    land availability, 62
    land boundary issues, 62
    land issue in Kenya, 62–63, 63n11
    land ownership, 62–64
Legal, Social and Economic Aspects of the African Refugee Problem (Addis Ababa 1967), 44
Lutheran World Federation (LWF), 45, 46, 76–78, 187

Malawi, 41, 48
Mogadishu, 29, 69
Moi, Daniel, 25, 61, 62, 62n8, 65, 151, 153–55, 154n48
Mozambique, 21, 50, 53, 66

Namibia, 21
National Christian Council of Kenya (NCCK), 77, 79–81, 156, 157–58, 190
National Resistance Army (NRA), 31
Ndadaye, Melchior, 31, 31n69, 33, 92

INDEX OF SUBJECTS 239

New Partnerships for Africa's
    Development (NEPAD), 200
Nimeiry, Jaafar, 23
non-refoulement, x, 45
Northern Frontier District Liberation
    Front, 65
Ntryamira, Cyprien, 31
Nyerere, Mwalimu Julius, 2, 174

Obote, Milton, 29, 139n3, 174
Ogaden region, 27, 34
OAU Convention Governing the
    Specific Aspects of Refugee
    Problems in Africa, 21, 44, 45,
    69, 70
Organization of African Unity (OAU),
    xvi, 21, 34, 35, 42, 44–45, 45n20,
    54, 65, 173, 190, 201

parastatal companies, 64, 64n12
Parousia, 111
pilgrim
    definition of pilgrim, xvii–xviii,
        204–6
    ecclesiology of pilgrims, 106, 109,
        111
    pilgrim identity, x, xviii, xix, 138,
        160, 164–65, 169, 171, 183, 188,
        196
    pilgrim motif, xv, 3, 6, 8, 9, 13, 94–
        137, 138–40, 146, 148, 149, 160,
        177, 183, 186, 188, 192–93, 197
pilgrimage, xvii, 11, 13
post-independence, 17, 21–22

refugee
    definition of refugee, 42–45, 45n20
    ethic for refugees, 1–14
    refugee assistance, 5, 55
    refugee camps, 3, 29, 32, 47–49,
        48n37, 53, 66, 69–75, 156,
        157n54, 162–63, 166–67, 185,
        192–97
    refugee status, ix, 34, 37, 43, 45,
        45n20, 71–72, 158, 199
Refugee Bill, 70, 70n29, 173, 190, 199
rehabilitation, 51, 55, 74, 77, 200
relief organizations, 24, 28
repatriation, 20, 30, 44, 47, 51, 53–54,
    57, 69, 73–74, 163, 187, 200
Rhodesia, 21
Rwanda, 30–33
    genocide, 21, 31–32, 31n69, 32n73,
        48, 171, 174, 198
    Rwandese Patriotic Front (RPF), 31

sabbatismos (creation rest), 107
Selassie, Haile, 27
slave trade, xv, 16, 18–20, 34, 37, 130,
    186
sojourners, 94, 108, 123, 126, 127n148,
    128n150, 129
South Africa, 21, 66, 167, 171, 190
Structural Adjustment Programs
    (SAPs), 36, 130, 167
Sudan National Movement (SNM), 29
Sudan People's Liberation Army (SPLA),
    24

Turkana people, 48, 49n39, 69, 72, 82,
    82n75–76, 83–84, 84n81, 84n83,
    85, 187, 192, 212
Tutsi, 30–33, 92, 161

United Nations High Commission for
    Refugees (UNHCR), ix, 1, 42,
    73–76
UN Refugee Convention, 20

wars of independence, 20
World Council of Churches (WCC), xvi,
    15, 46, 157, 160, 204
World Vision International (WVI), 45

Scripture Index

The Old Testament

Genesis

15:13	97
23:4	128

Exodus

20:8–10	98
22:21	172
22:21–23	98
23:9	172
23:12	98

Leviticus

19:9–10	97
19:33	172
19:34	172
25:23	97

Deuteronomy

10:19	172
14:28–29	97, 98
15:4	147
16:1–8	97
16:13–15	98
26:5	98
26:12	98

Psalms

38:13	128
87:1–2	116

Isaiah

43:19	195

Jeremiah

29:7	99

Wisdom of Solomon

11:10	121n127
11:15—12:37	121n127

4 Maccabees

16:16–23	121n127

The New Testament

Matthew

18:15	148
22:32	125
25:31–46	99

Luke

4:18	147
9:51	95n4
9:58	95n4, 135
22:25–26	145

Romans

12:9–13	99
15:1	99

1 Corinthians

14:26	148

Ephesians

3:6	147
3:10	141

Colossians

2:15	141

1 Timothy

3:2	99

Titus

1:2	99

Hebrews

1:1–14	118
2:1–2	118
2:1	114, 119
2:3	100
2:5	95n7
2:10	109
2:11	125
3–4	108, 116
3:1	119
3:5	119
3:7—4:13	102, 105, 110, 112
3:12—4:11	113n104
3:12–13	134
3:12	119
3:13	120
3:14	120, 134
3:16	114
3:19	119
4:1	113n101, 114
4:3	114
4:6	114
4:10–11	114
4:11	113n101, 126
4:14	113n101, 113n104
4:16	113, 113n101, 134
5:7	154n49
5:8	120
5:11	95n7
6:1	113n101
6:9	95n7
6:10–12	134
6:19–20	114
6:20	109, 132
7–10	116
7:19	114
7:25	113
8:1	95n7, 113n104
9–10	123
9:5	95n7
9:12–14	170
9:12	114
9:24–25	114
10:5	114
10:21	113n104, 116
10:22–24	113n101
10:22	113, 134
10:22–23	119
10:23	126
10:24–25	120
10:25	134
10:32–39	121
10:32–38	120
10:32–34	123
10:34	120
10:35–39	119
10:35	120
10:36—12:13	101
10:38–39	122
11–13	116
11:1—12:29	118
11	105, 108, 110, 118, 121, 121n127, 123n131, 134
11:1–40	119, 120, 121
11:1–2	121
11:1	110, 124
11:3–31	121
11:3–16	13
11:3–12	123n131
11:6	113
11:8–22	122, 122n130
11:8–12	124

11:8	114	12:28	110, 113n101, 113n104, 117
11:9–10	97	13	108
11:10	95, 96, 116, 125	13:1–4	149
11:11–17	xviii	13:1–3	120
11:13–16	96, 122n130, 123n131, 134	13:1–2	134
11:13	xi, 94, 124, 134	13:2	xviii, 99, 134, 174
11:14–15	126	13:3	135
11:16	96, 124, 126, 129	13:5–6	135
11:17–40	123n131	13:7	133
11:17–22	125	13:10	113n104
11:24–26	122n130	13:12–16	120
11:26	122n130	13:13–16	116
11:28	111	13:13–14	111
11:32	95n7	13:13	113n101, 114, 123, 133
11:35	125	13:14	106, 113n104
12	114, 122	13:15	113n101
12:1–4	120	13:16	120, 135
12:1–3	123, 125	13:23	100
12:1–2	120		
12:1	113n101, 115, 119, 121, 170	1 Peter	
12:2	109, 119n125, 122, 122n130, 129	2:11	99
12:3–4	119, 122	2 John	
12:3	120	10–12	99
12:4	120, 122		
12:18–24	121	Revelation	
12:18	113	12:11	133n168
12:21	154n49		
12:22	97, 113		
12:26–28	97		
12:28–29	154n49		

www.ingramcontent.com/pod-product-compliance
Lightning Source LLC
Chambersburg PA
CBHW050347230426
43663CB00010B/2026